Dealing
With Crisis

A licensed practising psychologist in the
state of North Carolina, LAWRENCE G. CALHOUN
is Assistant Professor of Psychology
at the University of North Carolina,
Charlotte.

JAMES W. SELBY, author of several papers
published in professional journals, is also
a licensed practising psychologist in North
Carolina.

H. ELIZABETH KING, Assistant Professor
of Psychiatry at Emory University Medical
School, is Director of Pediatric Psychology
at Grady Memorial Hospital and consultant
to the Rape Crisis Center in Atlanta,
Georgia.

Dealing
With Crisis

A Guide to Critical Life Problems

LAWRENCE G. CALHOUN

JAMES W. SELBY

H. ELIZABETH KING

A SPECTRUM BOOK

PRENTICE-HALL, INC., Englewood Cliffs, New Jersey 07632

Library of Congress Cataloging in Publication Data

Calhoun, Lawrence G.
   Dealing with Crisis

   (A Spectrum Book)
   Includes bibliographies and index
   1. Crisis intervention (Psychiatry)
2. Adjustment (Psychology)   I. Selby, James W.
joint author.   II. King, H. Elizabeth, joint
author.   III. Title
RC480.6.C34   362.8 '2   76–23422
IBSN 0–13–197723–7
ISBN 0–13–197715–6 pbk.

A Spectrum Book

19 18 17 16 15 14 13

Printed in the United States of America

Prentice-Hall International, Inc., *London*
Prentice-Hall of Australia Pty. Limited, *Sydney*
Prentice-Hall of Canada, Ltd., *Toronto*
Prentice-Hall of India Private Limited, *New Delhi*
Prentice-Hall of Japan, Inc., *Tokyo*
Prentice-Hall of Southeast Asia Pte. Ltd., *Singapore*
Whitehall Books Limited, *Wellington, New Zealand*

To our parents

Contents

Preface

This volume represents an examination of a number of situationally based psychological problems. Events like divorce, death, abortion, and suicide are thought of as critical life problems posing hazards for personal adjustment. The research findings concerning these and other critical life problems are reviewed in order to give the reader a picture of the current state of our knowledge about the kinds of psychological problems arising from them.

Throughout this book, the use of psychological jargon and technical terms is minimized in order to make the information available to the widest range of readers. Thus, the attempt is to make the relevant information derived from psychological research intelligible to the layman. In addition, the book is useful as either a primary or secondary text for undergraduate courses in psychology of adjustment, mental hygiene, abnormal psychology and the like. Finally, the book, with extensive references in the semi-technical and technical literature, will prove useful as a handbook for paraprofessionals and professionals who work in the field of psychological services.

In reading this book, it should be kept in mind that the authors have adopted a perspective in which the importance of situational problems is highlighted. The situations selected are those which affect many individuals either directly or indirectly, situations which seem to pose a significant hazard for the psychological well being of the individual, and situations for which empirical research is available. We believe the use of this approach fills a gap in the psychological literature, while at the same time it provides important knowledge for a variety of readers.

The authors would like to acknowledge the assistance of Ms. Sandy Smith and Ms. Ronnie Moon in typing this manuscript. Further, the authors would like to extend their appreciation to Mr. Michael Hunter and the other members of the Prentice-Hall editorial staff for their assistance in the preparation of this manuscript.

Contemporary Views of Adjustment

CHAPTER ONE

During the course of our lives, we all encounter difficult situations, with psychological distress and emotional turmoil as their frequent accompaniments. People are faced with marital discord, the death of a loved one, retirement, physical illness or handicap, illegitimate pregnancy, and similarly stressful situations. Experiencing such problems in living, laymen frequently turn to psychologists and other mental health workers for solutions. Yet often these people seem disappointed in the results, accusing psychologists of evasiveness. Certainly, many college freshmen enrolling in introductory psychology courses become disillusioned, feeling that psychology does not address itself to the problems they encounter. Psychology texts and courses have traditionally been organized around particular theories or basic processes, rather than typical problems of living. This book attempts to organize and present what is known about the critical problems themselves.

WHAT IS ADJUSTMENT? THE DESCRIPTIVE CRITERIA

In casual conversation about a psychological problem or concern, there is likely to be heard the rhetorical question, "So what is normal?" In such discussions, seldom does anyone seriously attempt to answer this question. Yet for psychologists, defining adjustment and maladjustment, or normal and abnormal, is an important problem. Both in popular parlance and in technical literature the pairs of terms *adjustment* and *maladjustment* and *normal* and *abnormal* are typically used interchangeably. Professionals from a number of different theoretical persuasions and backgrounds have offered definitions of these concepts. All of these, not too surprisingly, have some advantages and some disadvantages. An axiom worthy of note at this point states that if there are many alternative explanations for the same event or phenomenon, none of them is very satisfactory, and such seems to be the case in trying to define adjustment and maladjustment. Nevertheless, a brief review of some of the more prominent descriptive definitions may prove a useful way of introducing some of the critical issues in this area.

Statistical Definition

One approach, referred to as the statistical definition, focuses on the notion of degree. As Davidson and Neale (1974) point out, the basic idea is to measure a number of psychological characteristics of a large number of people and to regard the extremes of such characteristics as maladjusted. The average on the characteristics is then interpreted as adjusted. Thus, normal, or adjusted, is what most people do, think, or feel; abnormal, or maladjusted, is whatever is different from the majority. If we follow this definition closely either extreme of a behavioral characteristic would be included under the general category of maladjustment. Consequently, as Millon (1974) and Rosen, Fox, and Gregory (1972) point out, people having a very high IQ would be seen as abnormal, just as are mentally retarded individuals.

This statistical definition has some appeal, and certainly within any particular study or experiment the definition is easily specified. There are, however, a number of important questions to be considered. First, what set of psychological characteristics is to be included in the definition, and are all such characteristics to be viewed as equal in importance (Davison & Neale, 1974; Kisker, 1972; Sarason, 1972)? For example, is being extremely anxious of the same degree of significance as being extremely careless?

A second important consideration regarding the statistical definition involves its comparative nature. Within this approach, a particular individual is viewed as adjusted or maladjusted according to a comparison of him with some group of individuals, often called the reference group. The average characteristics of this group define normal. A question which immediately arises is, Who will constitute an appropriate reference group?" (Buss, 1966; Sarason, 1972). For example, according to automobile insurance rates, it is statistically abnormal to have an accident; however, if you are a single male between the ages of 18 and 26, it is less abnormal. As another example, for the population as a whole, it may be statistically abnormal to commit a crime. Yet for adolescent males living within a big-city ghetto it may be abnormal not to commit a crime. Would those individuals living within a city ghetto and committing crimes be comparable to individuals living outside of ghettos and also committing crimes? Essentially, the question here is, "Which reference group is appropriate for a given comparison?"

Any investigatory or mental health worker adopting this definition must, explicitly or implicitly, come to grips with two issues—which psychological characteristics are relevant, and who constitutes an appropriate reference group for any given individual?

Subjective Criteria in Defining Maladjustment

Another approach to the definition of maladjustment is based on subjective criteria, i.e., a person's self-report of psychological distress and discomfort (Millon, 1974). Usually, such reports involve declarations of unhappiness, anxiety, depression, or discontent. Indeed, it seems that many people receiving psychological care enter treatment with such complaints, and many therapists regard reduction in the frequency or intensity of such complaints as a sign of progress. From time to time, however, most people experience such unpleasant emotions; for most of us, such emotional experiences tend to be brief and only mildly disruptive. If such subjective reports are taken as a sufficient criterion of abnormality, then this definition would encompass many people for brief periods of time. Thus, according to this definition, maladjustment would be a transient state that most people experience (Millon, 1974). It may seem appealing to supplement this subjective definition with additional requirements, such as that the distress must be of such-and-such an intensity or duration (Buss, 1966). Certainly, such an addition would reduce the number of people defined as abnormal; however, such supplementary requirements typically introduce the statistical definition through the back door. How intense or prolonged must the discomfort be before constituting maladjustment? In such instances, the subjective discomfort expressed by the individual is merely the psychological characteristic to which the statistical definition is applied.

An additional difficulty with the subjective definition is inherent in its subjective character. Many psychologists question the relia- bility of subjective reports in general. Such skepticism rests on logical as well as pragmatic grounds. An observer can only hear the verbal statements of another and note his facial expressions and bodily movements. From such information, the observer may infer certain internal states of the other person; however, at best such inferences are only educated guesses. Likewise, verbal des- criptions of one's internal state may be influenced by many factors aside from the internal state itself (Ullman & Krasner, 1969). Such factors might include the situational context, the individual's verbal skills, his memory, and other like considerations. Finally, many psychologists and other mental health workers would argue that because an individual may be unaware of some of his feelings (Kisker, 1972) his self-reports would be inaccurate and incomplete, or that reports and indications of unusually bright and cheery states evidence maladjustment (Millon, 1972; Rosen, Fox & Gregory, 1972). These considerations taken together make reliance on subjective criteria alone for defining maladjustment rather hazardous.

Social Adaptation Definition

Within the social adaptation approach, adjustment is equated with being adapted to one's environment (Millon & Millon, 1974). This definition implies a dynamic process, focusing on the in- dividual's ability to meet changing conditions. It stresses the importance of a person's relationship with the external world, particularly his social milieu. Adjusted behavior is that which is seen as socially acceptable. Upon reflection, however, certain difficulties become apparent. For instance, being adjusted to one's social environment typically connotes social conformity. Within this definition adjusted individuals tend to be those who behave in ways expected by the social group, and maladjusted individuals are those who deviate from, or defy, such social norms. Such a criterion of social conformity poses two immediate problems. First, as Ullman and Krasner (1969) point out, our society is pluralistic, being made up of many different social groups with conflicting values and expectations. Conformity then involves adherence to some values that may be contradictory to others. Second, as Kleinmuntz (1974) points out, some societal values may be extremely destructive, e.g., those of Hitler's Germany. Would conformity to such societal values and expectations represent adjusted behavior?

Additionally, some deviation from whatever behaviors are expected is usually tolerated, and with such tolerance arises the question of degree once again. How much deviation will still be viewed as adjusted behavior? The issues inherent in the statistical approach become relevant, only without the benefit of data indicating the degree of conformity or nonconformity.

Likewise, adopting the social adjustment definition raises interpretive problems concerning the social reformer and the nonconformist. If through some act of God or miracle of nature, everyone were well-adjusted, there would be no social change generated from within a society. Everyone would be busy following accepted norms of conduct.

Abnormal As a Summary Term

Reflection upon the merits and limitations of each of the definitions of abnormal indicates how difficult it is to identify a statistical version of the concept. Part of the problem may reside in the fact that because the concept of adjustment includes a diversity of phenomena, various forms of maladjustment may rest on different definitions.

This diversity makes the task of developing a theoretically precise definition of maladjustment quite burdensome. Buss (1966) has argued that, from a practical point of view, several criteria are typically used in categorizing someone as maladjusted or abnormal. He suggests that the term is applied on the basis of three criteria—*subjective discomfort, bizarreness of behavior,* and *inefficiency.* These criteria borrow various parts of the previously considered definitions, and the shortcomings of each should be kept in mind.

By the term *subjective discomfort,* Buss includes physical complaints caused by psychological factors and enduring anxiety and depression. By the term *bizarreness of behavior,* Buss is referring to "abnormal deviations from accepted standards of behavior or deviations from consensually defined reality."

The latter aspect of this definition refers to such phenomena as hallucinations where the individual has a perception having only a minimal sensory basis, e.g., he hears voices when there is no one present. By the term *inefficiency,* Buss refers to the individual's inability to meet social responsibilities and duties. Further, he suggests that inefficiency can be used as a criterion either in terms of a large discrepancy between an individual's potential and his actual performance or in terms of the individual's inability to meet whatever requirements exist for his social status.

Although these criteria remain somewhat nebulous and imprecise, they do seem to provide a rough idea of the kinds of functioning generally included under the category of maladjustment. Consequently, as we keep the various limitations and difficulties in mind, these criteria will be employed within this volume as a working definition of maladjustment.

EXPLAINING ADJUSTMENT

Up to this point, the discussion has been focused on the criteria to be used in reaching judgments about *whether* a certain behavior pattern is most appropriately viewed as adjusted or as maladjusted. We now turn to the question of *why* certain individuals display adjusted behavior while other individuals display maladjusted behavior.

A frequently repeated anecdote about several blind men and an elephant may prove a useful introduction to our brief discussion. It seems that a very studious prince in ancient India wanted to have a better understanding of the elephant. As he could afford it, he commissioned the four wisest men in his domain to conduct an extensive study of the elephant. It so happened that all four of the wise men were blind. To make their task easier they decided to have an elephant brought to them, and each of them began to examine the elephant very carefully. Each one of the four sages positioned himself at a different part of the elephant's huge figure. One of the wise men concentrated on the front leg, another concentrated on the trunk, still another focused his attention on the elephant's huge side, and the last wise man focused his attention on the elephant's tail. In order to avoid any bias in his report, each of the four sages prepared an independent report on the elephant. The reports, of course, each reflected the particular way in which the sage had studied the elephant. The wise man who had studied the elephant's foot argued strongly that the elephant was very much like a tree trunk and should therefore be regarded as a plant. The wise man who had concentrated on the trunk argued that the elephant had much in common with the snake and further that it would make a useful addition to the palace plumbing system. The sage who focused his attention on the elephant's side suggested that the elephant was most like a wall and that elephants might be regarded most usefully as some form of simple architectural structure. Finally, the wise man who had studied the elephant's tail suggested that the elephant might be grown commercially as a source of rather low-grade broomstraw.

It is clear in the anecdote that each of the four sages adopted a distinctly different perspective, and the conclusions each drew about elephants in general were clearly influenced by the particular perspective from which he had examined the elephant. In trying to draw conclusions about the origins of adjusted and maladjusted behaviors, different psychologists have tended to approach the issue from somewhat different perspectives. Just as the wise men emphasized different aspects of the elephant, so different psychologists have emphasized different causal factors to explain the origins of behavior (Price, 1971; Zubin, 1972). We will briefly examine five of the most prevalent perspectives in contemporary clinical psychology: the ecological perspective, the humanistic perspective, the behavioral perspective, the biophysical perspective, and the psychoanalytic perspective.

The Ecological Perspective

Psychologists using the ecological perspective suggest that the-degree of adjusted behavior shown by a particular individual is a function of the ecological position the individual occupies (Goldenberg, 1973; Zubin, 1972). The effects of sociocultural factors such as socioeconomic status (Hollingshead & Redlich, 1958), the economy (Brenner, 1973), family patterns (Frank, 1965), and other factors have been related to varying degrees of adjustment. Psychologists looking at behavior from the ecological perspective have suggested that the social context of behavior is a major determinant in the decision to label certain behaviors as adjusted or maladjusted. Furthermore, once an individual has been labelled as maladjusted, sociocultural forces may play a major role in maintaining his maladjusted behavior (Scheff, 1966). Social forces are seen as playing a major role in the origin, in the decision to label behavior as adjusted or maladjusted, and in the maintenance of the behavior once it is initiated. From the ecological perspective, then, the degree of adjustment an individual demonstrates is seen as resulting from the interplay of sociocultural factors in a complex ecological net.

The Humanistic Perspective

Perhaps the most optimistic of the perspectives on adjustment, the humanistic viewpoint is focused on "growth" and the "realization of human potential." From this perspective all individuals are seen as being capable of fulfilling their inherent potential, and man is seen as basically good (Maslow, 1967; Rogers, 1961, 1965). When an individual exhibits behavior we would call maladjusted, the individual is viewed as having been exposed to an environment that somehow blocked that individual's innate tendency to grow and to fulfill his inherent potential. From this perspective, one of the major factors that may block an individual's growth is the denial or distortion of certain experiences because of their incongruence with his self-concept (Rogers, 1959). This distortion of experience can then provide the basis for behavior patterns the clinician would call neurotic or, in cases of extreme distortion, for behavior the clinician would call psychotic.

The humanistic perspective places a major emphasis on the study of "healthy" as opposed to "disturbed" persons (Maslow, 1954, 1965), and the perspective sees maladjusted behavior as the result of factors that impede the innate positive growth of which all individuals are capable.

The Behavioral Perspective

From the behavioral perspective behaviors whether adjusted or maladjusted, are viewed as originating in the individual's learning history. The behavioral perspective sees behavior as the result of three main factors: classical conditioning, operant conditioning, and imitation learning (Bandura, 1969; Mischel, 1968, 1971, 1973a). Although many proponents of the behavioral perspective do not ignore personality characteristics as a source of behavior (Mischel, 1973b), the main focus of the behavioral approach is on the critical role of environmental contingencies in initiating and maintaining behavior (Bandura, 1969; Mischel, 1968, 1971; Wolpe, 1973).

In attempting to understand why a particular individual exhibits either adjusted or maladjusted behavior, psychologists utilizing the behavioral perspective attempt to conduct a *functional analysis* of behavior. A functional analysis of behavior is simply an attempt to determine the environmental factors that change with changes in the behavior of interest (Mischel, 1971). In other words, the psychologist using this perspective is interested in determining observable events that happen before, at the same time as, and after the behavior of interest occurs. The basic emphasis of this perspective is that behavior, whether adjusted or maladjusted, is a function of past and present learning.

The Biophysical Perspective

From the biophysical perspective, maladjusted behavior is seen as the result of a dysfunction in the physical make-up of the individual as a result of heredity, biochemical disorders, or physical damage to the central nervous system. From this perspective, maladjustment is simply the behavioral manifestation of an actual physical dysfunction of some kind.

There are data which suggest that at least for some categories of maladjustment hereditary components play a significant role (Slater & Cowie, 1971; Rosenthal, 1970). Furthermore, there are data which suggest that biochemical and physical factors may play a significant role in some types of maladjusted behaviors as well (Costello, 1970). The evidence does not indicate that all instances of maladjusted behavior are necessarily caused by physical disorders, but the available data do suggest that the biophysical perspective receives support in many instances. The essence of the biophysical perspective is that behavior is viewed as primarily a function of the individual's biophysical make-up.

The Psychoanalytic Perspective

Sigmund Freud may well be the one individual who has had the most pervasive influence on the social sciences. His complex psychoanalytic theory has gone through countless revisions by other psychoanalytic theorists. From the psychoanalytic perspective, human beings are seen as continuously affected by the interplay and conflict of psychological forces, most of which are unconscious. Humans are born with certain basic motives, and these basic motives are the prime movers for all the behavior the individual manifests. According to the psychoanalytic perspective, all behavior is motivated. Slips of the tongue (Freudian slips), forgetting, word reversals, and every other behavior is caused by motives that usually are "unconscious," unknown to the individual manifesting the behavior.

Whether an individual displays adjusted or maladjusted behavior is also ultimately a result of the interplay of psychological forces. From the psychoanalytic perspective, the socialization patterns and child-rearing practices to which an individual is exposed play a crucial role in determining his prevalent behavior patterns, because an individual's background is crucial in determining the way in which the psychological forces within him will interplay. When behavior that we would call maladjusted occurs, the observed behavior is regarded as a surface manifestation of unconscious motives and conflicts. Hence, from the psychoanalytical perspective, both adjusted and maladjusted behavior are seen as the result of innate psychological forces, mostly unconscious, in conflict with the demands of social living (Maddi, 1972). The true cause of an observed behavior will be truly understood only when the unconscious factors that lead to the behavior are uncovered.

From the psychoanalytic perspective, the cause of maladjustment must be looked for within the individual, in the part of the individual's psychological make-up that is unconscious.

Brief Review

We have examined five of the most prevalent explanations of adjustment-maladjustment in contemporary psychology: the ecological perspective, the humanistic perspective, the behavioral perspective, the biophysical perspective, and the psychoanalytic perspective.[1] We began the discussion of casual perspectives by recounting the story of the four wise men and the elephant as an illustration of how perspectives can influence conclusions about the phenomenon studied. It was not our intention in using the elephant anecdote to suggest that psychologists of all perspectives are metaphorical blind men. Although most psychologists would

[1] As discussions of the various perspectives of adjustment have purposefully been brief, some oversimplification may have occurred. For further readings on these perspectives readers may find the following sources useful:

The ecological perspective—Price (1971), Scheff (1966), Zubin (1972).

The humanistic perspective—Maslow (1965), Rogers (1961).

The behavioral perspective—Bandura (1969), Mischel (1968, 1971), Wolpe (1973)

The biophysical perspective—Meehl (1962), Rosenthal (1971).

The psychoanalytic perspective—Hall (1954).

probably argue (depending on their own favorite perspectives) that some of the perspectives are more useful than others, it would seem that all of the perspectives discussed have at least some utility in explaining some forms of behavior.

Another perspective on adjustment, which does not replace but complements the others just discussed, is one the authors call the *critical problems perspective*.

THE CRITICAL PROBLEMS PERSPECTIVE

Each of the previous approaches identified a relatively stable and persistent source of influences on the individual. The critical problems perspective, on the other hand, focuses on more-or-less discrete situations and events which may potentially lead to subjective discomfort, bizarreness of behavior, or inefficiency. Thus, the emphasis is on problems which may be upsetting and troublesome for the people encountering them.

Writing under the general rubric of crisis theory, many psychologists and psychiatrists (Caplan, 1964; Farberow, 1967; Kalis, 1970; McGee, 1973) over the past decade have adopted this critical problems perspective. Clinics such as Benjamin Rush Center in Los Angeles and the Walk-In Clinic of the New York Medical College-Metropolitan Hospital Center, as well as emergency psychiatric services at many metropolitan hospitals, have been based on this approach. These centers, as part of a broad move in community psychology and psychiatry, have attempted to reach people during the period of their greatest distress. These centers and clinics have frequently been referred to as "walk-in" facilities, emphasizing their contrast with more traditional clinics that require appointments sometimes weeks in advance (Fensterheim & Schrenzel, 1967). At walk-in clinics, treatment typically concentrates on the situation or event bringing the individual into the clinic and on the way that individual has reacted to that circumstance. Therapists attempt to aid the person in regaining his former functioning, concentrating on what can be done at the moment to improve the individual's psychological state (Jacobson et al., 1965). Generally, the course of treatment is ten or fewer sessions. Beyond providing immediate relief, some crisis theorists have argued, such timely intervention reduces the chance that an individual will develop more prolonged forms of maladjustment (Langsley et al., 1968).

In developing crisis theory, authors have most heavily emphasized the nature of the individual's reaction to whatever stressful situation may have arisen. For instance, Dixon and Burns (1974) suggest that a crisis may be defined as a significant disruption such that an individual is not able to maintain normal functioning and must resort to new strategies or modes of coping. Such a state may yield some resolution, or it may result in a state of chronic dysfunction. Several stages in a crisis reaction can be identified, according to Dixon and Burns (1974). The first is marked by "a sharp rise in tension, followed by feelings of helplessness and confusion. The individual does not know how to think about his problem, how to evaluate the crisis or how to evaluate the reality of the situation. He cannot seem to marshal problem-solving resources." The second stage has been described as the use of new or unusual problem-solving mechanisms. Pasewark and Albers (1972) describe the development of disorganization, detachment, and apathy if there is no resolution.

According to Caplan (1964), situations or events leading to such reactions consist of various kinds of abrupt life changes—occasions when the individual's pattern of living is substantially altered. As several crisis theorists have noted, such life changes can be usefully divided into two categories, *maturational* crises and *situational* crises (Aguilera et al., 1970; Caplan, 1964). Aguilera et al. (1970) state that, "Maturational crises have been described as normal processes of growth and development. They usually evolve over an extended period of time, such as the transition into adolescence, and they frequently require that the individual make many characterological changes."

Situational crises, on the other hand, arise from external sources, such as the death of a loved one, severe physical illness or debilitation, illegitimate pregnancy, abortion, or divorce. As the term *crisis* has been closely associated with a focus on an individual's reaction rather than the situation or event giving rise to that reaction, it has seemed more appropriate within this book to refer to roughly the same situations and events as *critical life problems*.

Such critical problems are encountered by most people, directly or indirectly, during the course of their lives, and certainly they represent challenges to the psychological well-being of each individual. A listing of all potentially hazardous situations and events would be unmanageable and, in part, would depend on the personal history of each individual. We have attempted in this book to select a set of situations that appear to be of present concern for many, including clinicians, and for which the social sciences have provided some empirical evidence.

Thus, with the exception of a last chapter devoted to describing sources and forms of psychological help, each chapter focuses on one such critical problem. The nature and scope of the problem, as well as some of the ways in which people react to it, are described. Finally, where appropriate, some suggestions are made concerning what might be done to deal with such a problem constructively.

REFERENCES

AGUILERA, D. C., MESSICK, J. M. FARRELL, M. S. *Crisis intervention: theory and Methodology*. St. Louis: C. V. Mosby, 1970.

BANDURA, A. *Principles of behavior modification*. New York: Holt, Rinehart and Winston, 1969.

BRENNER, M. H. *Mental illness and the economy*. Cambridge, Mass.: Harvard University Press, 1973.

BURNS, J. L. & DIXON, M. C. Telephone crisis intervention and crisis volunteers: Some considerations for training. *Amer. J. Commun. Psychol.*, in press.

BUSS, A. H. *Psychopathology*. New York : John Wiley & Sons, Inc., 1966.

CAPLAN, G. *Symptoms of preventative psychiatry*. New York: Basic Books, 1964.

COSTELLO, C. G. *Symptoms of psychopathology: A handbook*. New York: John Wiley & Sons, 1970

DAVISON, G. C. & NEALE, J. M. *Abnormal psychology: An experimental clinical approach*. New York: John Wiley & Sons, 1974.

FARBEROW, N. W. Crisis, disaster and suicide: Theory and therapy. In E. S. Schneiderman (Ed.). *Essays in self-destruction*. New York: Science House, 1967.

FRANK, G. H. The role of the family in the development of psychopathology. *Psychol. Bull.*, 1965, *64*, 191–205.

HALL, C. S. *Primer of Freudian psychology*. Cleveland: World Publishing Co., 1954.

HOLLINGSHEAD, A. B. & REDLICH, F. C. *Social class and mental illness*. New York: John Wiley & Sons, 1958.

JACOBSON, E. *Depression: Comparative studies of normal, neurotic and psychotic conditions.* New York: International Universities Press, 1971.

KISKER, G. W. *The disorganized personality.* New York: McGraw-Hill, 1972.

KLEINMUNTZ, B. *Essentials of abnormal psychology.* New York Harper and Row, 1974.

LANGSLEY, D. G. & KAPLEN, D. M. *The treatment of families in crisis* New York: Grune & Stratton, 1968.

MADDI, S. *Personality theories: A comparative analysis.* Homewood, Ill: Dorsey, 1972.

MALIS, B. L. Crisis theory: Its relevance for community psychology and directions for development. In D. Adelson & B. L. Malis, (Eds.). *Community psychology and mental health.* Scranton, Pa.: Chandler, 1970.

MASLOW, A. H. Lessons from peak experiences. In R. Farson (Ed.). *Science and human affairs.* Palo Alto: Science and Behavior, 1965.

MASLOW, A. H. *Motivation and personality.* New York: Harper, 1954.

MASLOW, A. H. Neurosis as a failure of personal growth. *Humanities,* 1967, *3,* 153–170.

McGEE, R. *Crisis intervention in the community.* Baltimore: University Park Press, 1974.

MEEHL, P. E. Schizotaxia, schizotypy, schizophrenia. *Amer. psychol.* 1962, *17,* 827–838.

MILLON, T. *Theories of psychopathology and personality.* Second edition. Philadelphia, Pa.: W. B. Saunders, Co., 1973.

MISCHEL, W. *Introduction to Personality.* New York: Holt, Rinehart and Winston, 1971.

MISCHEL, W. On the empirical dilemmas of psychodynamic approaches: Issues and alternatives. *J. Abnorm. Psychol.* 1973, *82,* 335–344(a).

MISCHEL, W. *Personality and assessment.* New York: John Wiley & Sons, 1968.

MISCHEL, W. Toward a cognitive social learning reconceptualization of personality. *Psychol. Rev.* 1973, *80,* 252–283(b).

PASEWARK, R. A. & ALBERS, D. A. Crisis intervention: Theory in search of a program. *Social Work, 17,* 70–77, 1972.

PRICE, R. H. *Abnormal behavior—Perspective in conflict.* New York: Holt, Rinehart and Winston, 1971.

ROGERS, C. R. A humanistic conception of man. In R. Farson (Ed.). *Science and Human Affairs.* Palo Alto: Science and Behavior, 1965.

ROGERS, C. R. A theory of therapy, personality, and interpersonal relationships, as developed in the client-centered framework. In S. Koch (Ed.). *Psychology: A study of a science,* Vol. 3. New York: McGraw-Hill, 1959.

ROGERS, C. R. *On becoming a person.* Boston: Houghton Mifflin, 1961.

ROSEN, E., FOX, R. E. & GREGORY, I. *Abnormal psychology.* Second edition. Philadelphia, Pa.: W. B. Saunders Company, 1972.

ROSENTHAL, D. *Genetic theory and abnormal behavior.* New York: McGraw-Hill, 1970.

ROSENTHAL, D. *Genetics of psychopathology.* New York: McGraw-Hill, 1971.

SARASON, I. G. *Abnormal psychology: The problem of maladaptive behavior.* New York: Appleton-Century Crofts, 1972.

SCHEFF, T. J. *Being mentally ill: A sociological theory.* Aldine, 1966.

SLATER, E. & COWIE, V. *The genetics of mental disorders.* London: Oxford University Press, 1971.

ULLMAN, L. P. & KRASNER, L. A. *A psychological approach to abnormal behavior.* New Jersey: Prentice-Hall, 1969.

WOLPE, J. *The practice of behavior therapy.* Second edition. New York: Pergamon, 1973.

ZUBIN, J. Scientific models for psychopathology in the 1970's. *Seminars in Psychiatry,* 1972, *4,* 283–296.

Adolescence: A Period of Conflict and Transition

CHAPTER 2

IGNATIUS J. TONER

Few periods of life have been the object of such stereotypic conjecture as the period of adolescence. Adolescence has been commonly labeled as a period of increased immorality, political dissent, excessive alcohol and drug use, and sexual permissiveness. The term "infancy" suggests helplessness; "childhood" suggests innocence; "adolescence" suggests neither. Next to old people, adolescents probably suffer the greatest prejudice based on age of any group in this society. Yet, surprisingly, empirical data on how adolescents think and act are remarkably scarce. Even though the adolescent years comprise more than 10 per cent of the average life span, this period is the object of less than 2 per cent of all psychological articles since 1942. Before 1942, less than 1 per cent of articles in psychology were devoted to adolescence (L'Abate, 1971). Developmental psychologists have preferred to concentrate on the first dozen years of life and, indeed, the volume and quality of objective information on the early years (e. g., Hetherington & Parke, 1975) are a tribute to the ability of man to study himself. Clinical and social psychologists (e.g., Davison & Neale, 1974; Secord & Backman, 1964) have studied the post-adolescent years

The author gratefully acknowledges the valuable editorial assistance of Ms. Pamela Kidder in the preparation of this manuscript.

with equal fervor. Their research hero, the college sophomore, is generally regarded as a representative of normal adult thinking and behavior even though he/she can be equally considered as representative of normal adolescent thinking and behavior.

Adolescence is a period associated with difficulties not only for the individual growing up but also for adults who interact with the adolescent individual. Not only are physical changes occurring during this period, but more importantly the individual begins to develop new patterns of thought and social interaction. The goal of the present chapter is not to cover all of the possible problems associated with this critical period in life. The goal of this chapter is to serve as an introduction to the critical life problem of living through adolescence. In this chapter we will concentrate on four specific areas in which adolescents begin to develop new ways of thinking and acting: *morality, political thinking, drug use,* and *sexuality.*

Whereas in other chapters of this book our main concern is with the consequences and solutions for certain problem situations, in this chapter we will focus on the description of the situation itself, the critical problem of going through adolescence.

THE LIMITS OF ADOLESCENCE

The onset of adolescence is often considered to be the moment when reproduction is possible, generally between 10 and 15 years of age, depending on the individual. Adolescence is thought to come to an end when "full sexual maturity" has been achieved. However, the great variance in when particular individuals meet the criterion for onset and the great dispute over what "full sexual maturity" really means has led psychologists to adopt the layman's approach, it is now accepted that an individual begins his/her adolescent period when just about everybody starts considering him/her as an adolescent; the individual is no longer an adolescent when just about everybody starts considering him/her as an adult.

The period of adolescence is one of change from childhood to adulthood. When the changes are dramatic, as in the case of adolescent morality, political activity, drug use, and sexuality, they can lead to stressful personal conflict between the individual and the people and institutions affected by the changes. The problems brought about by changes in thinking and behavior are not unusual, as virtually all adolescents go through them. Perhaps it is more unusual if the changes do not occur in an adolescent or if the changes do not result in conflict between the adolescent and others.

THE DEVELOPMENT OF MORALITY

Adolescence represents a period of growing autonomy and independence for the individual. The social horizons of the adolescent are expanding and he/she is likely to be exposed to a diversity of values and expectations. Although such changes are viewed as important positive steps in development, they may also produce conflicts for the individual and his family. Potential family problems are described in Chapter 4.

For the individual much of the change occurring in adolescence may be viewed in terms of moral development. With an increase in freedom of behavior, the adolescent faces a variety of moral decisions in such areas as political beliefs, drug use, and sexual behavior, to name but a few. Thus, understanding moral development in adolescence will help us in understanding the behavior of adolescents in other areas.

The development of attitudes and behavior which involve judgments of right and wrong has been of considerable interest to developmental psychologists. Many of the writings of Sigmund Freud (e.g., 1923) are concerned with the feelings generated by the conflict between the powerful, pleasure-oriented motives and the need to prevent antisocial impulses from controlling the personality. However, Freudian theory has not generated as much research about moral development as have two other impressive theories of development, *the cognitive-development approach* of the famous Swiss psychologist Jean Piaget (e.g., 1932) and his American counterpart Lawrence Kohlberg (e.g., 1969) and *the social-learning approach* as exemplified in the research and writings of Albert Bandura and Richard Walters (e.g., Bandura & Walters, 1963). The research these two major approaches have generated has contributed much to our understanding of the development of morality. Furthermore, the theories are not neces-sarily mutually exclusive but rather address themselves to different aspects of morality. Cognitive-developmentalists study morality in terms of conscious prior *judgments* concerning the rightness or wrongness of specific courses of action. These psychologists look for the higher mental processes that underlie moral judgments.

Social-learning theorists, on the other hand, are more con-cerned with *what* people do than with *why* people act as they do. Morality, for the social-learning theorist, is regarded in terms of specific acts which society might label as right or wrong. The acts are established and maintained, as are virtually all other behaviors, through reward, punishment, and observational (or imitative) learning.

The Cognitive-Developmental Approach

Lawrence Kohlberg (e.g., 1969) and his colleagues at Harvard have proposed a highly detailed account of the development of moral judgments. Like Piaget, Kohlberg suggests a stage notion of development. However, Kohlberg's theory has six rather than two separate stages in the development of moral judgment. The six stages are age-related.

Kohlberg's first stage of moral reasoning is characterized by an obedience and punishment orientation. Judgments of right and wrong are based on a deference to superior authority, because punishment is feared if the authority is not obeyed. Judgments made at Kohlberg's first stage, as with Piaget's first stage, are based on the consequences of action.

The second stage of Kohlberg's sequence is characterized by a naive, pleasure-seeking orientation in which motivation to behave morally results from the self-centered desire to obtain rewards through conformity.

Stage three has been labeled the stage of "good boy/nice girl" morality. At this stage a person behaves morally in order to main-tain good relations with others and to gain their approval. Unlike people at the first two stages, those at the third stage may begin to judge behavior in terms of intention of the actor as well as in terms of consequences of the act.

The fourth stage is characterized by the motivation to do one's duty to keep the social order intact. Laws must be obeyed so that society may continue to function. Thus, morality is judged by adherence to the rigid rules set down by the society. Kohlberg believes that most adolescents and adults achieve stages three and four and than many, if not most, Americans remain in these stages with no further development.

Some people do progress beyond stages three and four. The attainment of more advanced stages is rare before adolescence because the final two stages of the sequence require very sophisticated cognitive abilities that usually are not fully developed before adolescence. Stages five and six are of special interest to our discussion because many adolescents appear to achieve the level of moral thinking characteristic of stage five and some adolescents appear even to attain stage-six moral thinking.

A person operating at stage five adheres to the morality of contract, individual rights, and democratically accepted law. Laws are to be obeyed, but obedience may be modified by a consideration of the welfare and rights of others. The law is not the final determinant of behavior because it may be changed at times to benefit the larger number of people.

Stage six, the highest of the sequential stages of moral thinking, is attained by very few people. Morality at this level is based on individual principles and individual conscience. Unlike earlier stages in which the law or the greater good is the basis of morality, in stage six the only judge is the self. Self-condemnation is to be avoided whether or not it corresponds to possible condemnation by others. Similarly, self-approval is sought rather than the approval of others. There is a reliance on such abstract principles as justice, equality, compassion and true respect for others. Such moral reasoning demands some of the most sophisticated cognitive abilities that man can possess.

Kohlberg (1963) has observed that about 30 per cent of a sample of 16-year-olds gave stage-four responses, and about 25 per cent of the sample gave stage-three responses when asked to verbally respond to a story depicting a moral dilemma. Only about 10 per cent of the 16-year-olds gave stage one responses and another 10 per cent gave stage two responses. Younger children (age 7) tended to make moral judgments at stages one and two. At the more sophisticated end of the moral judgment sequence, about 20 per cent of the 16-year-olds gave stage-five responses and about 5 per cent were judged to be at stage six. No thinking at stage four, five, or six was detected in 7-year-olds and none from stage five or six was found in 10-year-olds.

The implication that emerges is that adolescence is the earliest time of life in which individuals can be found at each of the six stages of moral judgment. Kohlberg has further noted that, after adolescence, there is relatively little likelihood of advancement to higher moral stages. The bases for judging right and wrong and the motivation for action changes throughout the early years of life, but the most dramatic changes occur during the adolescent years. Formerly held beliefs give way to new ways of thinking. Parents and other authority figures who had become accustomed to regular obedience when the individual was at the earlier stages of moral thinking are puzzled and challenged by the sophisticated moral philosopher that is the adolescent. Reasonable conflict with others is not in any way a negative influence on the adolescent's moral development. Indeed, such conflict may well impel the adolescent to new and higher levels of moral thinking. Although the cognitive-developmental position is being challenged by some researchers (Kurtines & Greif, 1974), certainly Kohlberg and Piaget have provided a refreshing perspective on the development of moral thinking in the individual. In both systems, the adolescent emerges as a self-governor of his/her own behavior.

Such changes in moral thinking will be accompanied by changes in the way in which adolescents approach the problem areas of politics, drugs, and sex. These problem areas can provide a significant source of conflict between the adolescent and others, including family, teachers, church, and police. These conflicts can facilitate the adolescent's moral development and are in fact necessary for such development to continue (Turiel, 1974).

The Social-Learning Approach

Although the cognitive-developmentalists have provided a theory that helps to explain the thinking that underlies adolescent behavior, it is the social-learning theorists who provide a theory that explains what specific behaviors the adolescent might demonstrate.

Social-learning theorists contend that what people do is more important than what they think. Researchers with this orientation attempt to account for ongoing behavior and to predict future behavior according to their understanding of the demands of the present situation as affected by the learning history of the individual. What people do is a function of what they have learned to do. The individual is likely to perform in the manner that he/she has been rewarded for in the past and is less likely to behave in a way that has been punished in the past. In addition, other people may serve as models of behavior for the developing individual.

Because reinforcement contingencies are not static but constantly changing, the period of adolescence with its typical exposure to new agents of reinforcement and new models often produces altered moral behavior. What was rewarded, punished, and modelled by parents and peers during early childhood may well be different from what new peers and the new, autonomous self of the adolescent reinforce and demand. It is not surprising that adolescents undergoing such changes may at times feel overwhelmed.

In the remainder of this chapter, general patterns of adolescent political thinking, drug use, and sexuality will be described. At the foundation of these new behavior patterns are the new reinforcement contingencies and the new models that the adolescent encounters, as well as the emerging moral philosophy of self-governance. This is a philosophy that demands that, for the first time in his/her life, the individual be the primary determinant of his/her action. In fact, adolescents who have achieved the higher stages of moral thought appear more resistant to the pressure of other's opinions than are adolescents at lower stages of moral thought (Fodor, 1972). Therefore, while adolescent behavior can be controlled to some extent by the reactions of others (LaVoie & Looft, 1973; LaVoie, 1973, 1974), their decisions and behavior are marked by dramatically increasing independence.

With this general framework in mind, we turn our attention now to three general areas that seem to be critical for the adolescent: political growth, drug use, and sexuality.

POLITICAL GROWTH IN ADOLESCENCE

Conflict is often observed between adolescents and their elders on political issues. A classic investigation by Adelson and O'Neil (1966) assessed the growth of political ideas in adolescents. In this study, the adolescent years appear to be critical ones in the development of a political philosophy in the individual. Political understanding increases throughout adolescence. The child and pre-adolescent display an incomplete and garbled sense of political order. These younger individuals know random politicians and party labels, but their understanding of politics is highly personalized and marked by "half-understood platitudes." However, by the end of adolescence, the individual has generally become well-acquainted with the political aspects of his society.

Consistent with more recent data (Hampden-Turner & Whitten, 1971), Adelson and O'Neill noted that the course of the development of political ideas closely parallels the emergence of more sophisticated moral judgments in the adolescent. There develops in adolescence a "sense of community," a sense of social and political collectivity (i.e., "the people"), as well as an increased awareness of organized government. Eleven-year-olds tend to evaluate government in terms of its effect on them personally, not in terms of the impact of government on the larger society. When challenged on their political philosophy, 11-and 13-year-olds were found to be unable to justify their political ideas beyond a simple statement of political preference. These younger pre-adolescents displayed respect for and submission to the power of government, which identified them as true moral realists. However, significant shifts were noted in the older adolescents who displayed more morally autonomous thinking in making political decisions. The political ideology of the older adolescent was characterized by a concern for the welfare of others and an appreciation of other people's views.

Whereas the pre-adolescent held an assortment of essentially unrelated and often inconsistent rules of governance, the older adolescent was more likely to have achieved a semblance of internally consistent and less fragile political and moral beliefs. The development of such a system is gradual, but Adelson and

O'Neil noted that the biggest changes in political thinking seem to occur between 11 and 13 years of age.

The changing nature of the adolescent's moral thinking may have a profound effect upon his participation in the social systems with which he/she becomes acquainted. Changing moral and political beliefs are likely to conflict with the beliefs of parents, teachers, and religious leaders who were accustomed to having the child mirror their ideas and opinions. The development of principles of self-governance in the adolescent is normal, and the negative reaction to this development by many elements of society is just as normal. This societal reaction may be heightened when the adolescent's political ideas lead to political action.

While many recent studies have attempted to provide a psychological profile of student activists (e.g., Winborn & Jansen, 1967; Feuer, 1969; Keniston, 1971; Kerpelman, 1972; Conger, 1973), the impact of political beliefs and action on the adolescent's interaction with others has never been properly investigated. Thus, while such research as Thomas (1971) and Kraut and Lewis (1975) indicates that liberal, politically active adolescents tend to come from liberal, politically active families, the question of whether the adolescent's political activity is a cause or an effect of his family's political philosophy remains untested. The determinants of the adolescent's political behavior remain unknown with the exception that the behavior is the product of a widening perspective on the world—a perspective that reflects the increasing moral sophistication of the adolescent.

ADOLESCENTS AND DRUGS

In his book *Adolescence and Youth* (1973), John Janeway Conger of the School of Medicine of the University of Colorado introduced his fine chapter on adolescent drug usage by noting that attitudes toward drug use may be the most significant area of disagreement between adolescents and their parents. Objective information is often difficult to find because of the emotionality involved on both sides of the question of whether drug use is to be allowed in our society. Marijuana research has been a special victim of such non-objectivity. Only recently have legitimate attempts been made to assess the effects of this psychoactive drug on the user (Consumer Reports, 1975a). To further aggravate an emotion-charged problem, the issue has been subject to political pressures that have impeded sound medical and psychological investigations.

An attempt will be made here to present objective, current data on drug use by adolescents. We begin with a discussion of adolescent use of one of the most commonly used psychoactive drugs, alcohol. Adolescent drinking trends seem remarkably like adult drinking patterns (Bacon & Jones, 1968). Surveys have indicated that, although only about 10 per cent of high school students drink regularly, 80 per cent of college students report regular use of alcohol. The consumption of alcohol appears to increase throughout adolescence.

Like the research on adolescent political activists, research on adolescent drinkers is almost always correlational; consequently, cause and effect relationships between drinking and family/personality variables are largely unknown. Furthermore, investigation of the reinforcement contingencies that maintain and strengthen drinking behavior is needed. The taste and effect of alcohol may be rewarding to many adolescents. However, there is little doubt that peer pressures and peer reinforcement contribute to alcohol usage (e.g. Alexander, 1964; Riester & Zucker, 1968; Eisenthal & Udin, 1972).

Most adults do not seem alarmed by the increased legal use of alcohol by adolescents, though the increased use of other drugs by adolescents has been disturbing to the older generation. It appears to many adolescents that adults are more concerned with the illegality of using certain drugs than they are with the potential harm involved in using the drug. Thus, the adult who smokes several packs of cigarettes a day, who has a cocktail or two before and after every dinner, and who takes tranquilizers to relax may find the occasional use of an illegal drug such as marijuana by his/her adolescent son or daughter highly disconcerting.

Marijuana usage in adolescents has been increasing rapidly, and marijuana is at present the most widely used of all of the illegal psychoactive drugs among adolescents. Recent surveys (Mizner, Barter, & Werme, 1970; *Playboy*, 1970; Gallup, 1972) have noted

that, whereas only 5 per cent of all college students had tried marijuana in 1967, the percentage had risen to 22 two years later, and
to 42 in 1970. In 1972, 51 per cent of all college students claim to
have tried the drug. For many adolescents, peer pressures appear
to stimulate marijuana usage, and it is rarely condoned by parents.
As in the case of research on political activism, specific information on how the use of marijuana affects the ongoing social
interactions of the user is needed.

Other drugs are used considerably less frequently than alcohol
and marijuana by adolescents and young adults. Young people
seem wary of such drugs as heroin, cocaine, LSD, and mescaline.
Student surveys published in *Playboy* magazine in 1970 and 1971
found that, while 13 per cent of college students claimed to be
frequent users of marijuana, 1 per cent or less of the sample
claimed to use barbiturates, LSD, or hard drugs frequently. As
with alcohol and marijuana, the use of "hard drugs" by high
school students seems less than the use of such drugs by college
students.

Adolescent drug usage can properly be viewed as both a cause
and an effect of conflict between the adolescent and his world. The
dramatic increase in the use of marijuana during the past decade
indicates that a true generation gap exists in this area. If marijuana
usage is as extensive as the surveys suggest, for many young
people who may already question the necessity of laws governing
their personal lives, each "puff" is reaffirming their legal "crimin-
ality" (Consumer Reports, 1975b). Further, drugs may be used by
adolescents as a means of escape from or avoidance of adjustment
problems and conflict. The cyclic relationship between drug usage
and adolescent conflict with authority figures demands increased
empirical attention.

ADOLESCENT SEXUALITY

Long before adolescence, the developing individual has fairly
well-defined ideas of what behaviors are considered appropriate
for his/her sex (Kohlberg, 1966), and he/she is generally behaving
in accordance with these considerations (Mischel, 1970). Within a
given culture, ideas as to what behavior is appropriate for men

and what behavior is appropriate for women are fairly clear-cut and consistent. For example, in most Western societies, females are usually expected to be warmer and more expressive than males while males are usually expected to be more controlling and assertive than females (Broverman, Vogel, Broverman, Clarkson & Rosenkrantz, 1972).

While the general area of sex-role development has been extensively treated by psychologists studying childhood (e.g., Hetherington & Parke, 1975), the emergence of sexuality has generally been left to psychologists studying adolescence. As noted earlier, the period of adolescence has been delineated by sexual markers, i.e., the onset of adolescence occurring when reproduction is possible and the ending of adolescence marked by the attainment of full sexual maturity. Sexual activity and interest in sexuality increases dramatically during the adolescent years. Some earlier research indicates that the "sex drive" is stronger for male than for female adolescents (Douvan & Adelson, 1966). However, recent research has questioned the notion of differing drive levels.

A recent survey (Hunt, 1970) revealed that only about 10 per cent of the adolescent females interviewed believed that "women have innately less capacity for sexual pleasure than men." Further, Masters and Johnson (1970) suggest that women often have a greater capacity to respond sexually than do men. The discrepancy with findings of past studies on the relative strength of the sex drive in adolescent males and females may well be due to changing cultural orientations toward male and female sexuality. The relative freedom of sexual expression for both men and women seems to be a fairly recent phenomenon. It is therefore not surprising that the more recent the study or survey, the more likely is the finding that male and female sex drives differ little in strength.

The attitudes of today's adolescents toward sexuality appear to differ from the attitudes of the previous generation. Adolescents seem to feel less guilt about their sexual behavior than their parents felt when they were adolescents (*Playboy*, 1971). There also appears to be an increasing concern among adolescents about the philosophical and ethical issues involved in their sexuality (Hunt, 1970). The emphasis of today's adolescent seems to be on openness, honesty, and a reliance on a personal moral system. Further, adolescents do not appear to be dominated by their sexuality. A recent study of the place of human sexuality in the hierarchy of adolescent interests (Kermis, Monge & Dusek, 1975), in fact, found that the adolescent is usually an individual with balanced interests in a variety of areas, including sexuality. Sexuality was not the dominant interest for any of the age levels of adolescent studied. The stereotype of the adolescent consumed by his newly acquired sex drive received no support. Instead, the normal adolescent of today appears to have as rational a perspective on sexuality as do normal adults.

There is strong agreement among researchers that the sexual behavior of today's adolescents reflects the changing attitudes of adolescents toward sexuality. All adolescent sexual behavior is not undergoing dramatic change, however. There is little evidence of significant changes in the incidence of masturbation in male and female adolescents over the past few decades (Pomeroy, 1969a, 1969b; Bardwick, 1971). Homosexual preferences remain infrequent, with 93 per cent of today's males and 91 per cent of today's females preferring exclusively heterosexual behavior (*Playboy*, 1971).

Change has been noted in other areas of adolescent sexual conduct. Petting behavior seems to be occurring earlier and more frequently for recent groups of adolescents than for the adolescents of the past (Kinsey et al., 1948, 1953; Packard, 1970; Luckey & Nass, 1969). There also appears to be a dramatic increase in premarital intercourse over the last three generations of adolescents (Lake, 1967; Playboy, 1970, 1971; Packard, 1970; Luckey & Nass, 1969). Moreover, females are increasingly more likely to report such behavior. There is additional evidence that such increased sexual behavior can rarely be labeled as promiscuous. Three out of four college males and females report that they have intercourse with only one partner and that they are emotionally involved with that partner (Packard, 1970; *Playboy,* 1971).

A recent study of sexual behavior in adolescents (Jessor & Jessor, 1975) focused on the transition from virginity to non-virginity in high school and college students. The authors note that the loss of virginity is still a significant event in the lives of most individuals. This event may signify the attainment of a more mature status, greater autonomy and independence, and the reaffirmation of the individual's own sexual identity. The prevalence of nonvirginity in the middle-class students was found to increase from 21 per cent for males and 26 per cent for females in the tenth grade to 33 percent and 55 percent respectively in the twelfth grade. Eighty-two per cent of college-age males reported that they had engaged in sexual intercourse, and 85 per cent of college-age women reported that they were not virgins. The finding of a high incidence of sexual activity by college males and females is consistent with data from other recent surveys (e. g., Kaats & Davis, 1970; Sorensen, 1972) and strongly suggests that the stereotype of a higher level of sexual activity by males is not accurate. Males and females are apparent equals with regard to the timing and frequency of sexual encounters. The Jessors also found that there was a rather permissive attitude regarding acceptable reasons for intercourse in their college sample. Sixty-four per cent of the college males and 44 per cent of the college females reported that it was acceptable "for two young people who are not married to engage in sexual intercourse if they both want to when they hardly know each other and have no special feeling for each other." It therefore seems that college students are accepting of casual sexual encounters in others, though they tend to refrain from casual encounters themselves (Packard, 1970; Playboy, 1971). High school students, in the Jessor study, were much less permissive, feeling that sexual intercourse was rarely if ever acceptable when the individuals are not emotionally involved.

Sexual behavior is, like most complex human behaviors, a multidetermined phenomenon. Whereas the level of personal morality certainly influences the timing and frequency of sexual intercourse, other factors contribute to the likelihood of sexual activity in youth. For example, a recent research effort by E. Mavis Hetherington (1972) has found that, when all other factors are held constant, the way in which adolescent girls who no longer have a father in the home interact with men is directly related to the cause of the father's absence. Girls whose fathers had died were characterized as inhibited around men, while girls whose fathers left the home because of divorce were clumsily erotic toward men. Such data suggest that psychologists have finally begun to investigate family variables which predict the sexual behavior of the developing child.

CONCLUSION

From the separate discussions of the issues of moral development, political thought and action, drug and alcohol usage, and sexual attitudes and behavior in the adolescent, some interrelationships can be discerned.

There is an accumulating body of evidence that strongly suggests that sexual behavior and drug usage are correlated in adolescents (e.g., *Playboy*, 1970; Jessor & Jessor, 1975). The Jessor study found that the use of marijuana and alcohol is significantly related to virgin-nonvirgin status. For high school males, 61 per cent of nonvirgins reported that they had used marijuana more than once, while only 28 per cent of the virgins reported such use. Similar differences in drug use were found between virgins and nonvirgins in the high school female sample and in the college male and female samples. Further, drinking behavior was likewise found to differ for virgins and nonvirgins in both high school and college males and females. Since these findings are correlational, one or more of three causal relationships might be at work: (1) drug use and/or drinking leads to an increased likelihood of sexual activity; (2) sexual activity leads to an increased use of alcohol and marijuana; or (3) a third factor leads to both an increased likelihood of sexual activity and an increased likelihood of alcohol and marijuana usage. While choices (1) and (2) are possible, option (3) lends itself to interesting speculation.

In the discussion of the data from their study, the Jessors noted that in adolescence there is an increasing likelihood that the individual will break from his/her early modes of thinking and behaving. When that break occurs, not a single behavior but rather an entire class of behaviors becomes more likely. It is as if the normal adolescent reaches a point at which he/she takes control of his/her own life. When this occurs, increasingly independent political thinking, more active political involvement, more experimentation with alcohol and drugs, and new sexual attitudes and increased sexual activity may all be more likely to occur. What contributes to reaching this point of transition? The cognitive-developmentalists may claim it is the natural development of moral thought. The social-learning theorists may claim it is changing reinforcement conditions. In all probability, both positions are right.

Adolescence is a period of transition because the adolescent is growing, experiencing conflict, and altering his/her own decisions and the actions of others in his/her world. Adolescence may not be a pleasant experience for all individuals, but it seems to be a necessary, though prolonged, rite of passage into maturity.

The best way to characterize the adolescent may be in terms of what he/she is not as well as what he/she is. The adolescent is not just an old child, possessing more of something than he/she had as a child. Likewise, the adolescent is not simply a young adult who has less of something than he/she will have as an adult. The adolescent is qualitatively different from both adults and children and should be treated as such.

Adolescence is a period in which major changes occur and in which individuals develop moral concepts, develop new political beliefs, develop new sexual views and behaviors, and are confronted with the issue of drug use. Our attention has been focused on these areas in the present chapter. The problems encountered by the adolescent are not limited to the topics covered here. However, the areas covered serve to illustrate that adolescence appears to be a stage of life accompanied by critical problems in living.

PROJECTS AND QUESTIONS

1. Discuss what the adolescent rebels of the late 1960s might be like today. Specifically, have they likely changed their political views, drug-use patterns, sexual attitudes, and/or sexual behavior?
2. Trace historical trends in the ways in which science and society have viewed the use of the psychoactive drugs by youth.
3. "Chastity in adolescents today is its own punishment." Do you agree? Discuss.

SUGGESTED READINGS

Popular Press

DAVISON, P., & DAVISON, J. Coming of age in America, *New York Times Magazine*, March 9, 1975, pp. 65–70. This article emphasizes the fact that because Western societies have largely eliminated specific "rites of passage" from

childhood to adulthood, adolescents are caught in a kind of ill-defined limbo.
Changing attitudes of youth on sex, patriotism, and work, *U.S. News and World
Report,* June 3, 1974, pp. 66–67. This article provides the data of a survey of
college and noncollege youth aged 16-25 in 1969 and 1973. It reveals that the
dissidence seen among college students of 1969 is less apparent in the college
students of 1973. Furthermore, dissatisfaction among noncollege youth, largely
unseen in 1969, has increased to bring dissent among noncollege youth of 1973 to
about the same level as that of college youth of 1969.

Violence in schools: Now a crackdown, *U.S. News and World Report,* April
14, 1975, pp. 37–40. This article provides an account of the dramatic rise in the
occurrence of criminal violence in public schools and recent attempts by many
administrators, teachers, and parents to solve this problem. Included is a special
section on the increased use of alcohol by adolescents.

Advanced Sources

J.J. CONGER. *Adolescence and youth: Psychological development in a changing
world.* New York: Harper and Row, 1973. One of the finest texts written on
the subject of adolescent development, this book provides excellent chapters on
drug use and sexuality in youth.

E. M. HETHERINGTON & R. D. PARKE. *Child psychology: A contemporary
viewpoint.* New York: McGraw-Hill, 1975. This book provides a developmental perspective on issues that affect adolescent growth. Chapters on moral
development and sex-role development are especially well written.

S. L. JESSOR & R. JESSOR. Transition from virginity to nonvirginity among
youth: A social-psychological study over time. *Developmental Psychology,* 1975,
11, 473–484. Up-to-date data on adolescent sexual attitudes and conduct is com-
bined with an intriguing perspective on the changes in adolescent behavior.

REFERENCES

ADELSON, J. & O'NEIL, R. P. The growth of political ideas in adolescence: The
sense of community. *J. personality and soc. Psychol.* 1966, *4,* 295–306.

ALEXANDER, C. N. Consensus and mutual attraction in natural cliques: A study
of adolescent drinkers. *Amer. Sociology,* 1964, *69,* 395–403.

BACON, M. & JONES, M. B. *Teen-age drinking.* New York: Crowell, 1968.

BANDURA, A. & WALTERS, R. H. *Social learning and personality development.*
New York: Holt, 1963.

BARDWICH, J. *The psychology of women: A study of bio-cultural conflicts.*
New York: Harper & Row, 1971.

BROVERMAN, I. K., VOGEL, S. R., BROVERMAN, D. K., CLARKSON, F. E. &
ROSENKRANTZ, P. S. Sex-role stereotypes: A current appraisal. *J. soc.
Issues,* 1972, *28,* 63.

CONGER, J. J. *Adolescence and youth: Psychological development in a changing
world.* New York: Harper and Row, 1973.

CONSUMER REPORTS. Marijuana: The health questions. March, 1975, pp. 143–149. (a)

CONSUMER REPORTS. Marijuana: The legal question. April, 1975b, pp. 265–266. (b)

DAVISON, G. C. & NEALE, J. M. Abnormal psychology: An experimental clinical approach. New York: Wiley, 1974.

DOUVAN, E. A. & ADELSON, J. The adolescent experience. New York: Wiley, 1966.

EISENTHAL, S. & UDIN, H. Psychological factors associated with drug and alcohol usage among Neighborhood Youth Corps enrollees. Devel. Psycho., 1972, 7, 119–122.

FEUER, L. S. The conflict of generations. New York: Basic Books, 1969.

FODOR, E. M. Delinquency and susceptibility to social influence among adolescents as a function of level of moral development. J. soc. Psychol., 1972, 86, 257–260.

FREUD, S. The ego and the id. London: Hogarth, 1923.

GALLUP, G. Survey of college drug use. New York Times, February 6, 1972.

HAMPDEN-TURNER, C. & WHITTEN, P. Morals left and right. Psychol. Today, 1971, 4, 39–43, 74–76.

HETHERINGTON, E. M. Effects of father absence on personality development in adolescent daughters. Devel. Psychol. 1972, 7, 313–326.

HETHERINGTON, E. M. & PARKE, R. D. Child psychology: A contemporary viewpoint. New York: McGraw-Hill, 1975.

HUNT, M. Sex education survey, Seventeen, July, 1970.

JESSOR, S. L. & JESSOR, R. Transition from virginity to nonvirginity among youth: A social-psychological study over time. Devel. Psychol. 1975, 11, 473–484.

KAATS, G. R. & DAVIS, K. E. The dynamics of sexual behavior of college students. J. marriage Family, 1970, 32, 390–399.

KENISTON, K. Youth and dissent. New York: Harcourt, Brace, Jovanovich, 1971.

KERMIS, M. D., MONGE, R. H. & DUSEK, J. B. Human sexuality in the hierarchy of adolescent interests. Paper presented at biennial meeting of the Society for Research in Child Development, Denver, April, 1975.

KERPELMAN, L. C. Activists and non-activists: A psychological study of American college students. New York: Behavioral Publications, 1972.

KINSEY, A. C., POMEROY, W. B. & MARTIN, C. E. Sexual behavior in the human male. Philadelphia: Saunders, 1948.

KINSEY, A. C., POMEROY, W. B., MARTIN, C. E. & GEBHARD, P. H. Sexual behavior in the human female. Philadelphia: Saunders, 1953.

KOHLBERG, L. The development of children's orientations towards a moral order. 1. Sequence in the development of moral thought. Vita Humana, 1963, 6, 11–33.

KOHLBERG, L. A cognitive-developmental analysis of children's sex-role concepts and attitudes. In E. E. Maccoby (Ed.). The development of sex differences. Stanford, California: Stanford University Press, 1966. Pp. 82–173.

KOHLBERG, L. Stages in the development of moral thought and action. New York: Holt, 1969.

KRAUT, R. & LEWIS, S. Alternate models of family influence on student political ideology. *J. personality and soc. Psychol.*, 1975, *31*, 780–791.

KURTINES, W. & GREIF, E. B. The development of moral thought: Review and evaluation of Kohlberg's approach. *Psychol. Bull.*, 1974, *81*, 453–470.

L'ABATE, L. The status of adolescent psychology. *Devel. Psychol.*, 1971, *4*, 201–205.

LAKE, A. Teenagers and sex: A student report. *Seventeen*, July, 1967.

LAVOIE, J. C. Punishment and adolescent self-control. *Devel. Psychol.* 1973, *8*, 16–24.

LAVOIE, J. C. Aversive, cognitive, and parental determinants of punishment generalization in adolescent males. *J. genetic Psychol.* 1974, *124*, 29–39.

LAVOIE, J. C. & LOOFT, W. R. Parental antecedents of resistance to temptation behavior in adolescent males. *Merrill-Palmer Quarterly*, 1973, *19*, 107–116.

LUCKEY, E. & NASS, G. A comparison of sexual attitudes and behavior in an international sample. *J. marriage Family*, 1969, *31*, 364–379.

MASTERS, W. H. & JOHNSON, V. E. *Human sexual inadequacy*. Boston: Little, Brown, 1970.

MISCHEL, W. Sex-typing and socialization. In P. H. Mussen (Ed.). *Carmichael's Manual of Child Psychology*. Vol. 2. New York: Wiley, 1970.

MIZNER, G. L., BARTER, J. T. & WERME, P. H. Patterns of drug use among college students. *Amer. Psychiat.*, 1970, *127*, 15–24.

NESSELROADE, J. R. & BALTES, P. B. Adolescent personality development and historical change: 1970–1972. *Monographs of the Society for Research in Child Development*, 1974, *39*, Serial No. 154.

PACKARD, V. *The sexual wilderness: The contemporary upheaval in male-female relationships.* New York: Pocket Books, 1970.

PIAGET, J. *The moral judgment of the child.* New York: Harcourt, Brace, 1932.

PLAYBOY, Student survey, September, 1970.

PLAYBOY, Student survey, September, 1971.

POMEROY, W. B. *Boys and sex.* New York: Delacorte, 1969. (a).

POMEROY, W. B. *Girls and sex.* New York: Delacorte, 1969. (b).

RIESTER, A. E. & ZUCKER, R. A. Adolescent social structure and drinking behavior. *Personnel and Guidance J.* 1968, *47*, 304–312.

SECORD, P. F. & BACKMAN, C. W. *Soc. Psychol.* New York: McGraw Hill, 1964.

SORENSON, R. C. *Adolescent sexuality in contemporary America.* New York: World, 1972.

THOMAS, L. E. Family correlates of student political activism. *Devel. Psychol.* 1971, *4*, 206–214.

TURIEL, E. Conflict and transition in adolescent moral development. *Child Devel.* 1974, *45*, 14–29.

WINDBORN, B. B. & JANSON, D. G. Personality characteristics of campus social-political action leaders. *J. Counseling Psychol.* 1967, *14*, 509–513.

Sexual Dysfunctions

CHAPTER 3

Perhaps none of the other critical problems in this book produce as much emotional reaction as do problems in sexual functioning. Television commercials, billboards, and popular magazines all tell us that sex appeal is one of the most important ways we have of being attractive to others. When we experience sexual failure, we may feel that we are somehow unattractive, worthless, or at least a good bit less than our perfect ideal.

The concept of sexual dysfunction should not be confused with "sexual deviations" or "sexual deviance." *Sexual dysfunction* refers to an impairment in the individual's ability to engage in fulfilling sexual activities; in general, the term implies either difficulty in being able to initiate sexual intercourse and/or difficulty in achieving an orgasm. The term *sexual deviation,* on the other hand, implies that the behavior in question is considered unusual and undesirable and that the object of sexual desire is inappropriate. Labels currently used to identify sexual deviations include voyeurism, fetishism, masochism, and several others. A sexual dysfunction is not a sexual deviation, and in this chapter we will be looking exclusively at sexual dysfunctions.

Estimates of the number of persons who have sexual dysfunctions are not precise, but there are indications that as many as 50 per cent of marriages will be subjected to sexual dysfunction in one or the other partner (McCary, 1973). Sexual problems are not uncommon in our society, and in this chapter we will look at some of the available information on sexual problems. We will examine the various *types* of sexual dysfunctions in males and females, look at some of the possible *causes* of sexual dysfunctions, and finally look briefly at the *treatment* of sexual dysfunction.

TYPES OF SEXUAL DYSFUNCTIONS

Although both males and females develop sexual dysfunctions, the specific forms that sexual problems take are different for males and females, and we will look at the two types separately.

Sexual Dysfunctions in Males

Perhaps the type of sexual dysfunction of males which comes to mind first is *erectile dysfunction.* This label describes the condition of the male who is unable to introduce his penis into the vagina of his partner because he is unable to achieve or maintain an erection. This type of sexual dysfunction has been called "impotence" by some authorities, (e.g., Masters & Johnson, 1970), but the term erectile dysfunction may be a little more precise and may produce a little less emotional reaction. Authorities on sexual dysfunction (Kaplan, 1974; Masters & Johnson, 1970) have distinguished between two general types of erectile problems. *Primary* erectile dysfunction describes the condition in which the male has never had a satisfactory erection, whereas *secondary* erectile dysfunction describes the situation where the individual has functioned well at some point in the past but currently experiences erectile dysfunction.

Premature ejaculation is also a term that has become familiar in recent years. This condition is one in which the male, when sexually aroused, ejaculates "too quickly." Masters and Johnson (1970) suggest that "too quickly" means an ejaculation that occurs too fast for the male to sexually satisfy his partner at least 50 per cent of the time.

Retarded ejaculation or ejaculatory incompetence is in many ways the opposite of premature ejaculation. Retarded ejaculation is the inability of the male to ejaculate, especially when the penis is contained in the vagina. This problem occurs less frequently than either premature ejaculation or erectile dysfunction.

It should be emphasized that these three types of male sexual dysfunction are defined in terms of very specific forms of sexual responses. The definition of these sexual problems should not be taken to indicate that individuals who experience these problems have lost their interest in sex or that they have become "oversexed." These problems are defined with reference to rather definite types of psychophysiological response patterns, and the presence (or absence) of a sexual problem should not be taken as an indication of the male's level of sexual interest.

Sexual Dysfunctions in Females

Just as the term *impotence* is the one most commonly associated with male sexual problems, the term *frigidity* is probably the one most commonly associated with sexual dysfunction in females. For the same reasons that impotence is not a good term (because of its lack of precision and its degrading connotations), frigidity is also not a good term. Perhaps the best common definition of frigidity is a label to women who fail to respond to the advances of a would-be seducer. Therefore, for our purposes, "frigidity" is not regarded as a meaningful description of any form of sexual dysfunction in females. However, there are several terms which are currently utilized to describe female sexual dysfunctions.

The term *general sexual dysfunction* describes a female who basically has no sexual feeling. She does not obtain pleasure from sexual stimulation, or if she does the pleasure is minimal (Kaplan, 1974).

Orgasmic dysfunction describes a condition in which the female is unable to experience sexual orgasm. As with the term erectile dysfunction, two general categories of orgasmic dysfunction are recognized: primary orgasmic dysfunction and secondary or situational orgasmic dysfunction. *Primary orgasmic dysfunction* describes the condition in which the female has never had an orgasm by any means. *Secondary* or *situational orgasmic dysfunction* indicates that orgasms are restricted to certain specific situations (e.g., masturbation with a vibrator) or that the individual has achieved orgasm in the past but does not at present.

A third category of female sexual dysfunctions is *vaginismus*. This category of dysfunction refers to a rather dramatic condition, in which there is an involuntary contraction of the muscles of the vagina, thus making intromission of the penis impossible (Ellison, 1972; Kaplan, 1974; Masters & Johnson, 1970). Careful note should be taken of the fact that the contractions are involuntary, and consequently the woman herself does not produce vaginismus at will. The condition cannot be altered simply by deciding not to contract the vaginal muscles.

Painful Intercourse

We have looked at three general categories of male sexual dysfunction and three general categories of female sexual dysfunction. Another form of sexual problem, which can occur to both men and women, is technically known as *dyspareunia* (Fink, 1972), but we will refer to the problem simply as *painful intercourse.*

The term describes the condition: Painful intercourse is the situation in which an individual, either male or female,[1] experiences pain during intercourse. A wide variety of physical causes can lead to painful intercourse, and although we include this problem in our description of sexual problems, the causes and treatment of sexual dysfunctions which we will discuss probably apply much more directly to the other six categories of sexual dysfunction than they do to painful intercourse.

CAUSES OF SEXUAL DYSFUNCTION

Physical Causes

As with any form of behavioral disorder, there are a wide variety of possible causes for sexual dysfunctions. Because sexual dys-

---

[1]Although some theorists restrict the term dyspareunia, i.e., painful intercourse, to females, we utilize the term to apply to both males and females.

functions clearly involve problems with certain areas of physical functions, it is not surprising that a wide range of physical problems can cause sexual dysfunctions. For example, painful intercourse can be caused by a variety of different types of infections, by physical trauma to the sexual organs, by lacerations caused by rape or childbirth, by hypersensitivity of certain tissues, and so on. Erectile dysfunction can be associated with early diabetes. Pearlman (1975) has cited several different types of trauma that can lead to erectile dysfunction, including injuries to the head and spinal cord, foreign objects in the urethra, and loss of the testicles. Alcohol abuse is also related to sexual problems (Viamontes, 1974). It is clear, then, that at least in certain cases physical factors may be responsible for sexual dysfunction.

Psychological Causes

Indications are, however, that most instances of sexual problems are caused not by physical factors but by psychological factors. Although estimates of the proportion of cases caused by physical problems must be regarded as guesses, only about 5 to 10 per cent of sexual dysfunctions are caused by physical factors. In other words, 90 per cent to 95 per cent of sexual dysfunctions are probably caused by psychological factors.

The particular type of psychological causes to be emphasized will depend on the theoretical perspective of the sexual therapist and the sexual researcher. As we noted in Chapter 1, several perspectives are currently utilized in attempting to explain the causes of psychological problems. For example, whereas a therapist using the psychoanalytic perspective might tend to emphasize unconscious factors, an individual using the behavioral perspective might be more interested in how a sexual dysfunction could have been learned. Keeping in mind that different therapists will tend to emphasize different categories of causes, we will turn our attention to some specific categories of psychological causes of sexual dysfunctions proposed by researchers and therapists (Ellison, 1972; Fink, 1972; Friedman, 1973; Kaplan, 1974; LoPiccolo & Lobitz, 1973; Masters & Johnson, 1970).

HISTORICAL FACTORS.

The history of a particular individual contributes to his sexual adjustment. The experiences which we had in the reasonably distant past may still have some influence on our current behavior, and the area of sexual dysfunction is no exception. Two specific types of historical factors may contribute to sexual dysfunction: (1) socialization and child-rearing and (2) traumatic early experiences.

The way in which individuals are brought up, particularly the way in which sex is viewed by the parents and other significant adults, may have an impact on later sexual problems. Individuals who are raised in an atmosphere in which sex is presented as something dirty, evil, and disgusting may be expected to have a greater potential for developing sexual dysfunctions than individuals who are raised to view sex as a desirable and integral part of life. Excessive religiosity where sex is concerned, with the presentation of sexual activity as something that is sinful and unforgivable, may help pave the road for later sexual dysfunction.

Early traumatic sexual experiences may also contribute to the development of sexual dysfunctions. The suggestion that early traumatic experiences with sex may increase the probability of adult sexual problems should not be confused with the popular notion that *all* kinds of very unpleasant experiences can lead to psychological difficulties later. The focus here is on traumatic experiences which are primarily sexual in nature. For example, an early experience with forcible rape or sexual assault may provide the foundation for future sexual problems. Strong embarassment associated with the first sexual experience, for example, has been reported in the history of some individuals with erectile dysfunction. Early sexual experiences that were associated with strong embarrassment, high levels of fear and anxiety, a high degree of pain, or other similarly unpleasant responses may provide the groundwork for future sexual dysfunction.

At this point, we need to make one more of those disclaimers for which psychologists are becoming famous. Although these historical factors may be found in the backgrounds of many persons who experience sexual dysfunction, it is very clear that not all individuals who have traumatic sexual experiences and not all individuals who have rigidly antisexual socialization will develop sexual dysfunction. What we are suggesting is simply that individuals who do develop sexual dysfunctions tend to have (on the average) histories with the types of experiences and childhood conditions we have described.

CURRENT, IMMEDIATE CAUSES.

Although the past history of the individual certainly plays a role in the development of sexual dysfunction, most authorities emphasize the importance of factors in the individual's current life. In other words, what is happening to the individual, at the present time, that causes his/her sexual dysfunction?

Ignorance can be one of the simplest causes of sexual dysfunction. The simple failure to engage in appropriate sexual activity may cause sexual dysfunction through insufficient arousal, inappropriate stimulation, lack of knowledge about sexual anatomy, and the like. The treatment of problems that result from ignorance can be rather dramatic, as it probably will consist simply of sex education designed for the individual with the sexual problem.

It is *anxiety,* however, which can be regarded as the most pervasive of all psychological causes of sexual dysfunctions. The word "anxiety" has been overused by psychologists, and it means many different things to different people. In the context of sexual dysfunction anxiety simply means worry about sexual performance, fear of failing sexually, fear of pain, fear of pregnancy, and so on. Most of the current treatment methods used for sexual problems tend to focus on reducing the anxiety associated with sexual situations. The idea is that if the anxiety, from whatever cause, can be reduced and perhaps eliminated, then the sexual dysfunction will be significantly helped. As we will see later in this chapter, the idea seems to be a good one.

The final cause of sexual dysfunctions that we will look at in this section is *relationship problems.* When two individuals are having trouble getting along with each other, it will come as no surprise to discover they may also have sexual problems. Problems in the relationship between two people may contribute to problems in the specifically sexual aspects of that relationship. Not only is it difficult to "make love to someone you hate," but the failure to tell each other what is and is not sexually pleasing may also contribute to sexual dysfunctions.

To summarize, sexual dysfunctions may be caused both by historical psychological factors and by current psychological factors. The child-rearing practices to which an individual was exposed and his/her early sexual experiences can contribute to sexual problems. Current factors most frequently emphasized are ignorance, anxiety, and relationship problems.

TREATMENT OF SEXUAL DYSFUNCTIONS—A BRIEF DESCRIPTION

The last chapter of this book is devoted to a general overview of sources of psychological help. However, as treatment methods developed specifically for the alleviation of sexual dysfunction have multiplied in recent years, we will briefly discuss two general treatment procedures.

Before we describe specific procedures, we must emphasize that the specific details of the treatment procedure vary. Masters and Johnson (1970) pioneered sex therapy and made the treatment of sexual problems a well-known method of psychological treatment. There are a wide variety of approaches that either are slight modifications of the Masters and Johnson procedures or represent major differences (Adelson, 1974; Ellison, 1972; Fuchs, et al., 1973; Ince, 1973; Lobitz & LoPiccolo, 1973; Murphy & Mikulas, 1974; Wilson, 1973). In general, most treatment programs developed for sexual dysfunctions have much in common: The procedures owe much to the techniques developed by Masters and Johnson, and the problems tend to be viewed from the behavioral perspective (see Chapter 1).

The treatment procedures described here were developed for the treatment of two different sexual problems: premature ejaculation, a problem unique to males, and vaginismus, a problem unique to females.

The Treatment of Premature Ejaculation

As with the treatment of any sexual dysfunction, the procedure usually begins with a relatively extensive assessment of the problem, considering information about the individual's sexual history, current sexual life, partner(s), current relationship(s), and so on.

Generally, the individual must have a willing sexual partner who agrees to cooperate for the duration of the psychological treatment. Once the assessment of the problem has been undertaken and the cooperation of a partner obtained, the couple is then given the assignment of performing a hierarchy of sexual tasks.

The sexual tasks are usually carried out by the couple in the privacy of their own bedroom. Usually, the couple describes to the therapist what happened, without therapist observation.

The typical sequence of sexual tasks used in the treatment of premature ejaculation begins with the couple engaging in mutual sexual pleasuring. Based on the instructions of the therapist(s) the couple engages in limited foreplay, without engaging in subsequent intercourse. It is the sexual stimulation of the male by the female partner that takes on critical importance in the treatment of premature ejaculation.

While the male lies comfortably on his back, his partner stimulates his penis until he achieves an erection. As ejaculation approaches, the female either squeezes the penis or lets the erection subside by stopping stimulation. Whether or not the squeeze is employed varies with the therapist's treatment procedures. The idea is simply to help the male partner learn to achieve an erection, without immediately ejaculating.

After some control of the erection is obtained with the "stop-start" method, the next sexual task is intercourse, but intercourse undertaken in a very specific way. The therapist usually will instruct the couple to engage in intercourse with the female in the superior position. With the female partner astride the male, the penis is introduced into the vagina, and the couple remains motionless. If the male should experience an imminent orgasm, he tells his partner, who elevates herself and either applies the squeeze technique or lets the erection subside. This sequence of events is repeated. After the male has achieved sexual union without immediate ejaculation, slow, gentle motions may begin after intromission of the penis is achieved.

Once the individual is able to initiate intercourse and maintain an erection without ejaculation, the treatment is complete. Reasonable control of ejaculation has been achieved. Although it is probably not necessary in all cases, the suggestion has been made that the couple occasionally again go through the stop-start sequence without ejaculating. Such a return to the techniques used in the therapeutic program is meant to insure that the male will continue to have good control of his ejaculatory reflex.

As with any attempts that psychologists make to help individuals with behavior problems, this exact sequence will not be used for all cases of premature ejaculation even by the same therapist. The techniques described, however, are used so extensively that this outline of the treatment sequence probably represents well the general approach that most clinical psychologists use in treating premature ejaculation.

The Treatment of Vaginismus

When the conclusion is reached after an initial assessment that the individual female's primary problem is in fact vaginismus, the treatment procedure usually follows a rather specific program.

The basic goal of the treatment of vaginismus is to decondition, to help the individual unlearn, the involuntary contractions of the muscles around the vagina. Just as with the treatment of premature ejaculation, the treatment of vaginismus is undertaken in a series of steps.

Most therapists assume that the contraction of the vagina can be eliminated, if the female goes through a hierarchy of tasks. The tasks are simple and specific, usually involving either the use of dilators developed especially for vaginal dilation or the use of the fingers. The basic idea is to help the individual become comfortable first with minimal dilation of the vagina and then gradually to increase the size of the dilation. The final goal is comfortable introduction of the penis into the vagina.

If dilators are used, the individual female begins by introducing into her vagina the largest dilator she can tolerate. Once she is comfortable with that one, she uses the next larger size, and so on, until dilators resembling the size of an erect penis can be comfortably accommodated in the vagina. Although a partner is not essential in the treatment of vaginismus, it probably will make the treatment procedure simpler if the female does have a partner who can help her.

If dilators are not used, the procedure can be carried out using one finger, then two. The sequencing is the same as with dilators. If dilators are not used, it is probably desirable for the female to have a male partner who will go through a prescribed hierarchy of tasks with her.

Once the individual can accommodate comfortably to vaginal insertion of either dilators or fingers, the next step will probably be very quiet intercourse. The final steps in the treatment of vaginismus are not unlike the treatment of premature ejaculation. Initially the penis is introduced, and the partners remain relatively motionless. As she feels comfortable, the female partner will begin gentle thrusting motions. Finally, regular intercourse can be enjoyed.

The whole sequence, from the initial session to the final sessions in which intercourse is successful (assuming treatment was helpful), probably will take several days. In most situations, where office visits to a professional occur once or twice a week, a successful treatment program will probably take a few weeks or a few months.

Although the specific treatment methodology will vary, the basic goal of most approaches to the treatment of vaginismus is to help the patient learn to become comfortable with vaginal insertion. Working through a program in which she learns to become comfortable with more and more vaginal dilation, the individual female should eventually become comfortable engaging in intercourse with the partner of her choice.

Does the Specific Treatment of Sexual Dysfunction Work?

The available data on the question of whether the specific treatment of sexual dysfunction works suggests that, in general, it does. If our goal is the elimination of the specific sexual dysfunction, then the available evidence suggests that the treatment of sexual dysfunction is in fact highly successful. For example, Masters and Johnson (1970) have reported a success rate of about 98 per cent with cases of premature ejaculation. The Masters and Johnson data indicate that for the other types of sexual dysfunction, the success rate is roughly about 80 per cent.

The lowest rate of success in the treatment of sexual dysfunction has been with cases of primary erectile dysfunction. Masters and Johnson (1970) have indicated that approximately 60 per cent of their cases were treated successfully. With the exception of primary erectile dysfunction, however, the available evidence indicates that the treatment of sexual dysfunctions has a good probability of success.

What about the Development of Other Symptoms?

One of the issues raised when behavioral treatment methods are designed to attack a problem directly is whether, if only the symptom is treated (for example, just the premature ejaculation), other problems will develop in its place?

One popular story about "symptom substitution" is of the individual who went to a hypnotist to try to stop smoking. As the story goes the hypnotist gives the individual a suggestion that he will no longer want to smoke. In fact, that happens, but the individual then develops a voracious need to bite his fingernails. The idea is that, because the underlying problem was not resolved, the elimination of one symptom will result in the "substitution" of a new symptom for the old.

This question about "symptom substitution" is frequently asked about the treatment methods for sexual dysfunction that we have briefly described here. If the sexual problem is dealt with directly, will not the individual then develop a new problem in the place of the sexual problem?

Although it is clearly not impossible for the direct treatment of sexual dysfunctions to cause further complications for the individual (Kaplan & Kohl, 1973), the evidence seems to clearly indicate that in the vast majority of cases no new symptoms will appear

(Kaplan, 1974; O'Leary & Wilson, 1975). Our conclusion, then, is that the direct alleviation of sexual dysfunction with the behavioral methods pioneered by Masters and Johnson tends to be effective and that these direct treatment methods do not result in the appearance of new problems.

SUMMARY

In this chapter we have looked briefly at the critical problem of sexual dysfunction. We have identified three major categories of sexual dysfunction in males: erectile dysfunction (primary and secondary), premature ejaculation, and retarded ejaculation. Three major categories of female sexual dysfunction were also identified: general sexual dysfunction, orgasmic dysfunction (primary and secondary), and vaginismus. Painful intercourse was identified as a sexual problem that can occur in both males and females.

The percentage of sexual dysfunction cases caused by physical problems tends to be small. Two general categories of psychological causes of sexual problems were discussed, historical factors and current, immediate causes.

The treatment of sexual dysfunctions of psychological origin was discussed. A brief description of the treatment of premature ejaculation and vaginismus illustrated current treatment methods. Finally, an evaluation of the treatment of sexual dysfunction was given, and the possibility of "substitute symptoms" was discussed.

A FINAL NOTE

We have said it many times in this book: Because specific problems vary and because individuals differ, the specific way in which a problem will be treated by any particular clinical psychologist, psychiatrist, or other therapist will vary with the client. It is our feeling, however, that the present discussion provides a brief but accurate description of contemporary views on sexual dysfunctions.

Now that we have reviewed information about sexual dysfunctions, we would like to make a plea: *Please do not attempt to treat yourself if you are experiencing sexual difficulties.* Attempts to change one's own pattern of sexual response can lead to a worsening rather than to an improvement of the sexual problem. By attempting to reduce a dysfunction without professional assistance, anxiety about fear of performance, failure to reach orgasm, and the like may be increased, thus leading to a possible worsening of the original sexual problem. We strongly urge that if you have a sexual problem, you should contact a qualified and properly licensed professional or clinic.

PROJECTS AND QUESTIONS

1. Although it is clearly not widely practiced or accepted (and unethical from many points of view), some of the more radical sex therapists actually demonstrate sexual techniques for their clients, observe the client engaging in sexual activity, and the like. From the point of view of the client of sex therapy, where do you think the sex therapist should "draw the line" in regard to his actual involvement in such activities as demonstrating or participating in sex with his/her clients?
2. Imagine a couple who are having sexual problems (for example, he experiences premature ejaculation). If the sexual problem is solved or cured, what positive consequences do you think this new sexual functioning will have on the relationship?
3. If there is a clinic in your area that conducts a reasonable amount of sex therapy, contact them and ask to interview an individual who actually conducts treatment of sexual dysfunctions. Interview that individual and report back to your group about the techniques, the therapist's training, the cost, and so on. If a clinic devoted to sexual problems only is not available, a mental health center, a university counseling clinic, a university psychology clinic, or a department of psychiatry of a medical school are all possible sources of further information. *Note:* For this project, make sure that you won't be charged for the interview!

SUGGESTED READINGS

Popular Press

F. BELLIVEAU & L. RICHTER. *Understanding Human Sexual Inadequacy.* New York: Bantam Books, 1970. A popularized but generally accurate "translation" of Masters and Johnson's much more technical book on sexual dysfunction.

H.S. KAPLAN. No-nonsense therapy for six sexual malfunctions. *Psychology Today,* 1974, October, 77–86. A readable summary of methods used to treat the most common forms of sexual dysfunction.

Advanced Sources

H. S. KAPLAN. *The New Sex Therapy.* New York: Brunner-Mazel, 1974. A current review of the treatment of sexual dysfunctions, incorporating many cases from the author's own clinical work. A good discussion of techniques as well as some theoretical issues.

W. MASTERS & V. JOHNSON. *Human Sexual Inadequacy.* New York: Little-Brown, 1970. A description of the treatment techniques developed by the authors and some discussion of outcome data.

REFERENCES

ADELSON, E. R. Premature ejaculation. *Medical Aspects of Human Sexuality,* 1974, *8,* 83–84.

BELLIVEAU, F. & RICHTER, L. *Understanding human sexual inadequacy.* New York: Bantam Books, 1970.

ELLISON, C. VAGINISMUS. *Medical Aspects of Human Sexuality,* 1972, *6* (8), 34–54.

FINK, P. J. Dyspareunia: Current concepts. *Medical Aspects of Human Sexuality,* 1972, *6,* 28–47.

FRIEDMAN, H. J. An interpersonal aspect of psychogenic impotence. *Amer. J. Psychotherapy,* 1973, *27,* 421–429.

FUCHS, K., PALDI, E. & ABRAMOVICI, H. Hypnodesensitization therapy of vaginismus. *Internat. J. Clinical & Experimental Hypnosis,* 1973, *21,* 144–156.

INCE, L. P. Behavior modification of sexual disorders. *Amer. J. Psychotherapy,* 1973, *27,* 446–451.

KAPLAN, H. S. *The new sex therapy.* New York: Brunner/Mazel, 1974.

KAPLAN, H. S. & KOHL, R N. Adverse reactions to the rapid treatment of sexual problems. *Psychosomatics,* 1972, *13,* 185–190.

LOBITZ, W. C. & LoPICCOLO, J. New methods in the behavioral treatment of sexual dysfunction. *J. Behavior Therapy & Experimental Psychiatry,* 1972, *3,* 265–271.

LoPICCOLO, J. & LOBITZ, W. C. Behavior therapy of sexual dysfunction. In A. Hamerlynch, L. C. Handy & E. J. Marsh (Eds.). *Behavioral change: Methodology, concepts, and practice.* Champaign, Ill: Research Press, 1973.

MASTERS, W. & JOHNSON, V. *Human sexual inadequacy.* New York: Little-Brown, 1970.

McCARY, J. L. *Human sexuality.* Second edition. New York: Van Nostrand, 1973.

McCARTHY, B. W. A modification of Masters and Johnson sex therapy model in a clinical setting. *Psychotherapy: Theory, research & practice,* 1973, *10,* 290–293.

MURPHY, C. & MIKULAS, W. Behavioral features and deficiencies of the Masters and Johnson program. *Psychol. Record,* 1974, *24,* 221–227.

O'LEARY, K. D. & WILSON, G. T. *Behavior therapy: application and outcome.* Englewood Cliffs, N.J.: Prentice-Hall, 1975.

PEARLMAN, C. K. Traumatic causes of impotence. *Medical Aspects of Human Sexuality,* 1975, *9* (6), 76–82.

PROCHASKA, J. O. & MARZILLI, R. Modifications of the Masters and Johnson approach to sexual problems. *Psychotherapy: Theory, research and practice,* 1973, *10,* 294–296.

VIAMONTES, J. A. Alcohol abuse and sexual dysfunction. *Medical Aspects of Human Sexuality,* 1974, *8* (11), 185–186.

WILSON, G. T. Innovations in the modification of phobic behaviors in two clinical cases. *Behavior Therapy,* 1973, *4,* 426–430.

Marriage and Family Discord

CHAPTER 4

Throughout the history of literature, novelists and playwrights have used the family as a setting for some of their most intense emotional dramas. In works like *Oedipus Rex, Hamlet,* and *Death of a Salesman,* the authors portray the emotional turmoil and entanglement embedded in family life. For centuries such literary works have contributed greatly to our understanding of the family. Although such artistic insights continue as an important source of intuitive understanding, the behavioral sciences in recent years have begun more systematic investigations. In the present chapter, some of the findings and ideas of such study, particularly as they pertain to troubled marriages and families, will be reviewed.

The clinical observation and theorizing of Sigmund Freud began focusing attention on the role of family relationships as a major factor in psychological development. In his view, interpersonal conflicts within the family became internalized in the child, with such internal conflicts playing a dominant role in emotional adjustment throughout life. Consequently, Freud (1963) developed a treatment, *psychoanalysis,* that focused exclusively on emotional conflicts inside the individual—on their origins in the person's past and on their present expressions. If a man had come into Freud's consulting room and said, "I just had a fight with my wife about money," Freud would probably have investigated how such a fight might have aroused old conflicts involving the man's relationship with his mother.

Within professional circles, this approach held sway for several decades until a growing number of investigators began to recognize its limits and to appreciate more fully the impact of social and situational factors on the psychological well-being of the individual (Horney, 1939; Sullivan, 1953). Such realization did not mean that the Freudian approach was no good but rather that Freudian theory alone was insufficient. It seemed much more reasonable to view man's behavior as determined by both his past experiences and the current situation. For almost everyone, past and present experiences involve other people and particularly family members. With this change in perspective, there has been a growing emphasis on the understanding and treatment of relationships among family members during the 1950s and 1960s (Ackerman, 1968; Langsley & Kaplan, 1968; Stuart, 1969; Toleman, 1969).

For our hypothetical man who comes into the consulting room describing a fight with his wife, the modern family-oriented therapist would likely wonder about their marital relationship in general. The therapist might wonder whether they had many fights, on what topics, what each partner expected and wanted from the other, how they communicated their hopes, desires, and fears to each other, how their fights were resolved, and what had been happening recently in their marriage and family. In trying to unravel such questions, therapists have made an all-important shift in their approach. No longer are therapists content to have the individual come in alone and sit in an easy chair to discuss the situation. With such a method the therapist is only hearing one side of a relationship; instead, the therapist is likely to involve the husband and wife and perhaps the children in treatment to work on their problems jointly under the therapist's supervision and direction (Cookerly, 1973; Eyberg & Johnson, 1974; Haley, 1972; Johnson, 1974; Patterson, Cobb & Ray, 1973; Revner, 1972). This shift in method and outlook represents the heart of what is referred to as family therapy.

In the present chapter, one of the prominent contemporary conceptual approaches to the functioning of the family will be outlined. Further, some of the individual characteristics correlating with marital stability and satisfaction will be described. Some of the more common threats to marital and familial satisfaction will be identified and discussed. Finally, a number of specific features, of marital and familial therapy will be reviewed.

MARRIAGE AND FAMILY PROCESS

In considering marital relationships, many investigators have attempted to identify the characteristics of an ideal marriage. In this vein, several workers have suggested that a successful marriage fulfills the personality needs of both members and provides them with personal satisfaction (Groves, 1941; Udry, 1971). Further, each person should be self-enhanced by the union and not corrupted by it (Burton, 1973). While such descriptions of how marriages should be may have some value, they lack the precision, specificity, and flexibility necessary for describing and understanding ongoing, changing actual marriages.

The Systems Approach. In attempting to develop a conceptual framework having such properties, a number of researchers and therapists have begun viewing marital and familial units as systems (Ackerman, 1969; Bowen, 1972; Haley, 1972; Jackson, 1970; Minuchin, 1974). Although these workers differ on specific issues, they share an over-all orientation and a number of key assumptions.

The family is seen as a network of relationships among the members, with such relationships being characterized by organized and repetitive ways of acting (Jackson, 1970). Thus, the family is made up of a set of relationships that are relatively stable: to some extent, the behavior and characteristics of each family member are determined by the family as a whole (Langsley & Kaplan, 1968; Lebovici, 1970). Since the family members are interdependent, change in one member affects the entire family. This interpretation is equally valid applied to the troubled behavior of any family member and leads to the view that family therapy is necessary for effective change (Burgess, 1972). As Ackerman (1970) points out, when such characteristic ways of interacting are interrupted, the family will through various means attempt to re-establish stable and predictable ways of interacting under the new conditions.

Viewing the family as a system aids in three major respects. First, attention is focused on the *interaction among individuals,* rather than on the characteristics of the individuals. Such characteristics of individuals are seen as products of past and present interactions with others and are of concern only in terms of how they affect present relationships. Second, the systems orientation changes the thinking about *causation* (Jackson, 1970). Instead of viewing causes as occurring in one direction, they are seen as operating in a circular fashion (Jackson, 1970). For instance, it may be that a husband's excessive drinking causes his wife to be depressed; however, her depression may also lead to his drinking as a means of coping with a depressed wife. Such situations, which have been referred to as "positive feedback loops" (Jackson, 1970), illustrate how troublesome behavior may be perpetuated within a family system. Third, the systems approach helps in viewing *the family as a social group,* although with the built-in age and sex characteristics of its members and certain functions, such as rearing of children, specified (Lidz, 1970). As such, the family might be expected to exhibit many of the principles evident in the functioning of most groups.

Agreements. In pursuing the systems approach, understanding the way in which relationships are established and maintained is very important. Jackson (1970) and Haley (1972) have provided assistance in this respect, proposing that a relationship consists of a set of agreements worked out between the two persons involved. The agreements contain the expectations and obligations of each person toward the other.

With a married couple, these agreements cover many areas of living together and concern what each person will or will not do. Some of these agreements are clearly spelled out, having been reached through deliberate discussion. For example, the couple may examine their budget together and decide that they can afford to go out to dinner once a month. Other agreements may not be so clearly articulated or reached in such a deliberate manner. Furthermore, the couple might not be aware of which agreement is operating but will recognize it when it is pointed out to them. Such an agreement might be that the husband or wife will talk to the other spouse whenever faced with a major career decision. Finally, there might be agreements which are apparent to an outside observer but denied by the couple. For instance, there may be an implicit agreement that the wife is a weak, fragile person who must be protected from bad news at all costs. The husband therefore attempts to hide any such news and the wife tries not to ask too many questions about potentially troublesome areas.

Agreements like these are worked out by couples in many areas of living, including their emotional responses to each other, their patterns of sexual intimacy, their finances, the place of children, friends, and in-laws, as well as routine tasks around the home. For convenience, the sum of such agreements may be referred to as the *marital contract* (Sager et al., 1968). Development of such a contract provides direction and guidance for the behavior of each partner, allowing their relationship to become more predictable and stable. Consequently, their living together becomes more comfortable and free of serious contention.

Using the idea of a contract allows us to understand more readily some of the common observations regarding marital discord. For instance, it is relatively easy to see that the first few years of marriage is a particularly difficult time, with many divorces occurring during this early phase. According to a number of studies (Baber, 1953; Blood, 1969; Kenkel, 1966; Ogg, 1965) approximately half of all divorces occur during the first six years of marriage, and almost one quarter of them occur during the first two years. This initial phase of marriage is when the couple must reach many agreements over a wide range of areas in a relatively short time, and as Haley (1972) points out, what might have been acceptable. to one spouse during courtship may suddenly become unacceptable. The extent to which the marital partners have not discussed specific expectations derived from their parents' relationships and have not accepted, rejected, or revised these expectations contribute significantly to marital breakdown.

Haley (1972) observes that immediately following the wedding a couple may go through a "psychological honeymoon." During this period, each partner may be tolerant of annoying behavior by the spouse. At some point, however, the couple is likely to have a fight in which grievances are expressed and agreements changed. Such arguments probably play an important role in redefining marital agreements and are probably a typical feature of good marriages. They represent one of the ways in which marital relationships change with changing conditions. Bach (1969), in an ironically entitled book, *The Intimate Enemy,* focuses his marital therapy around teaching constructive ways of arguing.

As the marital relationship endures and evolves, couples develop regular ways of resolving their disagreements. Such regular methods represent agreements about acceptable ways of resolving disagreements (Haley, 1972). Two of the more undesirable ways are contrasting styles: The first is to avoid talking about troublesome topics, and the second is to get into a power struggle in which both become argumentative. In some marriages both partners mutually agree, perhaps implicitly, to avoid talking about conflictful areas. If such an approach is used, then progressively more areas of living together are likely to be avoided in discussions, and the members become more isolated from one another. Such a method of resolving disagreements risks a loss of companionship, and according to Adams (1973) and Waller (1967) resentment may continue without ever being brought up.

On the other hand, confrontations between partners on many issues may also be highly detrimental to the marriage. Couples may become progressively more argumentative and combative, with disagreements in one area leading to disagreements in others. Each partner may be dedicated to having his own way in everything, maintaining a struggle for dominance or one-upmanship in the marriage. Of primary importance for the moment however, is the observation that couples also work out agreements concerning how conflicts are to be resolved (Jackson, 1970).

A final aspect of the agreement process described by Haley (1972) involves who in the marriage is to define the relationship in their various spheres of living together. Is one person to set all the rules in one particular area of living, or is it going to be an entirely shared process? For example, a wife is quite likely at some point to tell her husband that from now on he is to pick up his own clothes. Probably most people, including husbands, would agree that such a policy is reasonable. Yet, a particular husband may feel rather irritated, although he may not be able to identify the reason for such a feeling. His irritation is likely to be a response to her telling him what to do rather than to the nature of the request itself. He may refuse to pick up his clothes, claiming it is the principle of the thing. Jackson (1970) and Haley (1972) view disagreements involving *who* is to set the rules in a given area as the most difficult to resolve satisfactorily.

The marital contract needs to include agreements not only about what will happen in particular areas of living but also about who will set the rules, as well as agreements concerning how conflicts will be resolved. Additionally, a marriage contract is not a static document reached at one point in time and preserved throughout the remainder of the marriage. It is instead a constantly evolving set of agreements which need revision and elaboration as new situations are encountered.

Unusual Marital Contracts. As previously noted, viewing marriages from a systems approach assists in moving away from cultural sterotypes and idealistic notions of how such relationships ought to be. Such assistance is valuable in understanding unusual marital contracts. While most troubled marriages might be interpreted as involving an unusual contract, Langsley and Kaplan (1968) describe a specific type of unusual contract. They refer to this pattern as the "doll's-house marriage." It consists of an extremely unequal relationship in which one spouse's incompetence is required and even encouraged by the other. The doll, usually the wife, is described by Langsley and Kaplan (1968) as subservient, not making any independent decisions; and she is seen by her husband as helpless, dependent, and perhaps defective mentally or emotionally. She is cherished by him because of her limitations. The authors describe the husband as fearful of women, viewing himself as incapable of winning or keeping a real woman, although he may be comfortable in his dealings with other men. Their stable relationship is characterized by both partners viewing one of them as helpless, requiring the protection and constant supervision of the other. Langsley and Kaplan (1968) observe that although such marital relationships appear satisfying for the marital partners, they seem crisis-prone. According to the authors' clinical experience, the types of crisis most likely to disrupt previously successful doll's-house marriages include the arrival of a baby, financial hardship, and the intrusion of an adult attempting to make the relationship a more equal one.

Communication. Certainly, within marital and familial units communication is an important ingredient (Adams, 1973), particularly from the perspective of a contract (Haley, 1972; Jackson, 1967). Clear and meaningful communication would seem highly beneficial for establishing and revising interpersonal agreements. Bateson (1951), in some early work on communication, described two aspects of every communication message: a *report* component and a *command* component. The report refers to the factual information which can be evaluated for truth or falsity and can be viewed as the object of the communication. The command aspect indicates how this information is to be taken. The command aspect may be paraphrased as, "This is how I define the relationship within which the report takes place." This definition can be accepted, ignored, or countered by the person receiving the message (Jackson, 1970). The command feature may be illustrated by examining the following messages: "Get me a cup of coffee," or "Would you please bring me a cup of coffee?" In such instances, the report aspect, requesting coffee, remains the same; however, in the first statement, this report is presented as an order from a superior, while in the second it is presented as a request from a peer.

To further complicate the communication process, recent investigations have shown that such nonlanguage behavior as rate of speech, voice inflection and intonation, facial expressions, and physical gestures have communicative significance (Vetter, 1970). If these various aspects of the process are consistent with one another, the communication would seem most likely to be clear. Jackson (1970) and Haley (1972) have both noted that inconsistencies within the communication from one person enhances the difficulty of establishing agreements and resolving disagreements. Hence, communication in troubled individuals and families is more likely to be confused and contradictory and maladaptive (Jackson, 1966).

In viewing communication within the family, Sherman, Ackerman, Sherman, and Michels (1970) have described the role of nonverbal cues in the troubled families they have treated. From such experience, they suggest that nonverbal behavior such as gestures, sighs, and facial expressions may express attitudes and feelings contrary to those verbally expressed. As such, the nonverbal cues may elicit unexpected behavior from other family members and serve as stimuli for conflicts within the family.

A good communication process is not, however, a panacea for family problems. Even with the clearest communication among family members, individuals will differ in their desires, attitudes, values, and fears; and such differences may lead to disagreement and conflict. Although good communication may not eliminate such differences, poor communications seem likely to intensify and expand the difficulty. Consequently, clear communication among members may be a necessary but not sufficient condition for optimal family functioning.

Mate Swapping. In addition to individualized unusual contracts, there are other forms shared by substantial groups of couples. One such instance is represented by the practice of mate swapping. Whereas sexual exclusiveness has traditionally been seen as an integral part of marriage, some couples have worked out agreements eliminating this feature. Perhaps surprisingly, the research of Bartell (1971) and Smith and Smith (1974) present a descriptive picture of these couples similar to the nondeviant monogamous middle-class couples. According to one study (Smith & Smith, 1974), the swingers are mostly white respectable suburbanites, ranging in age from 18 to 70 years old. They tend to have higher levels of education than the general population, with 80 per cent having attended college and 50 per cent having graduated from college. The husbands tend to be primarily in white-collar and professional occupations. The couples have been married from three months to 30 years, with two to six years being most common (Smith & Smith, 1974). Such statistics emphasize the normality and conventionality of these couples, who apparently differ mainly in their ideas about sexual fidelity.

Comfort (cited in Bartell, 1971) suggests that such practice is beneficial to marriage, providing sexual variety without endangering the marriage itself; and Bartell (1971), in his research, found the divorce rate for "swingers" was lower than for couples who did not participate in mate swapping. The "swinging" couples identified what they saw as advantages to mate swapping, which included the fact that mate swapping was less time-consuming, expensive, less effortful, and provided more variety than having extramarital affairs. Further, swapping was seen as less emotionally entangling, and the opportunity existed for involving the spouse in the same activity, making it a family project.

As with more conventional marriages, mate-swapping couples develop agreements concerning sexual activity. The over-all thrust of such agreements about extramarital sex seem aimed at eliminating the emotional involvement typically accompanying sex in our culture. For instance, one marital partner is usually not allowed to attend a swinger's party without the other spouse. Parties involving more than three couples are usually preferred because they presumably lower the risk of emotional involvement. Participants are not supposed to make statements of emotional endearment, restricting complimentary remarks to the physical characteristics and sexual performance of others. Further, when a couple wishes to have a child, they drop out of mate swapping in order to insure that the husband is the father of the child. An important rule is that there be no concealment of sexual activity because, in their view, such deceit is the harmful aspect of extramarital sexual relations. One effect of such rules is to make contact with other couples relatively, brief leading to a constant search for new sexual partners. According to Smith and Smith (1974), these rules work relatively well, with only 34 per cent of the females and 27 per cent of the males reporting feelings of jealousy.

Thus, it would seem that having culturally unusual agreements as part of the marital contract does not necessarily hinder marital stability. The fact of such stability within an unusual contract is not a recommendation for the adoption of such marital practices.

INDIVIDUAL CHARACTERISTICS AND MARITAL SUCCESS

As we noted, individuals enter marriage with certain expectations concerning their spouse (Sager et al., 1968). The individual's expectations and his or her reaction to their not being fully satisfied are probably two of the major means by which personality factors affect marital stability and satisfaction. Groves (1941) suggests that a low tolerance for frustration and a lack of adaptibility are among the prominent personality factors contributing to marital breakdown. Further, Barnett (1968), in his clinical practice, has begun to describe how particular kinds of personality styles and associated emotional conflicts interact in various spheres of living to produce tension and dissatisfaction. Certainly, a number of theorists concerned with marital and family processes recognize the significance of such personality factors (Ackerman, 1970; Lebovici, 1970).

Many of the expectations within the marriage and family have been tied to sex-role stereotypes, with men expected to do certain activities such as providing the financial support, handling major financial interactions, and generally mediating between the family unit and the larger society. Women, in turn, have been expected to take care of the household, preparing the meals, cleaning the house, taking care of the children, and generally being atuned to the interpersonal relationships within the family (Lidz, 1970). Such differences in task assignment seem roughly consistent with frequently observed personality differences of women and men. Numerous studies summarized by Bardwick (1971) suggest that such differences are associated with differences in social learning and social pressure. Perhaps the most commonly observed differences include the greater passivity, dependence, and nurturence of women when compared with men, and the greater achievement motivation, agression, and assertiveness of men when compared with women (Bardwick, 1971). Such differences have lead to more or less standardized expectations of the roles of the wife and the husband (Lidz, 1970).

The development of the women's liberation movement has been focused on the elimination of such sex-role stereotypes (Bardwick, 1971). Consequently, it seems likely that more women and men are challenging these expectations about their role and function within the family. Certainly, the popular media have begun illustrating marriages and families radically altered by the changing conception of the role of women. Reducing the impact of such socially dictated expectations might lead to greater variety in the marital contracts worked out by modern couples.

Demographic Variables Correlating with Marital Stability

In searching for correlates of marital stability, social scientists have often employed the incidence of divorce as an index. While the incidence of divorce may be influenced by a number of factors in addition to marital stability, it is nevertheless highly visible and easily measured.

AGE

The age at which individuals are getting married has been declining over recent decades, and certainly the rate of divorce has been increasing over the same period (Carter & Glick, 1970). Further, as noted, half of the divorces occur during the first six years of marriage and over one fifth during the first two years (Baber, 1953; Blood, 1969; Kenkel, 1966; Ogg, 1965). These trends probably foster the observation of Kenkel (1966) that the rate of divorce, and therefore of marital instability, is considerably higher if the husband is under 25 and the wife under 20 years of age. Noting the frequency of such early divorces, Udry (1971) suggests that these young couples are less likely to tolerate unhappiness in their marriages.

In addition to the age of the individuals getting married, investigators have also examined the relationship between marital stability and the discrepancy in age between the husband and wife. Such investigations (Carter & Glick, 1970; Lance & Snider, 1962; Levinger, 1965) have found that the rate of divorce is lower when the husband and wife are approximately the same age than when there is a large age difference. Such findings support the popularly held belief that a large difference in age can result in marital dissatisfaction and difficulty.

RELIGIOUS AFFILIATION

Religious beliefs and affiliations have been factors traditionally viewed as important in marriage. Further, religious leaders of today at times have expressed concern that a loss of religious faith in many adults has resulted in a breakdown in marriage. A study by Blood (1969) has provided some empirical information consistent with such concern. He found that two to three times as many religiously inactive as devoutly religious men and women were involved in divorce. Further, a difference in the incidence of divorce has been found for different religious groups. Udry (1971) found that divorce is less likely among Roman Catholics than among Protestants. Levinger (1965) found that divorce was less likely if both marital partners were from the same faith than if they were from different faiths.

In viewing such relationships between religious affiliations and marital stability, particular care must be exercised. Organized religions tend to place a high value on marital stability, with the Roman Catholic faith not even recognizing divorce. Such social pressure is likely to keep the marriage intact, even though the individuals might be quite unhappy and dissatisfied with it. Consequently, the relative rates of divorce might present a somewhat distorted picture of marital satisfaction. Langner and Michels (1963) provide information somewhat consistent with this view, in that interfaith marriages seemed to produce no more emotional stress for spouses than marriages within one faith. These authors found no greater mental-health risk for individuals who married spouses of the same major religious faith. Further, the mental-health risk of adults was the same whether they came from homes in which their parents were of different major faiths or whether they came from homes in which parents were of the same major faith. Thus, the congruence of religious affiliations between the marital partners did not appear to enhance or detract from the apparent emotional well-being of the individuals involved. It might well be that religious belief significantly influences whether divorce is seen as an option for coping with marital and family problems.

ECONOMIC AND OCCUPATIONAL STATUS

Certainly economic resources and worries about such resources (Langner & Michels, 1963) play an important part in the psychological well-being of the individual and the family. Numerous studies (Blood, 1969; Kenkel, 1966; Lantz & Snyder, 1962; Ogg, 1965) have found greater marital instability (reflected in the rate of divorce) as socioeconomic level declines. Further, Levinger (1965) found that home ownership was positively associated with marital stability.

Apart from such indices, marital stability has also been examined in relation to occupational choices and attitudes toward occupational pursuits. As Lidz (1970) observes, providing the material requirements of the family traditionally has been defined as part of the male role. Scanzoni (1968) found that the attitudes of both the husband and the wife toward the husband's occupation were associated with the rate of divorce. He observed that in intact marriages the wife viewed her husband's job as sufficiently prestigious and adequate to support the family life style and aspirations. Such wives also viewed their husbands as satisfied with the job. In the dissolved marriages in which the husband had worked at a manual job, it did not provide sufficient satisfaction for the wife, even when their income may have been higher than that of the couples in the intact marriages. In the dissolved marriages, if the husband had a nonmanual job, the wife usually felt that he spent too much time fulfilling his occupational role. Scanzoni also found that the divorce rate is higher for women married to husbands in a lower socioeconomic position than that of their fathers. Presumably, such women expect more than their husbands can give, making the marital agreements unstable.

In addition to such attitudinal correlates, the divorce rate has been shown to vary with the category of occupation for both men and women. Contrary to the picture presented by the television soap operas, the work of Carter and Glick (1970) indicates that the highest divorce rates for men are among craftsmen, service workers, and laborers. The lowest divorce rates for men are among farmers, professional workers, managers, and sales-workers. For women, they found that the highest rate includes clerical workers and service workers, while the lowest rate includes farmers, professional women, and sales workers.

From such findings, it can be seen that marital stability is associated with a number of aspects of occupation and economic level. Such job related factors may be a continuing source of strain on the family's ability to maintain stable relations.

EDUCATION

Because in our culture educational attainment is correlated with occupational status and economic success, marital stability also varies with educational level (Carter & Glick, 1970). Taken as a whole, such data indicate that higher educational achievement is associated with greater marital stability (Blood, 1969; Carter & Glick, 1970; Lantz & Snyder, 1962). There are, however, some exceptions to this over-all relationship. For instance, college dropouts have a higher rate of divorce than do high school graduates who have not attempted college, and women who have gone to graduate school have a higher rate than women who graduate from college and do not attend graduate school (Blood, 1969).

REMARRIAGE

With the growing number of divorced individuals in our society, the psychological reactions to such an experience become all the more important. In the chapter on divorce, the effects of divorce on the individuals involved are examined. Undergoing a divorce does significantly affect subsequent attempts to achieve marital stability with another partner.

According to the findings of Carter and Glick (1970), if both members of the couple are entering into their first marriage, the duration of that relationship will be the longest. Udry (1972) studied couples waiting to get their marriage license, and in four out of every five cases the idea of divorce had not even occurred to them. Carter and Glick (1970) further found that if the present marriage is the first for the wife but a remarriage for the husband, the expected duration of the marriage is somewhat less than if it is the first marriage for both. The expected duration of the marriage continued to decrease if the present marriage is the first for the husband but a remarriage for the wife, and the expected duration reached the shortest when the present marriage was a remarriage for both partners.

Examining the mental-health risk of individuals who have remarried, Langner and Michels (1963) observed no detrimental psychological effects. They noted, however, that most of the people who had remarried within their sample were also in the high socioeconomic group, a factor shown to be beneficial to mental-health risk.

In a related sphere, Langner and Michels (1963) found that adults who came from homes broken by divorce were more likely to worry about their own marriage than individuals who came from intact homes. Further, these authors found that worrying about one's marriage, whatever the source of such worry, was highly related to the individual's mental-health risk. From their over-all results, they suggest that the divorce of parents sets the pattern for later marital problems and may be a specific precursor of these problems rather than a general trigger for all kinds of emotional troubles. The effect of divorce on the children involved is further explored in the chapter on divorce.

SUMMARY

This overview of demographic variables has identified a number of factors associated with marital instability. The (1) age of the individuals; (2) their religious affiliations; (3) their economic, (4) occupational, and (5) educational status; and (6) their marital histories have all been related to frequency of divorce. Consequently, it might be expected that such factors are sources of strain on the marital relationship. Perhaps these factors are best thought of as chronic conditions making the establishment and maintenance of working relationship agreements difficult. In the following section, some of the episodes occurring within family life that are also likely to strain such agreements will be considered.

PROBLEMS IN FAMILY DEVELOPMENT

Over the life span of a marriage, numerous changes alter the organization and functioning of the family system. Among the most common of such changes are the births, development and departure of children. The addition of children often requires rather substantial and rapid changes in the agreements between the husband and wife, as well as the establishment of new agreements between each parent and the offspring. Furthermore, a network of agreements must be developed among the siblings (Haley, 1972). Consequently, the family system becomes more complicated and subject to more influences with additional children.

The vast majority of couples within our culture probably view having at least one child as a desirable event, and the birth of the first child has not been associated with an increase in the incidence of divorce. In fact, couples with no children have a higher rate of divorce than couples with children (Lance & Snider, 1962; Levinger, 1965). Such findings, however, need to be interpreted with caution since couples with children may feel a greater need to stay together for the sake of the children.

Bowen (1972), from his clinical practice, describes a case illustrating the kind of dysfunction that may be associated with the introduction of children. In this case, the couple married when they were both approximately 22 years old, and he was beginning a career as an accountant. For the first three years of marriage, they were very devoted to each other, with each paying particular attention to the happiness, comfort, and well-being of the other. Each was particularly sensitive to the likes and dislikes of the other, and they achieved a considerable degree of marital satisfaction with each other. With the birth of the first child, less of the wife's energy was available for the husband, and their marital relationship became less satisfactory. With the birth of the second child, the situation worsened considerably. The wife became more absorbed with the children, and the husband spent progressively more of his time and energy at his work. The wife began developing dys-functional behavioral patterns, fatiguing easily, being depressed, and spending more time in bed. Initially, the husband tried to help out with the household chores and take a more active role in the care of the children; however, gradually he began to feel overtaxed and unrewarded for his efforts. The wife began feeling angry with an obstinate husband who demanded everything and gave nothing in return. He felt that the wife was so demanding that no one could please her, and he was bothered by her nagging and by her constant complaining and her dirty house.

The reaction of this couple to the addition of children probably represents an exceptional case. It may well be that their unusualness lies in the extent of their reaction and their inability to work out a new and more compatible set of agreements.

In addition to the mere presence of a new child, the characteris-tics of the particular child may be important. Several investigators (cf. Westman, 1973) have found wide variations among even very young children on a number of dimensions, and the characteristics of the child may or may not be compatible with the expectations of the parents. Chess and her associates (1970) have identified three general types of temperaments among infants, having dif-ferent implications for family functioning. The first such tempera-ment type is referred to as "easy children." They are characterized during infancy as quickly establishing predictable feeding and sleeping schedules, smiling at strangers, and readily accepting unusual foods. They usually evoke favorable responses in others and apparently experience the world as warm, tender, and accept-ing. Such children would seem to fit most readily into the expectations and desires of most parents and thus require the least modification of parental and marital agreements. Indeed, Chess (1970) notes that this group of youngsters develop the fewest behavior problems.

A second temperament type is referred to as *"difficult children."* As infants, they are characterized by much more unpredictable feeding and sleeping schedules, likely to reject new foods and toys, and require longer periods of adjustment to altered routines. Further, they are seen as more likely to fuss than express pleasure and more likely to respond to frustration with violent temper tantrums. In examining such children over a number of years, Chess (1970) found that they were the most likely to develop behavioral problems. She has suggested that such problems result from the child's inability to meet the demands and expectations of parents and later peers and school officials. She does suggest that such problems can be minimized if these demands can be modified and implemented in a slower step by step fashion.

The third temperament type is referred to as *"slow-to-warm-up children."* Such children are characterized by mildly negative reactions to new situations. There is a gradual adaptation accompanying repeated exposure to the stimuli. Pressure for quick adaptation typically intensifies the child's tendency to withdraw, and a negative child-environment interaction may be set in motion. Recognition of this disposition and patient encouragement often lead to an increase in interest and involvement from the child (Chess, 1970). In considering the significance of these temperament types, Chess emphasizes that such differences in themselves do not lead to behavioral disorders, but rather that the psychological problems of the child result from dissonant relationships within the family and the broader social matrix. Thus, the agreements worked out between parents and their children must recognize such individual differences in the children.

Adolescence

Erikson (1950), Sullivan (1953), and other theorists concerned with personality development have suggested that as children grow up, they go through a series of stages, with each stage having particular emotional issues and conflicts coming to the forefront. With such developmental changes, there is a need for changes in the family relationships. Adolescence might be seen as one period placing particular strain on existing family agreements.

The developmental process, moving from infancy to adulthood, can be thought of as a move from total dependence on the parents when the individual is an infant to virtual independence from parents when the individual is an adult (c.f., Hilgard, Atkinson & Atkinson, 1975). Adolescence is seen as a period when this process of growing independence is greatly accelerated. The individual becomes more and more oriented to the values, expectations, and behavioral patterns of his peer group as opposed to those of his family. This change in social orientation is accompanied by a number of other highly significant factors. For instance, within adolescence the individual achieves adult physical capacities, including secondary sexual characteristics, and sexual urges and desires become prominent. By virtue of such factors alone, the adolescent's ability to get into serious trouble would seem greatly enhanced. Further, adult roles with their accompanying obligations and privileges are withheld from adolescents, and they are encouraged to remain in school to acquire knowledge and skills seen as highly desirable within our culture. From the perspective of the family, the child becoming an adolescent would appear to introduce new problems for and arouse the parents. Coons (1971), from his counseling experience with adolescents and their families, suggests that in our youth-oriented culture, growing old often raises difficult feelings in the person—feelings of missed opportunities, disappointments, unattractiveness, and the like. He further suggests that such feelings become particularly marked for parents as their offspring move toward adulthood. Interestingly, a number of authors have reported a jump in the incidence of divorce after approximately 20 years of marriage, about the time children of the marriage would be approaching maturity. Certainly other factors may be at work; however, it seems likely that such an increase is in part at least related to such familial changes. Consequently, parents may be reluctant to recognize the growing competence and independence of their adolescents. At the same time, the adolescents themselves appear eager to try out and explore new activities, giving rise to problems for the individual (Freeman &

Coons, cf. Coons, 1971) as well as the family. It would seem that dependence versus independence is one of the main emotional issues around which family agreements need to be revised during this developmental stage.

A number of other emotional issues in adolescence have been viewed by mental health workers (Coons, 1971; Josselyn, 1971) as products of family functioning. Such issues included self-centeredness, intimacy, and escapism. Josselyn (1971) suggests that such attitudes result from a child-centered culture in which parents establish highly unequal contracts with their children. She maintains that a common element in parent-child interaction agreements is the idea that the child need not explore on his own for desired events and situations because they would be provided to him by parents who anxiously seek assurance that their services are satisfactory. In her characterization of such relationships, she appears to be suggesting that they are only minimally reciprocal, with very little being expected of the child. In her interpretation, such contracts lead to a continuing self-centeredness in which the individual expects such unequal agreements to continue with others; to difficulties in intimacy where more mutual and balanced agreements are seen as important; and to escapism from problem situations.

On a somewhat more general level, Langner and Michels (1963) found that adults who recalled frequent parental quarrels while they were growing up had a higher mental-health risk than those adults who recalled few parental quarrels during the same period. Furthermore, they found that if the adult respondents perceived both parents negatively, the respondent showed a considerably higher mental-health risk than if neither parent were perceived negatively. Finally, investigators questioned the respondents concerning their relationships with their own offspring. They found that, if the respondent reported having many problems with his children or indicated that the problems involved with rearing children outweighed the pleasure involved, there was a significant increase in the respondent's mental health risk. It would seem that family discord during adolescence is associated with the mental health of the family members.

One particular development occurring during late adolescence or early adulthood is the individual's departure from home. Paykel

(1973) has theorized that departing from interpersonal relationships, as well as entering new ones, are times of potential crisis for the individual. The adolescent leaving home would appear to represent an instance of such departure, as his contact with the other family members is likely to be greatly reduced in extent and intensity. Additionally, clinicians have seen interpersonal loss as a significant contributor to a variety of emotional troubles. Certainly, such departures would seem to disrupt the ongoing matrix of interpersonal agreements within the family (Jackson, 1970; Haley, 1972).

FAMILY THERAPY

As mental-health workers began recognizing the role of the family in the psychological well-being of individuals, appropriate techniques also emerged. The over-all aim for most of these approaches is to help change the way in which the family members interact (Ackerman, 1969; Haley, 1972; Minuchin, 1970). Therapists attempting to achieve this end have approached the problems with a wide diversity of specific techniques, ranging from a psychoanalytic background to a behavioral background (Patterson et al., 1973). Likewise, some therapists have addressed long-term chronic interferences with family functioning, while others have focused on crisis intervention techniques with the family (Eisler & Harrison, 1973; Langsley & Kaplan, 1968).

Although a general discussion of psychological resources is provided in Chapter 12, family therapy appears sufficiently specialized to merit consideration here, and some of the more common elements and techniques in such therapy are described. With the rapid emergence of such diverse treatment approaches, few systematic comparative studies of family therapy have been conducted, and our present knowledge rests, to a large extent, on clinical impression and description.

When couples and families seek professional help for their problems, it seems likely that they have either encountered an acutely disruptive crisis or that there has been a more gradual deterioration in the relationships involved. Within the systems framework, such problems are resolved through compromise or redefinition of parts of the contract (Haley, 1972); if one or both individuals are unwilling to make such changes in their relationship, the whole fabric may be threatened. Angry and painful interchanges may become more frequent and widespread (Eisler & Harrison, 1973), with both deriving progressively less satisfaction from the relationship.

Even when both partners earnestly desire to work out their disagreements, serious blocks may be encountered from a variety of sources, with one of the most important being the needs and fears of each person (Ackerman, 1970). Consider the following example. A wife presents to her husband, in a rather angry way, a notice from the bank indicating that they have significantly overdrawn their account. She may feel unhappy because for her being in debt is associated with unwanted dependence, and she feels angry with her husband because he got them in that position. On the other hand, the husband may feel a bit taken aback and threatened because providing financial security may have been defined as his responsibility, and he may search earnestly for some mistake in the checkbook. Interchanges between the two are likely to reflect such different emotional reactions; unless some common perspective can be reached, the interchange may lead to further distress between the two.

Despite such problems, most marriages seem to maintain stability without requiring professional help. Naturally, a question arises of when such help is necessary or desirable. There does not appear to be any research to help answer such a question; however, some guidelines on when to seek help are suggested. Professional help may be useful when one or both members of a couple feel progressively unhappy and dissatisfied with their marriage or family life despite efforts to change the relationship. Second, it may assist a couple that encounters a serious crisis that directly threatens the relationship or experiences recurrent crises without being able to establish a stable relationship. Third, therapy may be needed when one member of the family develops symptomatic behavior, like marked depression, recurrent headaches, or intense anxiety. Fourth, it is useful when a family breaks up after parental divorce. Therapy may often be useful at this point because even the most troubled relationships involve an entanglement of positive and negative emotion, and separations may have far-reaching consequences.

As couples come into therapy, each individual may want the

therapist to agree with him or her and to criticize the other. Each person seeks the therapist's support for his side of the conflict. Virtually all marital and family therapists recognize the importance of avoiding any fixed alliance (Ackerman, 1970; Haley, 1972). Occasionally, a therapist may provide one person with support and reassurance, but to be effective she should remain at some emotional distance in order to maintain an objective perspective. Resolving a conflict satisfactorily requires more than just ganging up on one side or another. The therapist will watch carefully how the individuals are interacting and communicating with one another and then point out such patterns to them. Additionally, the therapist may provide specific instructions or suggestions about ways to solve certain problems (Langsley & Kaplan, 1968), and Langsley and Kaplan, in treating families facing immediate crises, have found it useful to assign relevant family tasks.

The therapist, in his interaction with various family members, also serves as a model for the other family members. Eisler and Harrison (1973) have placed particular emphasis in this function, having the therapist explicitly identify particular interchanges as modeling. For instance, the therapist might say to the family as a whole, "Now, when John gets nervous and upset as he is now, the best way to ask him particular questions is. . . ." Aside from such explicit modeling, the therapist is involved with the same activity when he behaves kindly to a provoking teenager or when he insists on an answer to an emotionally laiden question. As Bowen (1972) points out, such interchanges have another value as well. From his experience, Bowen believes that other family members can understand some emotionally laiden messages better when they are directed toward the therapist's questions. Thus, a husband may be better able to find out what is bothering his wife when the therapist asks her, "What are you crying about?" and she responds, "John is always late for dinner, and all my work preparing the meal is wasted." John, asking the same question, may begin reacting to the potential accusation in her voice, leading to an argument. Listening to his wife explaining her problem the therapist allows (presumably) him to understand her disappointment and feeling of futility.

One technique recently developed in working with individuals has particular usefulness in working with couples and families.

This technique of *behavioral contracting* (Eisler & Harrison, 1973) is based on the idea that "If you scratch my back, I'll scratch yours." The therapist focuses attention on some small aspect of the present difficulties, perhaps a wife's complaint that her husband doesn't put up his coffee cup. An effort is then made to have the couple form an explicit contract with one another: "If you'll put away your coffee cup, I'll not leave my hair curlers all over the bed." The couple is then encouraged to carry out such a contract. As such interactions are carried out successfully, the therapist will move to more substantial agreements on more emotionally pro- vacative topics. As Eisler and Harrison point out (1973), the idea is to interrupt a cycle of negative experiences and to allow each to experience more positive benefits through the marriage. Such initial small changes can have an over-all effect on the family system, because they represent accomplishment and give rise to feelings of hope.

Despite the best efforts of all concerned, improvement in marital and familial relations is not inevitable. Improvement would appear to require a sincere commitment, maturity of emotions and judgments, and a patient persistent effort from everyone.

PROJECTS AND QUESTIONS

1. Divide the group into men and women, and ask each to develop terms they would want in a marital contract. Such agreements should include the areas of finances, child-rearing, work of each parent, sexual relations, the role of friends and in-laws, and distribution of chores around the home.
2. Select several major marital changes, some desirable changes and some un- desirable changes. Desirable changes might include the birth of a wanted child, promotion in a job, a desired move to a new town. Undesirable changes might include the birth of a defective child, an unwanted pregnancy, the loss of a job, a child in significant trouble with the law, or the occurrence of a major illness. Form one or more small groups and have the members role-play the situation, portraying how they think the individuals would feel and how such feelings might affect family life. Have the remainder of the group observe the role-played situation and then discuss what has happened.
3. In small groups, discuss how a marital contract between two homosexuals might differ from a marital contract between two heterosexuals. Consider, in particular, the effect of societal prejudices and pressures on such a deviant contract.

4. In small groups, discuss how marital contracts might differ from other inter-personal contracts at work or at school.

SUGGESTED READINGS

Popular Press

Swinging future. *Time, 101* (Jan., 1973), 34–35.

J. FLAHERTY. In defense of traditional marriage. *Life,* 1972, *73*, 59ff.

W. J. LEDERER & J. CRIST. Marriage: for and against *Harper's Bazaar,* 1972, *105*, 110–11.

Advanced Sources

C. J. SAGER, H. S. KAPLAN, R. H. GUNDLACH, R. L. KREMER & J. R. ROYCE, The marriage contract. In C. J. Sager & H. S. Kaplan (Eds.). *Progress in group and Family Therapy.* New York: Brunner/Mazel Pub., 1972.

J. R. SMITH, & L. G. SMITH, *Beyond monogamy.* Baltimore: John Hopkins University Press, 1974.

REFERENCES

ACKERMAN, N. W. Family psychotherapy and psychoanalysis: Implications of difference. In N. W. Ackerman, (Ed.). *Family process.* New York: Basic Books, Inc., 1970.

ACKERMAN, N. W. The growing edge of family therapy. In C. J. Sager & H. S. Kaplan (Eds.). *Progress in group and family therapy.* New York: Brunner/Mazel, Pub., 1972.

ACKERMAN, N. W. *The psychodynamics of family life.* New York: Basic Books, Inc., 1969.

ADAMS, JAY E. *Competent to counsel.* Philadelphia: Presbyterian and Reformed Publishing Co., 1973.

BABER, R. E. *Marriage and the family.* New York: McGraw-Hill Co., Inc., 1953.

BACH, G. R. *The intimate enemy.* New York: Morrow, 1969.

BARDWICK, J. M. *The psychology of women.* Harper & Row: 1971.

BARNETT, J. Cognitive thought and affect in the organization of experience. In J. Masserman (Ed.) *Science and psychoanalysis,* Vol. VII. New York: Grune and Stratton, Inc., 1968.

BARTELL, G. *Group sex.* New York: Peter H. Wyden, 1971.

BATESON, G. Information and codification: A philosophical approach. In J. Reusch & G. Bateson. *Communication: The social matrix of psychiatry.* New York: Norton, 1951.

BLOOD, R. O. *Marriage.* New York: Free Press, 1969.

BOWEN, M. Family therapy and family group therapy. In H. I. Kaplan & B. J. Sodock, (Eds.). *Group treatment of mental illness.* New York: E. P. Dutton, 1972.

BURGESS, E. W. The family as a unity of interacting personalities. In *Family therapy: An introduction to theory and technique.* California: Brooks/Cole Pub., 1972.

BURTON, A. Marriage without failure. *Psychol. Reports, 32*(3), Pt. 2, 1199–1208, 1973.

CARTER, H. & GLICK, P. C. *Marriage and divorce: A social and economic study.* Cambridge: Harvard University Press, 1970.

CHESS, S. Temperament of children at risk. In E. J. Anthony and C. Koupernik (Eds.). *The child in his family,* New York: John Wiley & Sons, 1973.

COOKERLY, J. R. The outcome of six major forms of marriage counseling compared: A pilot study. *J. Marriage Family,* 1973, *35 (4),* 608–611.

COONS, F. W. The developmental tasks of the college student. In S. C. Feinstein, P. Giovacchini, & A. A. Miller, (Eds.). *Adolescent Psychiatry,* Vol. I. New York: Basic Books, Inc., 1971.

EISLER, R. M. Crisis intervention in the family of a fire setter. *Psychotherapy, theory, and practice,* 1972, *9*(1), 76–79.

EISLER, R. M. & HARRISON, M. Behavioral techniques in family-oriented crisis-intervention. *Arch. Gen. Psychiat.,* 1973, *28,* 111.

ERIKSON, H. *Childhood and society.* New York: W. W. Norton, 1950.

EYBERG, S. M. & JOHNSON, S. M. Multiple assessement of behavior modification with families. *J. Consulting and Clinical Psychol.,* 1974, *42,* 594–606.

FREUD, S. *The basic writings of Sigmund Freud* (translated by A. A. Brill). New York: Random House, 1938.

FREUD, S. *Therapy and technique.* New York: The Macmillan Co., 1963.

GROVES, E. R. *Marriage.* New York: Henry Holt, 1941.

HALEY, J. Family therapy. In C. J. Sager, & H. S. Singer (Eds.). *Progress in group and family therapy.* New York: Brunner/Mazel Pub., 1972.

HILGARD, E. R., ATKINSON, R. C. & ATKINSON, R. L. *Introduction to Psychology.* Sixth edition. New York: Harcourt, Brace, Jovanovich, Inc., 1975.

HORNEY, K. *New ways in psychoanalysis.* New York: Norton, 1939.

JACKSON, D. D. The marital quid pro quo. In G. Zuk and I. Boszormenzi-Nagy (Eds.). *Family therapy for disturbed families.* California: Science and Behavior Books, 1966.

JACKSON, D. D. The study of the family. In N. W. Ackerman (Ed.). *Family Process.* New York: Basic Books, Inc., 1970.

JOSSELYN, I. M. Etiology of three current adolescent syndromes: A hypothesis. In S. C. Feinstein, P. Giovacchini, & A. A. Miller (Eds.). *Adolescent Psychiatry,* Vol. I. New York: Basic Books, Inc., 1971.

KENKEL, W. F. *The family in perspective.* New York: Appleton-Century-Crofts, 1966.

LANGER, T. S. & MICHELS, S. T. *Life stress and mental health.* New York: The Free Press, 1963.

LANGSLEY, D. G. & KAPLEN, D. M. *The treatment of families in crisis.* New York: Grune and Stratton, 1968.

LANTZ, H. B. & SNYDER, F. C. *Marriage: An examination of the man-woman relationship.* New York: John Wiley, 1962.

LEBOVICI, S. The psychoanalytic theory of family. In E. J. Anthony & Koupernik, C. (Eds.). *The child in his family.* New York: John Wiley & Sons, 1970.

LEVINGER, G. Marital cohesiveness and dissolution: An integrative review. *J. Marriage Family,* 1965, *27*(1), 19–28.

LIDZ, T. The family as the developmental setting. In E. J. Anthony, & C. Koupernik (Eds.). *The child in his family.* New York: John Wiley & Sons, 1970.

MINUCHIN, S. *Families and family therapy.* Massachusetts: Harvard University Press, 1974.

MINUCHIN, S. The use of an ecological framework in the treatment of a child. In E. J. Anthony & C. Koupernik (Eds.). *The child in his family.* New York: John Wiley & Sons, 1970

OGG, E. *Divorce.* New York: Public Affairs Pamphlet #380, 1965.

PATTERSON, G. R., COBB, J. A. & RAY, R. S. A social engineering technology for retraining the families of aggressive boys. In H. E. Adams & I. P. Unikel (Eds.). *Issues and trends in behavior therapy.* Springfield, Ill.: C. C. Thomas, 1973.

PAYKEL, E. S. Life events and acute depression. In J. P. Scott & E. C. Senay (Eds.). *Separation and depression: Clinical and research aspects.* Washington: American Association for the Advancement of Science, 1973.

SAGER, C. J., KAPLEN, H. S., GUNDLACH, R. H., KREMER, R. L. & ROYCE, J. R. The marriage contract. In C. J. Sager and H. S. Kaplen, (Eds.). *Progress in group and family therapy.* New York: Brunner/Mazel Pub., 1972.

SCANZONI, J. A social system analysis of dissolved and existing marriage. *J. Marriage Family, 30,* August 1968, 452–461.

SHERMAN, M. H., ACKERMAN, N. W., SHERMAN, M. H., & MITCHELL, C., Nonverbal cues and reenactment of conflict in family therapy. In N. W. Ackerman (Ed.). *Family Process.* New York: Basic Books, Inc., 1970.

SMITH, J. R. & SMITH, S. G. *Beyond Monogamy.* Baltimore: Johns Hopkins University Press, Co., 1974.

STUART, R. Operant-interpersonal treatment for marital discord. *J. Consulting and Clinical Psychol.* 1969, *33,* 675–682.

SULLIVAN, H. S. *The interpersonal theory of psychiatry.* New York: Norton, 1953.

TOLMAN, W. *Family constellation.* New York: Springer-Verlag, 1969.

UDRY, J. R. *The social context of marriage.* Philadelphia: J. P. Lippincott, 1971.

VETTER, H. *Language behavior and psychopathology.* Chicago: Rand McNally and Company, 1970.

WALLER, W. *The old love and the new.* Carbondale, Ill.: Southern Illinois University Press, 1967.

WESTMEN, C. F. (Ed.). *Individual differences in children.* New York: John Wiley & Sons, 1973.

The Handicapped Child

CHAPTER 5

MARY LYNNE CALHOUN

A child who is developmentally disabled, who is limited physically or mentally to such an extent that he requires extensive special services and support to make use of whatever potential is his, faces some very serious problems in life. Depending on the nature and severity of his handicap, he may face such obstacles as never developing skills of daily living such as feeding or dressing himself, never developing adequate speech and communication skills, never being able to function independently as an adult. Even if his physical or mental impairment is mild, he may suffer from a lack of social acceptance or from limited opportunities for personal growth or development. The hazards to personal adjustment for a physically or mentally handicapped young person are enormous.

In recent years there has developed in the helping professions an increasing awareness that the hazards to personal adjustment do not exist for the handicapped young person alone. Special demands are made on the family with a handicapped child. These demands range from the need to readjust the parents' hopes for the child in terms of the realities of the handicapping condition (Farber, 1960) to increased physical and financial responsibilities as a severely handicapped child grows older (Ehlers, 1966). These special demands, which vary from one time to another in the lifespan of a particular family, can indeed be considered critical life problems. Hutt and Gibby (1976) state categorically that parents of handicapped children are likely to show some significant emotional reactions to the fact that their child is handicapped.

This chapter will focus on the critical life problems of families with handicapped children. The scope of this chapter will be limited to the reactions of families with children who are *mentally retarded* or *physically handicapped*. It would be useful for us to define these conditions. *Mental retardation,* according to the American Association on Mental Deficiency (Gressman, 1973), refers to significant subaverage intellectual functioning existing along with impairment in adaptive behavior. The mentally retarded child, then, has trouble functioning adequately in society because of intellectual limitations. The degree of limitation varies tremendously. A helpful way of considering the degrees of limitation is to think in terms of mild, moderate, and severe mental retardation. A mildly retarded child may have a real struggle mastering academic tasks at school but may be able as an adult to hold a job, care for a family, and be a responsible member of the community. A moderately retarded person will probably never be able to live independently as an adult but often can learn to speak well, to feed, dress, and toilet himself, to play with other children, and to be a functioning member of a family. A severely retarded child will need a lifetime of support; this child will rarely learn to walk or talk and will be quite limited in his responsiveness to other people.

Physical handicaps refer to neurological, muscular, skeletal, and general physical disabilities. Conditions such as cerebral palsy, muscular dystrophy, spina bifida, and hydrocephalus are included in this category. The research on children with physical handicaps cited in this chapter will deal only with those conditions severe enough to affect the developmental process significantly. It should be noted that severe developmental disabilities often involve both physical and mental impairment. For example, 75 per cent of children with cerebral palsy, a neurological impairment affecting motor control, have IQ's below 70 and would therefore be classified as mentally retarded (Kirk, 1972). It is important to realize that it is difficult to compare families who have mentally retarded children to families with physically handicapped children because

often severely handicapped children are indeed multiply handicapped. Both conditions, of course, can and do occur independently. Because a child is physically handicapped, it is certainly
not reasonable to assume that he is mentally retarded as well, or
vice versa.

Although there are many other categories of children who are
developmentally different (i.e., speech-impaired, emotionally
disturbed, deaf, blind, learning-disabled, gifted) and although
their families also often have special problems in adjustment, we
are focusing our attention on the conditions of mental retardation and physical disability.

Our interest will be on how families react to the special demands
of a handicapped child, what variables influence the family's adjustment, the adjustment problems of brothers and sisters of
handicapped children, and finally what services and support
families have found helpful in dealing with the critical life problem
of a handicapped child in the family. In this chapter, the term
handicapped refers to a child who is either mentally retarded or
physically handicapped.

In reviewing the research in the behavioral sciences on this critical life problem, certain limitations become apparent and should
be specified. As Wolfensberger (1967) has pointed out, there are
many philosophical statements about the problems of families
with handicapped children but remarkably few carefully designed
research studies. The research studies that do exist rely heavily on
interviewing techniques and questionnaire data. Although these
methods certainly have value, they rely heavily on the respondents'
ability to remember events and feelings from the past, and it is
difficult to verify the accuracy of these memories. Many studies
deal with parents whose children are enrolled in programs for the
handicapped (community mental health centers and the like); the
reactions of these parents may not be generalizable to parents who
have not chosen to use such services or who have not had the opportunity to do so. Finally, most studies seem to deal with the
reactions of mothers, although the fathers' adjustment is also
important. These research limitations must be kept in mind so that
conclusions drawn from the research cited will be considered with
caution.

PATTERNS OF REACTION IN FAMILIES WITH HANDICAPPED CHILDREN

The reactions of families to the presence of a handicapped child vary markedly from family to family and may vary within one particular family from time to time. Certain patterns of reaction have, however, been identified in families with handicapped children that seem to reflect the difficulties many families experience in dealing with this critical life problem.

One of the most consistent research findings is that the family's participation in community and social activities is often drastically limited by the presence of a severely handicapped child. Holt (1958a), in a survey of families with severely mentally retarded children in England, found that 40 per cent of parents did not go out together and a smaller percentage of families reported that they were unable to take a vacation. In a study of Australian families with a severely retarded child, Schonell and Rorke (1960) report that about half the families interviewed said that their visits to friends' homes and their shopping arrangements were affected by the presence of the handicapped child. Meyerowitz and Farber (1966) investigated the families of 120 mildly retarded children in Illinois and compared the family patterns with those of 60 families of comparable income and occupational status but with no handicapped children. All families were from lower economic levels. The families with mildly retarded children seemed to be more isolated from their community than the contrast group in that they had less participation in voluntary organizations, less church attendance, and less contact with friends and relatives.

In addition to this relative social isolation, another important finding is that of a greater incidence of problems in family relations with handicapped children. A study of the mental health of near relatives of 20 multihandicapped children in Scandinavia by Berggreen (1971) found higher-than-expected rates of divorce, desertion of the family by the father, and hospitalization of one or both parents for psychiatric reasons. While the sample of 20 families is too small to allow much generalization, similar results have been found elsewhere. Testing and interviews with 65 cerebral-palsied children and their families (Podeanu-Czehofsky, 1975) led one researcher to conclude that 80 per cent of the families with a physically handicapped child showed some sort of family problem such as overt rejection of the child, excessive spoiling, or identifying the handicapped child as the scapegoat, the one who is to blame for other problems. The Meyerowitz and Farber (1966) survey found a greater amount of remarriage in families with mildly retarded children that in the contrast group of similar social status. The *Index of Marital Integration* was developed by Farber (1959) to explore the status of marriages in families with severely handicapped children. Following a survey with this index of families in Chicago, Farber (1959) concluded that marital integration is affected negatively by the presence of a severely mentally retarded child within the family structure.

A profound effect on families with handicapped children would seem to be the restriction of fertility. 201 families in England with retarded children were studied by Holt (1958b). While additional pregnancies were theoretically possible in 160 of the families, 101 of the families reported that they did not want any more children. In 90 of these families, this decision was attributed directly to the presence of the retarded child in the family.

Another pattern of reaction is the presence of physical or psychological problems in the mothers of handicapped children. Cummings, Bayley, and Rie (1966) report that middle-class mothers of mentally retarded children showed more physical signs of personal stress than did mothers of chronically ill children. In a review of the literature regarding mothers of cerebral-palsied children, Collins (1965) reports that much data suggests that mothers of physically handicapped children show more signs of depression than other mothers. Farber's (1963) survey of 268 mothers of severely retarded children found a higher-than-expected rate of physical symptoms and nervous complaints among these mothers.

The Critical Life Problems Perspective

These reaction patterns would seem to indicate that families with handicapped children experience some degree of stress and disharmony. Major researchers and theorists have attempted to account for these patterns from a crisis perspective. This perspective is congruent with the critical life problems perspective presented in Chapter 1 of this book. Perhaps the major theoretical work, based on extensive research, has been carried out by Bernard Farber, a University of Illinois sociologist. Several of Farber's studies have been cited previously. In studying the effects of a retarded child on the mother, Farber (1963) developed a theory of two types of crisis that occur in families with a handicapped child—the "tragic crisis" and the "role organization crisis." A "tragic crisis" is a situation or event that destroys the hopes for the expected development of a family member. The reliable diagnosis of a child as mentally retarded would be a tragic crisis because the family's hopes of an educationally, financially, and maritally successful life for that child may be destroyed. A "role organization crisis" is a situation or event that requires a change in existing roles (or expected behavior) in the family. Examples of role organization crisis would include that of a father who must continue to provide full financial support for a young retarded adult long past the time when most young people would be independent and self-supporting. Another example would be that of a younger sister who must assume much responsibility for the physical care of an older retarded sibling.

It is Farber's (1963) contention that the type of crisis the family is experiencing, "tragic" or "role organization", will determine to some extent the kinds of problems the mothers of retarded children will experience. He postulates that the psychological response to the impact of tragic crisis is "nervousness" while the complaint of "poor physical health" is the response to role organization crisis. He interviewed 268 mothers of severely retarded children and investigated such variables as the physical demands of the mentally retarded child on the mother, the initial emotional impact of the diagnosis of mental retardation, the state of the mother's health, and her history of treatment for "nervous conditions." The results of this study support Farber's (1963) hypotheses. Mothers who had received help for psychological problems reported a greater initial emotional impact of the diagnosis of mental retardation than did control-group mothers, and mothers who reported not being in good health perceived the mentally retarded child as making more demands (therefore leading to a role organization crisis) than did control-group mothers.

A further careful development of the crisis or critical life problem perspective has been carried out by Mercer (1966). She studied a group of patients who had been placed in institutions for the mentally retarded by their families and who were later released to their homes at their families' request. She compared the family patterns of this group with the patterns of families who had placed their handicapped children in residential facilities but who had not requested their release. Members of these two groups of families were interviewed to determine their perception of the severity of the problems prior to institutionalization. It was her hypothesis that the nature and severity of the crisis a family endured in the time preceding the institutionalization of the mentally retarded child would affect the family's willingness to have the child in the home again.

The results of the interviews support Mercer's (1966) hypothesis. She found that children still in residential facilities had frequently produced a severe preinstitutional crisis. There was a heavy burden of physical care for the child as well as interpersonal stress that was attributed to the presence of the handicapped child. In these cases, the family members seemed to agree that institutionalization was their best course of action. By contrast, the preinstitutional crisis of the released mentally retarded child more typically included behavioral problems on the part of the child but no excessive demands for physical care. Almost half of the families of children discharged had been divided on the issue of institutionalization. The preinstitutional crisis of families of released patients differed, then, from the crisis of families of children who remained in residential facilities.

Time-Limited Crisis

The theory that some crisis in families with handicapped children are time-limited, that is, limited to a specific point in time when a particularly stressful event occurs or some difficult decisions must be made (Mercer, 1966), is a useful framework for looking at some problems in families with handicapped children.

We will focus now on two particular time-bound crises: the crisis the family faces at the time of diagnosis of the handicapping condition and the crisis a family faces at the time a decision is made to institutionalize a handicapped child. Neither of these crises is maturational in nature, that is, neither occurs at one particular point in the lifespan of the child nor the lifespan of the family. The diagnosis of mental retardation, for example, can occur within days of the birth of the child but frequently occurs months or years later. The decision to institutionalize a child could be made at the time of diagnosis or at a point in time many years later or not at all.

THE TIME OF DIAGNOSIS AND REDEFINITION

Counselors experienced in dealing with handicapped children (Ross, 1964; Stewart, 1974) have stated that families often experience reactions not unlike grief when they learn that their child will probably be limited in his physical or mental development. Researchers have explored these clinical impressions and found support for them. In a 1960 study, Farber found that the higher the socioeconomic status of a family, the greater the initial grief impact of the diagnosis of mental retardation. This finding was explained by suggesting that families with higher socioeconomic status place a real premium on education and intellectual achievement. When they learn that their child will not make his mark in these highly desired areas, the loss in terms of expectation and hopes for the child is great.

Although Farber (1960) found that higher-status families experienced a greater emotional impact at the time of diagnosis, it must be noted that this is certainly a difficult time for families in all social strata. Ehlers (1966) conducted an intensive study of the reactions of 24 mothers of moderately and severely retarded children. These mothers were from lower-middle-class families. The mothers sought help for their children from physicians or others because they suspected that something was physically wrong with the child. He did not sit up or crawl when he should; he was slow in learning to talk. When the more accurate diagnosis of mental retardation was made, the mothers reported feeling shocked or disbelieving. They reported that fathers often responded angrily, insisting that there was nothing wrong with the child, that the mother simply was not a good mother. An interesting finding of this study is that the mothers reported that sometimes they were given information about their child regarding mental retardation by professionals, and they simply did not understand the implications. For example, two mothers reported being told that their child was a mongoloid at the time of the child's birth. Mongolism, or Down's syndrome, is a chromosomal problem that usually produces moderate mental retardation as well as a collection of physical characteristics that to Western laymen give the impression that the child is Oriental or "Mongoloid." When these mothers later expressed concern about the slow development of their children, they were shocked to learn that mental retardation is an expected aspect of Down's Syndrome. Clear, useful information does not always come at the time of diagnosis, and this lack of information can complicate the family's adjustment.

The time of diagnosis, Farber (1963) suggests, is the beginning of the family's need to "redefine" the child, to look at the child in terms of realistic hopes rather than the ideal expectations that were present before the diagnosis of mental retardation. Examples of this process of redefinition can be found in several studies which examine parents' perceptions of the child's intellectual and social abilities.

Zuk (1959) found that parents tend to overestimate the social ability of handicapped children and that this tendency is most pronounced when the child is normal in motor functions. Similarly, Condell (1966) found that parents' attitudes about the child's ability were very different from those of professionals working with the children. It would seem, then, that some parents have difficulty with the process of redefinition. It has been suggested, however, by Jensen and Kogan (1962) that the tendency to overestimate a child's ability decreased over time. In a study of children with cerebral palsy, they found that parents tended to overestimate the abilities of young children but became more realistic as the children grew older. Schulman and Stern (1959) found that a group of parents was moderately accurate in their estimates of the intelligence of their retarded children but that some parents overestimated the child's ability while others underestimated the intelligence quotient.

Redefinition of the child would seem to be an ongoing process, as is illustrated in Meyerowitz's (1967) study of parental awareness of mental retardation. He interviewed 186 families, divided into three groups. One group had first-grade children with intelligence in the average range. The second and third groups had first-grade children with intelligence in the borderline and the mildly retarded ranges. The children in the second group were in regular classes; the children in the third group in special education classes for the mentally retarded.

Each family was interviewed three times during the child's first two years in school; the interviews focused on the parents' awareness of the intellectual abilities of the children. There were some indications that the parents of the retarded children had some awareness of retardation. For example, they described the children as behaving immaturely and expected their children to complete fewer years of formal education than did the parents of nonretarded children. However, the parents' expectations for the retarded children when they reached adulthood showed no redefinition. The professional and occupational expectations for the retarded children were not statistically different from the parental expectations for nonretarded children.

The time of diagnosis of a handicapping condition in a child is seen then as a time-limited crisis that produces immediate effects of shock, disbelief, or grief-like reactions and demands a more long-term process of redefining the hopes and dreams for the child in light of this new and disturbing information.

THE DECISION FOR INSTITUTIONALIZATION

Full-time residential care for mentally retarded children has not been the primary nor even the most common treatment in the United States, nor is it likely to be. As Hutt and Gibby (1976) point out, only about 5 per cent of the mentally retarded persons in this country are ever in a residential facility for the retarded at a given time. The decision to institutionalize a mentally retarded child is by no means, then, the decision every family reaches or even considers. This topic is selected for discussion, however, because it is a good example of a time-limited crisis, a time in which a family must reach a decision about the best way to deal with the needs of the handicapped child and the needs of the family. Other similar time-limited crises might include decisions involving appropriate educational services for the child, how to handle a mentally retarded adolescent's desire for independence or feelings of sexuality, or how to make custodial or guardianship arrangements for the time when parents will not be able to care for the handicapped person.

As Mercer (1966) pointed out, the decision to institutionalize the handicapped child, that is, to assign the major responsibility for the child's care to a residential facility, is a decision that is often not made easily or comfortably. Her study indicated that families that later requested the return of the handicapped child to the home had experienced some real disagreement about the decision at the time placement was made. Grossman (1972) found in clinical interviews that the decision to institutionalize the child was often the cause of as well as a response to marital discord; the mother and father could not agree on this decision.

Numerous studies have found that the decision to place a child in an institution is usually made when the family is undergoing additional kinds of stress, such as economic pressure or marital discord, or when the child presents a series of complicated problems. Wolf and Whitehead (1975) found that the decision to institutionalize is related to the sex of the handicapped child and to the state of the parents' marriage. Male handicapped children are more likely to be institutionalized than female, and if the presence of the handicapped child is seen as a disruption of the marriage, institutionalization is more likely. The mothers in Ehler's (1966) study reported a desire to keep the retarded children at home as long as possible but were more willing to seek a residential placement if there were complications such as hyperactivity or lack of toilet training. When the child demands a heavy burden of physical care, placement is more likely (Mercer, 1966). Fotheringham, Skelton and Hoddinott (1971) found that institutionalized children were more likely to have been disruptive at home and at school and that their families seemed less capable of managing the children than the families of handicapped children who remained at home. Of 103 families with children with Down's Syndrome, the families that applied for institutionalization were the least economically stable and had the most problems in family relations (Stone, 1967).

The same pressures that operate to make residential placement more likely seem to influence the family's relationship with the child after placement. Twenty-two biographical and psychological variables were examined in 200 families who had children in a state institution for the retarded to determine which were related to the families' continued contact with the child or lack of it (Anderson, Schlottman & Weiner, 1975). The families' involvement with the handicapped children was measured by the number of visits to the institution and by attendance at parent conferences. Six variables were found to be related to the noninvolvement of parents with the institutionalized handicapped child: the presence of physical anomalies in the child, low occupational level of the father, maintenance payments not required from the family, a large discrepancy between the child's chronological age and his mental age, the parent with custody of the child having been divorced and remarried, and the distance from the institution.

The placement of a mentally retarded child in an institution has been seen by some researchers as a desirable solution to some of the special problems faced by families with handicapped children. Tizard (1964), for example, studied two groups of families in London. One group of 150 families had a severely retarded child who lived with them and the other group consisted of 100 families whose mentally retarded children had been placed in institutions. Tizard (1964) concluded that families who kept their mentally retarded children at home experienced more problems in adjustment than those whose children were institutionalized and that the problem of retardation tended to lower the quality and standards of life in the home significantly.

In recent years, however, other researchers have questioned whether institutionalization is the best solution for the problems of many families with handicapped children. Braginsky and Braginsky (1971) have raised questions about the development of children in institutionalized settings following their studies of such children. Grossman (1972), in her study of the brothers and sisters of retarded children, does not support the notion that normal siblings are better off when the handicapped child is out of the home. Fotheringham Skelton, and Hoddinott (1971), in a one-year follow-up study of institutionalized retarded children and their families, found no significant changes in the adjustment of families whose children were institutionalized, although some parents expressed considerable relief.

Although residential placement will probably continue to be sought by families with children with complicated problems and by families in economic or personal distress, alternatives to full-time residential placement will be discussed in the final section of this chapter, *What Helps?*

There Are Positive Reactions, Too

The preceding portions of this chapter have looked at certain family reaction patterns to the stress of having a handicapped child in the family. Reactions such as social isolation, marital discord, decisions to limit the size of the family, and physical symptoms of the mother were identified, and these reaction patterns were placed in a critical life problem perspective. It was noted that certain problems are time-limited, specific to a certain point in time in the life of the family.

If all one knew about families with handicapped children were the studies cited, it would seem certain that the presence of a handicapped child in a family is an unmitigated tragedy, and that families in this situation are universally overwhelmed by this unhappy circumstance. This is emphatically not the case. As stated earlier, reactions vary dramatically from one family to another and within one particular family over time. Although many families report stress reactions, many of these families report positive influences of the handicapped child within the family. Berggreen's (1971) study of the mental health of the near relatives of multihandicapped children in Scandinavia found that a high number of family members reported a strong desire to enter human services professions and attributed this desire to the presence of the handicapped child in the family. In Grossman's (1972) extensive study of 83 college students who had a mentally or physically handicapped brother or sister, 45 per cent of the college students were judged by the interviewers to have benefitted rather than been harmed by having a handicapped sibling. Tolerance, compassion, sensitivity to prejudice, and a strong appreciation of their own good health and intelligence were among the positive aspects reported. The reaction to the presence of a handicapped child in the family is not necessarily a negative one. The next section of this chapter will explore variables that influence a family's reaction to a handicapped child.

VARIABLES THAT INFLUENCE FAMILY REACTION PATTERNS

The question of what aspects of the family have an influence on the family's acceptance of a handicapped child is one that has interested several researchers. We will look now at some variables that have been identified as possibly having some bearing on the family's reaction to this critical life problem. These variables are (1) the social class of the family and the severity of the child's handicap, (2) the religion of the family, (3) the differences between mothers and fathers, and (4) the sex of the handicapped child. We will look also at the special problems of brothers and sisters of handicapped children.

Social Class of the Family and the Severity of the Child's Handicap

We will look first at two seemingly unrelated variables: the social class of the family and the severity of the handicap. Research seems to indicate that some families in all social strata show a high acceptance of the handicapped child while other families in all social classes show a low acceptance of the handicapped child. Grossman (1972) found no significant differences in the coping abilities of upper-class families and lower-middle-class families but did find striking differences in the aspects of their situations that made a difference in their ability to cope adequately with a handicapped child in the family. The most striking aspects seem to be the relation of the severity and nature of the child's handicap to the social class of the family. We will look now at that relationship.

The majority of cases of mild mental retardation seem to have a cultural basis, that is, the great majority of mildly retarded children do not seem to be the victims of organic brain damage or identifiable diseases but instead come from backgrounds that are best described as impoverished (Hutt & Gibby, 1976). A large number of social and cultural factors such as malnutrition and lack of language stimulation in the home have been suggested as possible causes of mild mental retardation in children from impoverished backgrounds. For severely mentally retarded children, no such cultural bias exists. Severe mental retardation is associated with identifiable organic causes much more frequently than mild mental retardation and seems to strike families of all social classes in equal proportion. It is interesting therefore to look at differences in family reactions to severely handicapped children in light of the social class of the family.

Farber (1964) found that upper-class families have more difficulty in adjustment than lower-class families when the handicapped child does not require an inordinate amount of physical care but primarily represents a frustration of the aspirations for the family. Similarly, Grossman (1972) found that for upper-class men, the more serious the physical handicap, the better their acceptance of the handicapped child. It would seem, then, that for upper-class families, children with physical handicaps who require a great deal of specialized physical care present a more clear-cut need for help than children who are mentally retarded but who have no physical evidence of disability. The family with a physically handicapped child seems to have less confusion about its role in caring for that child than the upper-class family with a less obviously handicapped child and is therefore better adjusted. The upper-class family with a less obviously handicapped child must go through the tragic crisis of giving up dreams of success for the child but having a less clear-cut notion of how to help the child. This family therefore has more adjustment problems.

For lower class-families who do not have the financial resources to care for the physical demands of a severely handicapped child comfortably, the presence of a physical handicap makes adjustment more rather than less difficult for the family. Mercer (1966) reports that extraordinary burdens of physical care in lower-class families are a contributing factor in a family's decision to have a child remain in an institution. Farber (1959) found that a role organization crisis due to physical care demands was a more common response than a tragic crisis in lower-class families. In studying sisters of handicapped children, Grossman (1972) found that lower-class women (who were given a great deal of responsibility for the care of their handicapped sibling) were better adjusted when no physical handicap was present.

An interesting interaction seems to exist, then, between the social class of the family and the nature and severity of the child's handicap. For the upper-class family, adjustment seems to be easier when an obvious physical disability is present. For the lower-class family, the presence of a physical handicap with the accompanying demands for physical care make adjustment more difficult. Grossman (1972) summarizes these findings by noting that the adaptation of lower-class family members seems to be related to various real or concrete aspects of their experiences with the handicapped child such as the degree of his retardation or physical handicap. In contrast, upper-class family members seemed more influenced by their feelings about the handicapped child rather than the actual physical characteristics.

Religion

The religious affiliation of the parents of a handicapped child has been seen as having bearing on the acceptance of the child in the family. While some studies have found no relationship between a parent's religious affiliation and the acceptance of the handicapped child (Ehlers, 1966; Stone, 1967), several studies have found consistent religious differences. Stubblefield (1965) reports that Roman Catholic parents are more accepting of a mentally retarded child than either Protestant or Jewish families and explains this finding by commenting that the Catholic religion specifies that parents need not feel guilty about bearing a mentally retarded child but rather should see themselves as being specially chosen for a special task, the care of a child who needs special treatment. Zuk, Miller, Bartrum, & Kling (1961) also found Catholic mothers to be more accepting of a handicapped child, and those who were more faithful in church attendance showed an even greater acceptance. Adams (1966) studied that relationship of religious affiliation to the adjustment of adolescent siblings of handicapped children. Adams (1966) found that while Protestant siblings of handicapped children showed poorer psychological adjustment than Protestant adolescents who did not have a handicapped brother or sister, Catholic teenagers with a handicapped sibling showed greater adjustment than Catholic teenagers who did not have a handicapped brother or sister.

The evidence presented here is somewhat contradictory. Although some studies show no relationship between religion and the adjustment of the family with a handicapped child, others present evidence that Roman Catholic families seem better adjusted to this critical life problem than families with other religious affiliations. Two weaknesses in these studies might help account for the contradictory results. First, the studies focused for the most part on religious affiliation, that is, how people identify themselves in terms of religion, rather than the intensity of religious commitment. It might be that the depth of religious conviction is actually more related to acceptance of a handicapped child than the particular affiliation, and this factor was not explored in most of the studies. Second, as Zuk et al. (1961) point out, the measures of maternal acceptance employed in these studies differ from one another and may tap different aspects of the family's adjustment or acceptance of the handicapped child. Most parents are somewhat ambivalent about their feelings: They feel good about certain aspects of their life with the handicapped child but they are resentful or unhappy about other aspects. The different measures of family acceptance may explore different aspects of the family's adjustment and will therefore come up with differing results.

Differences Between Mothers and Fathers

As was noted at the beginning of this chapter, most research on the family with a handicapped child has focused on the attitudes and problems of mothers while very little attention has been paid to the reactions of fathers. What data are available suggest that mothers and fathers respond to the problem of a handicapped child in the family in different ways. For example, Ehlers (1966) reported different reactions at the time of diagnosis of mental retardation. Mothers reported feelings of shock, disbelief, and grief while fathers were described as expressing anger at the diagnosis, insisting that nothing could be wrong with the child. Another difference was found by Capobianca and Knox (1964), who evaluated parents' estimates of the intellectual level of their mentally retarded children. It was found that fathers were more accurate in their estimates than mothers. The mothers tended to overestimate the intellectual level of the child.

A questionnaire was developed by Gumz and Gubrium (1972) to elicit information about the attitudes, perceptions, and beliefs of mothers and fathers about mentally retarded children. Particular emphasis was placed on parents' attitudes toward the crisis of having a handicapped child, how they viewed the child in situations outside the realm of family life, and what future roles they foresaw for their child. Differences were found between the attitudes of mothers and those of fathers. There was a tendency for a father to perceive his child in terms of specific goals—helping the child develop independence, appropriate job opportunities, and so on. The mothers were more likely to think of their roles in interpersonal terms; they saw themselves as managing tensions among different family members.

The Sex of the Handicapped Child

Whether the handicapped child is a boy or a girl has an influence on the family's adjustment. The evidence strongly suggests that the presence of a male handicapped child is more disruptive to family harmony than the presence of a female handicapped child. As has been noted earlier, Wolf and Whitehead (1975) found that the sex of the handicapped child influenced the family's decision to institutionalize a mentally retarded child: Boys were found to be more likely to be institutionalized than girls, and boys were seen as more disruptive to the parents' marriage. Farber (1959) reports that parents seem to have less trouble getting along with a mentally retarded girl than a mentally retarded boy.

The initial stress that parents experience when they learn their child is handicapped appears to be somewhat sex-linked (Farber, Jenne, & Torgo, 1960). The mother indicates a markedly greater impact if the retarded child is a boy. Eventually, however, there is a shift. Mothers of mentally retarded boys report more adjustment problems than mothers of mentally retarded girls. After the initial impact of diagnosis, then, both parents report more difficulty with mentally retarded boys than with girls.

Theorists (Farber, 1959; Farber, Jenne, & Torgo, 1960) attempt to explain these findings by pointing out that cultural expectations still differ somewhat for boys and for girls. The boy is expected to achieve status in terms of education and financial success at least equal to that of his father. As many families do not have such high expectations for girls, it may not be quite so difficult for them to adjust to impaired intellectual functioning in girls.

Brothers and Sisters

We have focused thus far on variables that have affected the adjustment of the family in general to the handicapped child. Attention will now be paid to the adjustment of brothers and sisters to a handicapped child in the family. Perhaps the major research in this area has been done by Grossman (1972), whose work has been cited previously. She is a clinical psychologist who organized and worked with a group of normal siblings of handicapped children and then formulated a program of systematic research to investigate issues raised by the clinical work with these brothers and sisters. The five-year research project involved systematic interviews and questionnaires given to 83 college students who had a physically or mentally handicapped brother or sister. Part of the group of college students came from upper-class backgrounds while others came from lower-middle-class backgrounds. Many of the findings to be cited regarding the personal adjustment of brothers and sisters of handicapped children will be drawn from this work. Variables to be discussed include the responsibility of normal siblings for their handicapped brothers and sisters, sex differences, birth order and family size, and whether it is better for the normal siblings for the handicapped child to be at home or to be removed from the home.

RESPONSIBILITIES OF SIBLINGS

One hazard to the personal adjustment of the siblings of a handicapped child is that parents sometimes expect the sibling to assume an inordinate amount of responsibility for the care of the handicapped child. In an important study, Shere (1955) investigated 30 pairs of twins, each of which had one twin who had cerebral palsy and another twin who was not handicapped. Shere (1955) found some differences in the behavior of parents toward the handicapped and nonhandicapped twins. The parents generally expected the nonhandicapped child to assume more responsibility and to act older than age capabilities would warrant, and the parents tended to be more responsive to the problems of the cerebral-palsied child. The parents also tended to overprotect the handicapped twin and didn't permit him much independence in his activities.

Sex differences have been found in the demands parents place on the brothers and sisters of handicapped children. Grossman (1972) reports that brothers are usually not expected to assume major responsibility for the physical care of the handicapped children but that sisters, especially those from lower-class backgrounds, frequently are expected to assume major share of this responsibility.

SEX DIFFERENCES

Other sex differences have been noted in the adjustment of brothers and sisters. Both sexes express more embarrassment about having a handicapped sibling when that sibling is of the same sex, that is, boys are more embarrassed by having a handicapped brother while girls are more embarrassed by a handicapped sister (Grossman, 1972). Farber (1959) found that older sisters were more adversely affected by the presence of a handicapped child in the home than were older brothers. This finding could certainly be related to the evidence that sisters are assigned more responsibility for physical care than are brothers.

BIRTH ORDER AND FAMILY SIZE

The number of brothers and sisters in the family and whether the handicapped child is older or younger than his siblings has some effect on the personal adjustment of brothers and sisters of handicapped children. Older brothers and sisters were found to earn consistently higher coping scores than younger brothers and sisters of handicapped children (Grossman, 1972). Similarly, Graliker, Fishler, and Kock (1962) found that mentally retarded children caused few adjustment problems for brothers and sisters who were considerably older (i.e., a 10-year difference in age). It might be speculated that a younger handicapped child causes fewer role-organization problems because he functions as the youngest family member both in birth order and in fact. A brother or sister who has an older handicapped sibling, on the other hand, might be expected to function in very responsible ways before being developmentally ready for such responsibility.

Grossman (1972) also found that the greater number of children in the family, the greater the coping scores of the nonhandicapped brothers and sisters. It would seem that a large number of children in a family often protects one brother or sister from excessive responsibility for the care of the handicapped child.

HOME VERSUS INSTITUTION

It is sometimes suggested that it is wise to remove the handicapped child from the home situation for the sake of the non-handicapped brothers and sisters. Farber (1959) developed the *Sibling Role Tension Index,* which was administered to brothers and sisters of mentally retarded children. He concluded that role tension of siblings is higher when the mentally retarded child is in the home than when he is out of the home. Grossman's (1972) findings contradict this. Although individual family circumstances will of course vary, she found that when the family resources are sufficient to cope with the physical care demands of the handicapped child without placing undue hardship on the brothers and sisters, the brothers and sisters express less guilt and discomfort when the handicapped child is at home than when he is in an institution.

WHAT HELPS?

We have looked at the reaction patterns of families to the critical life problem of having a handicapped child and at the social and psychological variables that influence the family's adjustment and acceptance of the handicapped child. We will conclude this discussion by looking at factors identified by families and by researchers as helping to make the adjustment to this problem more comfortable and more positive. These factors will be discussed in terms of information and services.

Information

The need of parents for clear, sympathetic information about the child's handicapping condition has been expressed by many families. The mothers in Ehler's (1966) study rated the provision of good information as a critically important service they wished professionals would render. These mothers reported that all too often information about the child's diagnosis or progress was presented in an off-hand, unclear manner, and the mothers reported being confused and upset after such encounters with professionals.

A good understanding of the child's handicapping condition seems to have a pay-off in terms of the family's acceptance of the handicapped child. Stone's (1967) investigation of 103 families families with young children with Down's Syndrome produced this finding: Parents who knew more about the nature and characteristics of this condition were significantly more accepting of the child and were less likely to consider institutionalization.

A similar finding is reported in the study of brothers and sisters of handicapped children (Grossman, 1972). The college students who described their families as having been more open in permitting and encouraging questions about the handicapped child scored significantly higher on coping measures than brothers and sisters who reported that curiosity about the handicapped child and his condition was discouraged.

It would seem then to be the responsibility of professionals working with handicapped children and their families to be skilled in providing appropriate information about the child's handicap in an sympathetic manner, for the availability of good information seems to have a relationship to the family's acceptance of the handicapped child. One helpful resource for professionals is the guide compiled by Atwell and Clabby (1971) to 231 fundamental questions asked by parents about handicapped children. Included are such questions as these: What is the cause of the child's mental retardation? Is it safe to have another child? How can we explain our child's handicap to friends and relatives?

Services

In addition to the helpfulness of good information, certain services offered by agencies working with handicapped children have been identified by researchers as being of particular help to parents: parent groups, respite care programs, and practical home-training programs.

Parents of handicapped children report feeling more competent in meeting the needs of their children and report increased feelings of self-worth as the result of participating in organizations for parents of handicapped children (Warfield, 1975). Although many parents report friends as being considerate and sympathetic (Farber, 1959, for example, found that only 10 per cent of mothers of retarded children reported feeling ostracized by friends), there seems to be a special sense of support gained by getting together with mothers with similar problems. Ehlers (1966) reports that mothers of retarded children expressed a strong need to get together with other such mothers and felt a special sense of friendship when that opportunity was available. In addition to the help to mothers, parent groups such as the National Association for Retarded Citizens have excellent records of lobbying for legislative support for programs for the handicapped and for starting many local model programs (Hutt & Gibby, 1976).

Adolescent siblings of handicapped children report similar enhanced feelings of self-worth and good support when they are given the opportunity to meet with other teenagers in similar circumstances (Grossman, 1972). One group project conducted by Grossman (1972) involved having a group of adolescent siblings of handicapped children do volunteer work for a program for the mentally retarded. The opportunity to see mental retardation in a broader perspective and to get to know other teenagers in the process was seen by the adolescents as being very helpful in their acceptance of their handicapped brother or sister.

Services for handicapped children in communities have received strong endorsement from parents who express a need for a "breather" in the day-to-day care of handicapped children but wish the child to remain at home rather than in a residential facility (Ehlers, 1966). Aanes and Whitlock (1975) report on a parent relief program that is being conducted by a state facility for the mentally retarded. Instead of offering only full-time placement, this program offers short-term placement for handicapped children in times of parental stress (e.g., when the family is moving or there is a temporary money problem or the parents really need a vacation together) or in times of major family crisis such as the death of a parent or divorce. Another alternative to full-time care offered by the institution is supervision of the handicapped child for parts of days or evenings so that parents can make business or personal plans on a regular basis at that time. The short-term placement typically lasts for less than 60 days, and the child then returns to the family home. Aanes and Whitlock (1975) report that referrals to this program are on the upswing, and parents find this kind of crisis-centered, short-term care to be very helpful in time of stress.

Another community program that gets a strong endorsement is home-training programs for parents of handicapped children (Ehlers, 1966; Neifort & Gayton, 1973). In this kind of program, a home visitor, often a public health nurse or teacher, visits the home on a regular basis and offers the mother instruction on how to help her handicapped child with such self-care skills as feeding, dressing, and toileting and on how to provide stimulating learning activities for the child at home. Mothers report that not only do they get practical help with everyday problems in such a program but that they have a regular opportunity to talk informally with an interested professional, which makes adjustment easier.

A variety of community services for handicapped children and their families are currently being developed, and as has been seen, some have been identified by parents as being particularly helpful to families as they adjust to the critical life problem of a handicapped child in the family. A useful model for matching appropriate services to families who need them has been developed by Karnes and Zehrback (1975). In this model, professionals are to have a positive developmental view of children and their families and should view their role as consultative; parents should be involved in decision-making about their child and should have access to a number of alternatives for helping the child and the family.

SUMMARY

A handicapped child in the family has been seen as a critical life problem, making special demands on the psychological adjustment of the family. Certain aspects of this critical life problem are time-limited; they occur at a particular point in the life of the family. The success of the psychological adjustment of families varies from family to family, and certain variables have been identified as influencing that adjustment. Upper-class families tend to show better adjustment when the child has physical as well as intellectual problems; lower-class families have fewer problems when there is no excessive burden of physical care. Families with handicapped girls seem to have an easier time than families with boys. There is a tendency for Roman Catholic families to have higher adjustment scores than families of other religions. Brothers and sisters of handicapped children show better personal adjustment when they are older than the handicapped child, are part of a large family, and are not assigned an inappropriate amount of responsibility for the handicapped child. In terms of what helps families, the results are not surprising. Clear, sympathetic information from professionals, support from other parents, and good programs for the children all contribute to the psychological adjustment of families. The research in this area is somewhat tentative at present, and more careful study is needed on many aspects of this critical life problem so that more families can meet the needs of handicapped children and of other family members in positive, accepting ways.

QUESTIONS AND PROJECTS

1. Interview students in your college who have physical handicaps. What types of challenges do they face—architectural, academic, and personal?
2. Invite a representative from the local National Association for Retarded Citizens to speak to your class. Ask her to discuss changes in services for the retarded over the last 20 years and what local needs still exist. Explore parents' role in lobbying for services.
3. Visit a local class for the mentally retarded or physically handicapped. Ask the teacher to share her perception of the needs of families with a handicapped child.
4. Discuss the goals of genetic counseling and the impact of this kind of counseling for parents of handicapped children.

SUGGESTED READINGS

Popular Sources

V. APGAR, & J. BECK. *Is my baby all right? A guide to birth defects.* New York: Trident Press, 1973. A discussion of life before birth, what can go wrong, and why.

H. E. BLODGETT. *Mentally retarded children: What parents and others should know.* Minneapolis: University of Minnesota Press, 1971. Includes levels of mental retardation and relates them to child development and behavior. Supportive suggestions for parents' own psychological adjustment.

J. BLUMENFIELD, P. E. THOMPSON & B. S. VOGEL, *Help them grow: a pictorial handbook for parents of handicapped children.* Nashville: Abington Press, 1971. A guide to the development of self-help, social, and communication skills.

N. HUNT. *The world of Nigel Hunt.* New York: Garrett Publications, 1967. A young adolescent with Down's Syndrome describes his interests and feelings.

S. B. STEINS. *About handicaps: An open family book for parents and children together.* New York: Walker & Company, 1974. The story is of two children, one with cerebral palsy and one nonhandicapped, and deals with their questions in a warm, nonthreatening manner.

Advanced Sources

R. KOCH, & J. C. DOBSON, (Eds.). *The mentally retarded child and his family: A multidisciplinary handbook.* New York: Brunner/Mazel, 1971. 26 contributors from 17 disciplines have written an encyclopedic guide to the problem of mental retardation.

R. L. KROTH, *Communicating with parents of exceptional children.* Denver: Love Publishing Company, 1975. Good appendix of selected readings.

H. B. ROBINSON, & N. M. ROBINSON. *The mentally retarded child.* New York: McGraw Hill, 1965. Strong introduction to the psychological aspects of mental retardation.

REFERENCES

AANES, D. & WHITLOCK, A. A parental relief program for the mentally retarded. *Mental Retardation,* 1975, *13,* 36–38.

ADAMS, F. K. Comparisons of attitudes of adolescents towards normal and retarded brothers. *Dissertation Abstracts,* 1966, *27,* 622–623.

ANDERSON, V. H., SCHLOTTMAN, R. S., & WEINER, B. J. Predictors of parent involvement with institutionalized retarded children. *Amer. J. Mental Deficiency,* 1975, *79,* 705–710.

ATWELL, A. A. & CLABBY, D. A. *The retarded child: Answers to questions parents ask.* Los Angeles: Western Psychological Services, 1971.

BERGGREEN, S. A study of the mental health of the near relatives of 20 multi-handicapped children. *Acta Paed. Scand.* 1971, *9,* 16–23.

BRAGINSKY, D. D. & BRAGINSKY, B. M. *Hansels and Gretels: Studies of children in institutions for the mentally retarded.* New York: Holt, Rinehart & Winston, 1971.

CAPOBIANCO, R. J. & KNOX, S. IQ estimates and the index of family integration. *Amer. J. Mental Deficiency,* 1964, *68,* 718–721.

COLLINS, H. A. Introversion and depression in mothers of cerebral palsied children. *Missouri Medicine,* 1965, *62,* 847–850.

CONDELL, J. S. Parental attitudes toward mental retardation. *Amer. J. Mental Deficiency,* 1966, *71,* 85–92.

CUMMINGS, T., BAYLEY, H. C. & RIE, H. E. Effects of the child's deficiency on the mother: a study of mothers of mentally retarded, chronically ill, and neurotic children. *Amer. J. Orthopsychiatry,* 1966, *36,* 595–609.

EHLERS, W. H. *Mothers of retarded children: How they feel; where they find help.* Springfield, Ill.: Charles C. Thomas, 1966.

FARBER, B. Effects of a severely retarded child on family integration. *Society for Research in Child Development Monographs,* 1959, *24.*

FARBER, B. Family organization and crisis: maintenance of integration in families with a severely mentally retarded child. *Monographs of the Society for Research in Child Development,* 1969, *25.*

FARBER, B. Some effects of a retarded child on the mother. In M. B. Sussman (Ed.). *Sourcebook in marriage and the family.* Boston: Houghton Mifflin Company, 1963.

FARBER, B. *Family: Organization and interaction.* San Francisco: Chandler Publishing Company, 1964.

FARBER, B., JENNÉ, W. C. & TORGO, R. Family crises and the decision to institutionalize the retarded child. *Council for Exceptional Children, NEA Research Monograph Series,* 1960, *A-1.*

FARBER, B. & RYKMAN, D. B. Effects of severely mentally retarded children on family relationships. *Mental Retardation Abstracts,* 1965, *2,* 1–17.

FOTHERINGHAM, J. B., SKELTON, M. & HODDINOTT, B. A. *The retarded child and his family: the effects of home and institution.* Toronto: The Ontario Institute for Studies in Education, 1971.

GRALIKER, B. V., FISHLER, K. & KOCH, R. Teenage reaction to a mentally retarded sibling. *Amer. J. Mental Deficiency,* 1962, *66,* 838–843.

GROSSMAN, F. K. *Brothers and sisters of retarded children.* Syracuse: Syracuse University Press, 1972.

GROSSMAN, H. J. (Ed.). *Manual on terminology and classification in mental retardation.* American Association on Mental Deficiency, Special Publication No. 2, 1973.

GUMZ, E. J. & GUBRIUM, J. Comparative parental perceptions of a mentally retarded child. *Amer. J. Mental Deficiency,* 1972, *77,* 175–177.

HOLT, K. S. The home care of the severely mentally retarded. *Pediatrics,* 1958, *22,* 744–755. (a)

HOLT, K. S. The influence of a retarded child on family limitations. *J. Mental Deficiency,* 1958, *2,* 28–36. (b)

HUTT, M. L. & GIBBY, R. G. *The mentally retarded child: Development, education, and treatment.* Boston: Allyn & Bacon, Inc., 1976.

JENSEN, G. D. & KOGAN, K. L. Parental estimates of the future achievement of children with cerebral palsy. *J. Mental Deficiency,* 1962, *6,* 56–64.

KARNES, M. B. & ZEHRBACH, R. R. Matching families and services. *Exceptional Children,* 1975, *41,* 545–549.

KIRK, S. A. *Educating exceptional children.* Boston: Houghton Mifflin Company, 1972.

MERCER, J. R. Patterns of family crisis related to reacceptance of the retardate. *Amer. J. Mental Deficiency,* 1966, *71,* 19–31.

MEYEROWITZ, J. J. Parental awareness of retardation. *Amer. J. Mental Deficiency,* 1967, 637–643.

MYEROWITZ, J. H. & FARBER, B. Family background of educable mentally retarded children. In B. Farber (Ed.). *Kinship and family organization.* New York: Wiley, 1966.

NEIFERT, J. T. & GAYTON, W. F. Parents and the home program approach in the remediation of learning disabilities. *J. Learning Disabilities,* 1973, *2,* 85–89.

PODEANU-CZEHOFSKY, I. Is it only the child's guilt? Some aspects of family life of cerebral palsied children. *Rehabilitation Literature,* 1975, *36,* 308–311.

Ross, A. O. *The exceptional child in the family.* New York: Grune & Stratton, 1964.

Schulman, J. L. & Stern, S. Parents' estimate of the intelligence of retarded children. *Amer. J. Mental Deficiency*, 1959, *63*, 696–698.

Schonell, F. J. & Rorke, M. A. A second survey of the effects of a subnormal child on the family unit. *Amer. J. Mental Deficiency*, 1960, *64*, 862–868.

Shere, M. O. Socioemotional factors in families of one twin with cerebral palsy. *Exceptional Children*, 1955, *22*, 197, 206, 208.

Stewart, J. C. *Counseling parents of exceptional children.* New York: MSS Educational Publishing Company, Inc., 1974.

Stone, N. D. Family factors in willingness to place the Mongoloid child. *Amer. J. Mental Deficiency*, 1967, *72*, 16–20.

Stubblefield, H. W. Religion, parents, and mental retardation. *Mental Retardation*, 1965, *3*, 8–11.

Tizard, J. *Community services for the mentally handicapped.* London: Oxford University Press, 1964.

Warfield, G. J. Mothers of retarded children review a parent education program. *Exceptional Children*, 1975, *41*, 559–562.

Wolf, L. C. & Whitehead, P. C. The decision to institutionalize retarded children: comparison of individually matched groups. *Mental Retardation*, 1975, *13*, 3–7.

Wolfensberger, N. Counseling parents of the retarded. In A. A. Baumeister (Ed.). *Mental Retardation.* Chicago: Aldine Publishing Company, 1967.

Zuk, G. H. Autistic distortions in parents of retarded children. *J. Consulting Psychol.*, 1959, *23*, 171–176.

Zuk, G. H., Miller, R. L., Bartrum, J. B. & Kling, G. F. Maternal acceptance of retarded children: A questionnaire study of attitudes and religious background. *Child Devel.*, 1961, *32*, 525–540.

Abortion and Rape: Problems Unique to Women

CHAPTER 6

ABORTION

Until the very recent past, abortion was viewed only in negative terms in the United States. In fact, until 1967, when Colorado became the first state to liberalize its abortion laws, abortion was forbidden unless "necessary to preserve the woman's life." This did not mean that women did not obtain abortions. Fleck (1970) estimated that abortions outside of medical channels occurred a million times a year or for one out of every four pregnancies. Illegal abortions were frequently utilized even though they were not usually performed by physicians. Some women even attempted self-induced abortions, using coat-hangers, hatpins, and other implements (Guttmacher, 1973). These methods usually caused serious medical complications because of infection or perforation of the uterus. The majority of the illegal abortions performed were on poor women who were desperate enough to risk the serious consequences (Guttmacher, 1973; Hardin, 1974).

The more affluent woman was in a somewhat better position in that she was able to go to another country where abortion was legal or was able to obtain a "therapeutic abortion" from a private gynecologist in a good hospital. Fleck (1970) estimated that 10,000 abortions were performed annually on psychiatric grounds, because the woman was judged to be in danger of committing suicide. The practice of psychiatrically justified abortions has always been problematic and controversial. Decisions regarding suicide are very difficult, and in this situation the woman knew that she must be designated as suicidal to obtain an abortion. The woman and her psychiatrist were both put in especially difficult positions because they could not maintain the usual doctor-patient relationship. As there were no guidelines on the probability of suicidal risk necessary for a woman to deserve an abortion, most psychiatrists based their decisions on their own personal opinions concerning abortion. Psychiatric attitudes ranged from very anti-abortion stands, such as, "The author asks his colleagues to . . . concern themselves mostly with a search for contraindication rather than for indications to therapeutic interruption of pregnancy" (Bolter, 1962), to very proabortion stands, such as "After several such interviews [with a woman who became pregnant accidentally], one is hard pressed to maintain the view that the abortion decision should be made by anybody other than the pregnant woman" (Schwartz, 1973).

Although the psychiatric community condoned abortion for many women, abortion remained difficult to obtain and was viewed very negatively by society in general. Even after the 1973 Supreme Cout decision that abortion in the first three months of pregnancy is a decision to be made by the woman, many difficulties remain for the woman with an unwanted pregnancy.

Anti-abortion Views

The issue of abortion is highly emotional, and few people are neutral about it. There is a general cultural prohibition against abortion that stems from Judaic-Christian teachings involving the responsibility ethic. People are expected to be responsible for the consequences of their acts, and the woman is expected to be responsible for her pregnancy regardless of her capability to deal with it.

Motherhood is highly valued in Western culture and is often seen as a woman's sole purpose or her only means of fulfillment. The woman who obtains an abortion may be seen as rejecting motherhood and may consequently be rejected.

Stronger opposition to abortion comes from people who believe that abortion is murder. Some religious groups, the Catholic church being the most notable, are opposed to abortion on the grounds that the embryo should be considered a human life from the moment of conception. It is interesting to note, however, that both the English law and the Roman Catholic Church have altered their judgment as to the time that an embryo should be considered a human life; the removal of the embryo before this time was not considered abortion or murder. For people with strong religious beliefs about abortion, there is no question concerning abortion: however, many people remain unsure as to the wisdom of abortion for society in general as well as the individual woman.

Pro-abortion Views

The right of every woman to decide when and if she wants to be a mother is a major factor in the pro-abortion stand. A woman's right and legal means to control her body are becoming more possible with the influence of the woman's liberation movement. Many proponents of abortion argue that a woman should not lose her rights simply because she becomes pregnant.

Family planning and population control are also reasons given for the necessity of abortion. No one would disagree that contraception is preferable to abortion; however, the failure of a woman to use contraceptives may be due to factors other than unconcern or carelessness. Women fail to use contraceptives because of ignorance or unavailability (Schwartz, 1973). Failure to use contraception may also be due to the spontaneous nature of the sexual activity. Finally, contraceptive failure does occur. Many women cannot or will not take the pill for health reasons, and all of the remaining contraceptive methods—the IUD, diaphragm, foam, and condom—have failure rates of at least 2 to 3 per cent per year (i.e., for every 100 users, two or three will become pregnant each year) (Schwartz, 1973). Even the most careful and responsible approach to contraception does not guarantee that conception will not occur. Thus abortion is a method of population control and family planning, giving the current failure rates of most contraceptives and their lack of use by that segment of society who can least afford an unwanted pregnancy, i.e., the young, the poor, and the illiterate.

Pro-abortion advocates are concerned with the child's right to be wanted, rather than the child's right to life. Their contention is that the quality of life is crucial and that forcing a woman to have an unwanted child can have serious and detrimental consequences for the child as well as the mother.

Most people in the field of mental health are very aware of the problems of the unwanted child. In the majority of cases when rejection, whether overt or covert, occurs the child's concept of himself and his self-worth suffers as a result. Many women decide to continue a pregnancy about which they are ambivalent, and the consequences to their children may not be serious. However, the situation in which a woman's feelings are so negative that she requests an abortion is radically different, and these children may suffer significantly.

One study may allow some initial tentative statements to be made regarding these children. Forssman and Thuwe (1966) conducted a 21-year follow-up study of 120 children whose mothers had been denied an abortion. These children were assessed in terms of mental health, social adjustment, and educational level. They were compared to a control group composed of the very next same-sexed child born at the same hospital or in the same district. Thus the control group was selected on the basis of proximity of birth in time, geography, and sex of the child. The results of the study demonstrated that unwanted children were worse off in every respect. They had a higher incidence of many kinds of behavioral maladjustments; they required more psychiatric care, were arrested more often for antisocial and criminal behavior and drunkenness, received welfare assistance more frequently, and failed to achieve as high a level of schooling as did the control group.

The mental health of the woman is also a concern of the advocate of abortion. The rate of psychological difficulties is relatively high with about 4,000 documented cases of postpartum depression or psychosis requiring hospitalization in the United States each year (Hamilton, 1962). This is a little less than two per 1000 deliveries.

There are no statistics to indicate that the same high percentage of psychosis is occurring post-abortion. We turn our attention now to the psychological consequences for the woman who has an abortion.

Psychological Reactions to Abortion

The objective data concerning the reactions of women following abortion demonstrate a surprisingly low incidence of psychiatric complications. A frequently quoted study of aftereffects was done by Ekblad (1955) in Sweden. Using working capacity to measure the degree of difficulty following abortion, Ekblad found that five of the 54 women he studied (10 per cent) experienced impaired working capacity in connection with the abortion. Although he noted feelings of guilt and self-reproach in many women, these feelings seldom interfered with their working capacity. Further, he found that both personality type and the influence of others on the woman to obtain the abortion were related to feelings of self-reproach. Women diagnosed as abnormal and women who experienced coercion concerning the abortion were likelier to experience serious self-reproach. He commented that the greater were the psychiatric reasons for the abortion, the greater was the probability of unfavorable psychiatric consequences after the abortion. He further stated that these women would probably have had unfavorable psychological reactions if the pregnancy had not been terminated.

Other studies from Scandinavia report similar findings, and two, Kilstad (1957) and Brekke (1958) report an even lower incidence of psychiatric consequences, perhaps because these two studies were conducted in Norway, where the regulations concerning abortion are most liberal.

In the United States several types of studies have been conducted regarding the woman's reaction to abortion. Kummer (1963) conducted a survey of thirty-two psychiatrists and found that during an average of twelve years in practice only 25 per cent had encountered significant consequences to either illegal or legal abortions, and this only rarely. In contrast, 75 per cent had never seen a patient with any moderate or severe psychiatric after-effects of abortion.

Niswander and Patterson (1967) sent out questionnaires to 132 patients and received replies from 116 (87.9 per cent). These patients were women who underwent therapeutic abortion in 1963, 1964, or 1965. The results indicated that two thirds of the patients said that they felt better immediately, and they indicated that they felt even better as time passed. Few women regretted having the abortion (N = 6) and their regrets tended to disappear by the time of the eight-month follow-up examination.

Peck and Marcus (1966) and Simon, Senturia, and Rothman (1967) both conducted studies concerning women who had had therapeutic abortions for medical as well as psychiatric reasons. Simon, Senturia and Rothman (1967) contacted women from two months to 10 years after the abortion. Forty-six of the 65 women contacted (71 per cent) were interviewed and completed psychological tests and a questionnaire. The results of this study indicate that 50 per cent of the women felt immediate relief following the abortion. Thirteen women (28 per cent) felt mild or marked feelings of depression. It appears that many women were experiencing a transient "mourning reaction" to the loss of wanted pregnancy. Guilt was also examined, and 65 per cent of the women reported little or no conscious guilt. The 35 per cent who reported moderate or marked guilt also noted that this feeling decreased with time. Only one woman was noted to have serious psychiatric consequences because of the abortion. The authors concluded that although psychological problems do occur after abortion, they are typically not related to the abortion itself, but are the result of pre-existing problems.

Peck and Marcus (1966) interviewed women pre- and post-abortion (three to six months following surgery). These women formed two distinct groups based on the reason for abortion. Half of the abortions were for psychiatric reasons and half because of rubella. Of all the women only one was worse post-abortion and she improved quickly (three therapy sessions). This woman was pressured by her husband into the abortion, which was in conflict with her religious beliefs. The results concerning depression and guilt were similar to those of the Simon, Senturia, and Rothman (1967) study. The most interesting finding of the Peck and Marcus (1966) study is that 68 per cent (16) of the psychiatric group and 20 per cent (5) of the rubella group were considered psychiatrically improved at follow-up. Further, 49 of the 50 women would obtain the abortion if they had it to do again.

The psychological consequences of an abortion for psychiatric or medical reasons seem to be relatively minor. Review articles by Walter (1970) and Osofsky and Osofsky (1972) both conclude that the available evidence suggests that there are few serious after-effects to an abortion and that women who are refused an abortion may have serious difficulties post-partum. Extreme reactions to abortions are rare, and when they occur they are generally associated with problems existing prior to the abortion. Typically the findings suggest that mild to moderate feelings of guilt, regret, or remorse follow abortion and diminish over time (Peck & Marcus, 1966; Simon, Senturia & Rothman, 1967). This does not mean that the woman does not also experience positive emotions as a result of the abortion. On the contrary, the data suggest that the majority of women report feeling happy and satisfied with their decision and that this feeling increases over time (Niswander & Patterson, 1967).

With the changing of state laws and the 1973 Supreme Court ruling that abortion is the choice of the woman, a new group of women were able to obtain abortions. It is possible that the response of these women to abortions would be even milder than those reported in the earlier studies we have examined. One could hypothesize that a woman who does not want a pregnancy and has had no previous psychological difficulties will react to an abortion with a minimum of negative emotions and with a great deal of positive feelings.

A few studies conducted since abortion became more available should be helpful in assessing the psychological reactions of normal women to an unwanted pregnancy.

Fingerer (1973) conducted an interesting study to determine if the negative psychological aftereffects to abortion predicted by psychoanalytic theory actually occur. She utilized four groups of subjects: (1) abortion patients, (2) people accompanying abortion patients, (3) graduate students of psychoanalytic orientation, and (4) graduate psychology students who were asked to role-play the abortion situation. The group of abortion patients were asked to fill out the questionnaires measuring anxiety both pre- and post-abortion. The other groups were asked to fill out the same questionnaire. The results confirmed that the students whose theory predicted a severe reaction on the part of abortion clients rated the predicted reaction as severe. The role-playing group of students rated the expected reaction as significantly less severe than the psychoanalytic students, but significantly more severe than either the abortion patients or their friends. The abortion patients and their friends predicted only minor psychological discomfort, mainly of a depressive nature. Of significance is the fact that the patients after their abortions scored the lowest on the tests—significantly lower than their own pre-scores. Thus the abortion resulted in relief rather than anxiety and depression. These results must be interpreted with caution, however, in that half of the women did not return their results the day following the abortion, and Fingerer noted that some women who did return the results reported feeling very anxious and depressed. It is only on the average that there was little expected anxiety and depression and no immediate negative psychological aftereffects.

Osofsky and Osofsky (1972) conducted a study of the reactions of women in New York who were obtaining abortions. They noted moderate to very happy reactions in 64.6 per cent of the patients, with only 14 per cent displaying a moderate to extreme sadness. Guilt was not felt by the majority of women (76.2 per cent), and 78.7 per cent of the women were happy with their decision. There were some difficulties with this study, as on some of the scales subjects had to choose between two feelings which were not mutually exclusive. For example, one five-point scale had "negative—much guilt" at one end and "positive—much relief" at the other. It is possible that a woman may in fact feel much relief and some guilt following an abortion. In spite of these difficulties Osofsky and Osofsky made several pertinent points. They noted that women who had had difficulty with the decision to abort also reported more feelings of guilt following the abortion. Thus it is important to look at the decision-making process concerning the abortion to understand a woman's reaction to the procedure. For the woman who has made the decision and discussed it with those closest to her, her feelings post-abortion are likely to be more positive than the woman who has not explored the reactions of her friends and family.

Bracken, Phil, Hachamovitch, and Grossman (1974) conducted a study to examine the decision-making process and the social and interpersonal situation in which the decision was made. They were concerned with two specific variables, (1) knowledge about the abortion by partner and parents and (2) the degree of support which the partner and parents are perceived as giving toward the decision to have an abortion. Their findings support those of previous studies in that the over-all short-term reaction to the abortion was quite positive. They also found significantly more favorable reactions to the abortion in married and in older women. Finally, the greater the amount of support a woman perceived herself as receiving for the abortion, the more favorable her reaction to the abortion. The effect of partner support was significant among the older group of women, while the parental effect was significant in the younger age group.

Adler (1975) was concerned with clarifying the dimensions that underlie emotional responses of women to abortion and the relationship of the dimensions to background variables. Adler makes several interesting points. Emotional responses to abortion do not fall along a simple positive-negative dimension. After an abortion a woman experiences a variety of emotions, both positive and negative. Further, the negative emotions appear to center around two separate issues associated with the abortion—a "socially based" negative emotion composed of guilt, shame, and fear of disapproval and an internally based negative emotion based on the meaning of the pregnancy and the abortion for the woman. Adler found that the positive emotions were experienced most strongly of the three factors, and that happiness and relief following abortion appeared to be shared by the majority of women.

In summary, the psychological reaction of a woman following an abortion is a complex phenomenon affected by several variables. The woman who has experienced severe psychological difficulties in the past is the most likely to have a severe negative reaction to the abortion; however, the studies reviewed suggest that for the majority of these women the abortion is followed by feelings of relief and happiness. There is also evidence to suggest that psychological functioning is not impaired and may be improved following the abortion. The woman who has not experienced psychological difficulties in the past and who is obtaining an abortion for medical reasons is typically going to experience a mild and transient depression, which is probably a mourning reaction to the loss of a wanted pregnancy. The psychologically normal woman who is obtaining an abortion because she does not want the pregnancy is likely to experience relief and happiness following the abortion. She may experience negative emotions due to norm violation if her social situation is one in which the decision to abort is likely to be disapproved. The data reviewed support the notion that the possibility of negative psychological reaction to abortion has been greatly exaggerated and that there is no reason to believe that women will experience psychiatric difficulties following an abortion.

RAPE

Although more than 55,000 American women reported being raped in 1974, and official estimates of unreported rapes range from three and one-half to ten times this figure, most people have been unaware of the problem until very recently. The women's movement has played a major role in making rape a public issue, and societal attitudes as well as the specific medical, psychological, and legal problems facing the victim are being examined.

Attitudes Toward Rape Victims

Interest in the rape victim was stimulated by the writings of feminists and by the personal accounts of rape victims that indicated that the rape victim was viewed with much less than sympathy. Many professionals involved with treating the rape victim had begun to voice their concern over this problem in articles, books, and journals. Hayman, Lewis, Stewart, and Grant (1967), Williams and Williams (1973), Burgess and Holstrom (1974, 1975), Calhoun, Selby, and Warring (in press), Rotter and King

(1975), and King, Rotter, Calhoun, and Selby (1975) all address themselves to the problems a victim may encounter. They describe a variety of negative reactions ranging from coldly ignoring the victim to blaming the victim for having been raped.

A review of the literature suggests that these negative attitudes may have been perpetuated by most authors addressing themselves to the topic of rape. The literature regarding rape is sparse, and most of it concerns only the medical aspect of care. Halleck's (1962) is one of the few articles to address itself to psychological reactions of the rape victim. Although the body of the article is concerned with the reactions of the victim to the rape, Halleck comments, "A major factor . . . is the question as to whether rape actually did occur. In many instances in which it is known that force was used in obtaining sexual intercourse, this may have been brought on by the provocativeness of the victim. The problem here is different from that of the unwilling victim." (p. 273).

These two questions, (1) Did the rape actually occur? and (2) Was the rape brought on by the provocativeness of the victim? are recurrent themes throughout the literature.

Falk (1964) states that "Many so-called sex crimes never occurred at all. Often these sex crimes are the products of the imagination of women and children who accuse innocent men. . . . Many men are convicted on purely uncorroborated testimony. Complaints of this nature are often unfounded and many men have been 'railroaded' on sex offense charges by disturbed children and spiteful women" (p. 616).

The literature and data from Rape Crisis Centers (King, Rotter, Calhoun & Selby, 1975) and police departments (McDonald, 1971) indicate that the probability of false accusation is minimal. On the contrary, the concern for the falsely accused is so great that current laws regarding rape are very biased in favor of the accused; therefore, convictions in rape cases are notoriously low, the national rate being estimated at only 9 per cent (FBI, 1973). In spite of the fact that the legal system is so heavily biased in favor of the accused, the rape victim is still looked on with suspicion.

Given that rape occurred, the second question—did the victim precipitate the rape by her seductive or provocative behavior?— remains. Most of the articles on rape imply that this is the case.

Amir (1972), a sociologist who has written extensively about rape victims, has formulated a theory of "victim-precipitated" forcible rape. It should be noted that the rapist's belief that the victim has a bad reputation is regarded as victim-precipitation in his theory. He concludes that both by "(1) acts of commission when the victim enters the criminal situation as active participant. . . . and (2) acts of omission of preventive measures. . . . the victim becomes functionally responsible for the offense" (p. 155).

More recent studies indicate that the rape victim continues to be viewed as precipitating the rape incident by her behavior. Calhoun, Selby, and Warring (in press) report that college students believe that 33 per cent of all rapes are precipitated by the victim. Although King, Rotter, Calhoun, and Selby (1975) found a similar percentage for physicians (30 per cent), volunteer counselors in a rape crisis center estimated that victim precipitation occurred 15 per cent of the time. Thus when a woman is raped it is often viewed as her fault, even by the people assisting her following the rape.

There is reflected throughout the literature—medical, legal, and sociological—a bias against viewing the rape victim in the same sympathetic and compassionate light in which the victims of other violent crimes are seen. The prevalence of negative attitudes toward the rape victim cannot be minimized—nor can the effects of these attitudes on her psychological reactions following the rape incident.

Psychological Reactions of the Victim

Rape victims suffer a significant degree of physical and emotional trauma not only during the rape and immediately afterward, but for a considerable period of time following the rape. Burgess and Holmstrom (1974) noted that certain symptoms are exhibited by most victims and they termed this cluster of symptoms the "rape trauma syndrome." They described two stages. In the first or immediate stage, the victim finds her entire life style disrupted. Stage two is the long-term process in which the woman reorganizes her disrupted life style.

Although noting many of the same symptoms, Sutherland and

Scherl (1970) describe three stages: (1) acute reaction, (2) outward adjustment, and (3) integration and resolution. They note a middle stage in which many victims may demonstrate a good adjustment after the immediate issues surrounding the rape have been temporarily settled. They suggest that this is only a pseudo-adjustment and that the final resolution of the trauma will occur after a second period of upset or depression on the part of the victim.

Notman and Nadelson (1975) view the victims' responses as a stress reaction and note four stages: (1) anticipatory or threat phase, (2) impact phase, (3) post-traumatic recoil phase, and (4) post-traumatic reconstitution phase. In the threat phase, the anxiety of the potential victim may facilitate her perception of a dangerous situation so that it may be avoided. During the "impact phase" the degree of trauma as well as the coping mechanisms of the woman will determine the amount of disintegration that occurs. The victim may exhibit a wide range of fear responses during the acute situation. It is in the "post-traumatic recoil" phase that behavioral control and emotional expression are regained. The woman's view of her ability to cope may not only affect the way she handles this trauma, but it may affect her capacity to cope with future stresses. The "post-trauma reconstitution" phase may also affect the woman's future adjustment, because many of the self-reassuring defenses are lost. During this period the victim may respond maladaptively and blame herself for not having avoided or better handled the situation.

As the victim's reaction to rape has only recently begun to be studied, definitive statements regarding the process and stages of the woman's reaction are premature. *The most useful approach appears to be to view the rape as a crisis situation* in which the victim is faced with an extreme environmental trauma. The victim's response is the result of an interaction between the life-threatening stress and her coping mechanisms. Thus there will be situational, cultural, and personality-style differences in responding to the stress.

The victim may exhibit a wide variety of reactions in her initial reaction to the rape. Some women are tearful, others are hysterical, and others are apparently calm. Burgess and Holmstrom (1974) describe two major styles of reacting, "expressed" or "controlled." In the "expressed" style the victim evidences her anger, fear, and anxiety, whereas in the "controlled" style her feelings are masked or hidden. She appears calm, composed, and has a subdued affect. The majority of victims will demonstrate *variable responses* that are not at either extreme. There appear to be, however, some reactions common to many rape victims.

EMOTIONAL RESPONSES

The primary reaction is one of *fear*—fear of death, physical injury, or mutilation. This fear is an acute reaction to the threat of being killed and is probably the basis for many of the symptoms in the syndrome. Many victims are terrified of being alone, especially if the rape occurred in the home. Feelings of fear and panic are easily evoked in the victim in other situations. For example, she may become tearful at the sight of a car similar to the one in which the incident occurred. In some cases the fear may be so great that the woman may refuse to go to certain places or to be in certain situations. This can cause many problems as in the case of a victim who was raped by someone she thought was a physician. She became extremely upset if she was near a hospital or physician's office and consequently became very ill with a medical problem unrelated to the rape before she would obtain medical care.

Loss is another feeling that the rape victim experiences. Metzger (1975) states "Rape is loss. Like death, it is best treated with a period of mourning and grief" (p. 4). A woman may experience the loss of her self-worth, her autonomy, her trust in others, and her ability to control her life. She may also feel isolated or estranged from her friends and family, thus compounding her feelings of loss. When support from others is available, she may not feel so overwhelmed. If the rapist is known to the victim, the loss of trust will be more severe and, depending upon their relationship prior to the rape, may prove to be a serious obstacle to her future interpersonal relationships.

Guilt and *shame* are experienced regardless of the circumstances surrounding the rape. The victim may feel that she should have resisted more or that she should have known better than to be in the particular situation in which the rape occurred. The fact that society views rape as a sexual crime and often views the victim as having provoked the rape by seductive clothing or provocative behavior may further enhance the victim's feelings of guilt and shame.

Interestingly, *anger* does not seem to be a major component of the victim's initial reaction. She appears to feel responsible in spite of her feelings of helplessness and fear. Thus, at least initially, her anger may be directed inward, which is of course not surprising in our society where cultural restrictions on anger are strong. Chessler's (1972) book *Women and Madness* presents the thesis that it is these cultural restrictions on the outward expression of anger by the female that may account for the significantly greater incidence of depression and other types of mental illness in women.

The woman's emotional responses to the rape incident are complex. It appears that responses such as fear may be mediated by external or situational variables while other responses such as guilt and shame may be mediated more by internal variables which are culturally determined.

DISTURBANCES IN FUNCTIONING

Almost all victims report a disturbance in their *sleep* patterns. They have difficulty falling asleep or may wake up in an acute state of anxiety and be unable to go back to sleep. Screaming out in their sleep is not uncommon, nor are nightmares. The nightmares are initially a reliving of the rape experience or a situation which is very similar.

A decrease in *appetite* is a general finding as is a weight loss in the weeks immediately following the rape. Some victims may also report stomach pains or may become nauseated if they think of the assault. Disturbance in the eating pattern is typically not extreme, and it is an indication of a severe reaction if a significant weight loss occurs.

Sexual dysfunction is not uncommon. Bart (1975) reports that 32 per cent of the women she surveyed who were raped by strangers were affected sexually. If the woman had known the attacker she was even more likely to experience sexual difficulties. Forty-six percent of women raped by their dates were affected sexually, while 73 per cent of the women raped by their husbands were affected.

Thus there appears to be a relationship between the intimacy of the relationship before the attack and the degree of the victim's sexual disturbance.

CHANGES IN LIFE STYLE

Many victims experience changes of a major proportion in their life style (Burgess & Holmstrom, 1973). They may feel the need to get away and turn to friends or parents, which may signal a return to a more dependent state. Other women change their phone numbers, move to a new residence, or change jobs. This of course means a loss of familiar surroundings, neighbors, and acquaintances as well as a new adjustment that may be especially difficult for the older victim, who may leave her home of 20 or 30 years. Thus one of the major reactions to rape produces a need for readjustment in and of itself.

After a month or two the victim appears to be adjusting. She may resume work, have a decrease in nightmares, and may seem to have resolved many of her feelings about the rape. Sutherland and Scherl (1970) describe this as a pseudo-adjustment and note that more problems may follow. This phase appears to be based on the victim's denial or suppression of the events and of her emotional reactions to it. She is attempting to return to her previous way of life and may attempt to suppress those feelings which are disruptive to her functioning. The victim may briefly terminate contacts with her counselor or therapist during this phase. She may assume an attitude of acceptance, saying that "this could have happened to anyone" or that the rapist couldn't help himself because he was "sick." The victim is not interested in understanding her own reactions to the situation at this point. It is only after she begins to resolve the experience that she will focus upon her own reactions and feelings.

The resolution of the rape experience may be foreshadowed by a depression. A depressive reaction at this point is normal, but the possibility of more serious problems should not be overlooked. The depressive state may begin with a recurrence of nightmares, an increase in fears, or a decrease in the victim's ability to cope with her daily routine.

In this final phase two things are necessary. The victim must first obtain a realistic understanding of her part in the incident, then integrate the rape experience into her self-perception. The victim must deal with her anger toward the rapist as well as resolve her feelings of lost self-worth. Although it will never be insignificant, the rape incident will be incorporated as a life experience rather than continually experienced as a failure or as a stigma.

If a good resolution is not accomplished, many long-term problems can occur. Anxiety in situations reminiscent of the rape incident or even phobias can result. Disruption of sexual functioning is not uncommon, nor is a disruption of interpersonal relationships with men.

COUNSELING

Crisis counseling appears to be the most appropriate means of assisting women through the rape experience. It is currently available in most metropolitan cities through Rape Crisis Centers, Women's Centers, and Community Mental Health Centers. With the recent interest in rape and current books such as *Rape Victims in Crisis* (1975) and *Against Our Will: Men, Women, and Rape* (1975), more professional and personal understanding will probably be afforded the victim.

For women who have experienced personal difficulties that have required professional assistance, the rape experience may be a serious hazard emotionally. For these women crisis counseling will probably not suffice, and longer-term intervention is usually advisable. This is probably also true for the woman who had a previous rape experience that she has never divulged. These victims have had a "silent reaction to rape" (Burgess and Holmstrom, 1975) and may need to come to terms with the first experience before they are able to resolve the most recent experience.

Rape of a Child or Adolescent

Adolescents and younger children are frequently the victims of rape. Peters (1975) reports that 30 per cent of the rape victims in his study were adolescents (13 to 17 years old) and 15 per cent were children (12 years old and younger), and statistics from the Rape

Crisis Center in Atlanta are similar (Grady Memorial Hospital, 1975).

The behavioral reactions of children to rape are much less severe than those of either adolescents or adults. It may be that the lack of violence experienced is a contributing factor. Another reason may be the fact that the child has not become autonomous and independent; therefore, the loss of control experienced by adult victims may not be as significant a factor for the child victim. The loss of self-esteem and feelings of worthlessness so commonly experienced by the adult victim may not be as frequent in children because they may not have internalized the typical attitudes toward rape.

The child's immediate reaction may *appear* less severe because of developmental limitations, both cognitive and verbal, which hinder her ability to report the distress experienced. Additionally, children often tend to become emotionally withdrawn under stress, which could be a factor in their less-apparent immediate reaction (Peters, 1975).

The immediate reaction of the adolescent to the rape incident is much more obvious than that of the child but appears less pronounced than that of the adult victim (Peters, 1975). The increase in the severity of the reaction appears to be correlated with an increase in the likelihood that violence was associated with the rape. Adolescents reported difficulties in appetite, sleep, and interpersonal relationships as well as problems with school. Transfer to another school is sometimes helpful in preventing the adolescent from dropping out if peer support from schoolmates is not forthcoming.

The emotional distress of the family may hinder the child or adolescent's ability to cope with and resolve the rape experience. Families typically have strong emotional reactions to the rape incident that may increase the victim's feelings of guilt and shame. Further, the family usually needs to blame someone for the experience and sometimes blames the victim or themselves. When this occurs or when the assailant is a close friend or family member (Peters, 1975, found that 78 per cent of the offenders were known by the child victim), the effect on the family unit can be very severe. In these cases the parents as well as the victim need professional assistance in order to appropriately resolve the rape experience.

The long-term effects of the rape are probably much more serious for the child or adolescent than for the adult. Although there are no data to support this contention, it would seem that the rape experience could seriously hinder or affect the various developmental tasks yet to be mastered by the young victim. The disruption to the child's development has not been studied extensively, but there is evidence from clinical case studies that the rape experience may be very harmful. Katan (1973) reports that the rape experience can be "completely overwhelming and shattering" (p. 209) and that her adult patients who had been raped as children "felt keenly that the trauma had caused irreparable damage" (p. 222).

In summary, rape appears to be a crime in which the victim undergoes significant physical and emotional trauma both during the attack and in the weeks following it. There is evidence of both a negative physical and psychological impact on the victim. Although there are some reactions common to most victims, there is a great deal of individual variation. Rape is a crisis situation in which the woman is faced with a severe trauma. The majority of victims appear to need and to benefit from crisis counseling. When more serious reactions occur, the woman may benefit from professional assistance on a longer-term basis.

QUESTIONS AND PROJECTS

1. Visit a Rape Crisis Center and interview some of the volunteer counselors there. Focus particularly on the following topics:
   a. Do the counselors consider it a particularly difficult task to counsel victims of rape?
   b. Do the counselors feel they were adequately trained to deal with the physical and psychological consequences of rape?
   c. Would the counselor press charges if she were raped?
2. Visit a hospital that performs first-trimester abortions and ask physicians, nurses, and social workers about their views on abortion. Do opinions differ depending on how much the individual is directly involved in the abortion?
3. Interview an individual who counsels persons who seek abortions. Planned Parenthood or other such agencies may be a source of persons for your interview. Do the counselor's views on the consequences of abortion agree with the data summarized in this chapter?
4. This chapter has dealt primarily with abortion and rape—events that affect

women primarily. Are there critical life problems that affect men primarily? What are these problems?

5. One of Brownmiller's major conclusions in her book *Against Our Will* is that rape is essentially a powerful weapon used by men to continue to dominate women. Read the book and discuss this particular point.

SUGGESTED READINGS

Popular Sources

G. HARDIN. Abortion vs. right to life: The evil of mandatory motherhood. *Psychology Today,* 1974, *8* (November), 42–50 + . Presents the view that although abortion is not desirable in itself, it is preferable to forcing a woman to have an unwanted child.

Revolt against rape. *Time,* October 13, 1975, 48–54. A discussion on rape, focusing on Susan Brownmiller's book *Against Our Will.*

J. SELKIN. Rape. *Psychology Today,* 1975, *8* (January), 70–72 + . A discussion on how rapists conduct and plan their rapes and how to resist.

Advanced Sources

A. W. BURGESS, & L. L. HOLMSTROM. *Rape: Victims in Crisis.* Maryland: R. J. Brady Co., 1974. A description of the authors' views on rape and its consequences, based on their observation of rape victims.

H. J. OSOFSKY, & J. P. OSOFSKY. *The abortion experience: The psychological and medical impact.* Hagerstown, Md.: Harper & Row, 1973. This volume reviews the literature on abortion through 1972.

D. S. WALBERT, & J. D. BUTLER (Eds.). *Abortion, society and the law.* Cleveland: Case Western Reserve Press, 1973. An edited book offering chapters on various aspects of abortion.

REFERENCES

ADLER, N. E. Emotional responses of women following therapeutic abortion. *Amer. J. Orthopsychiatry,* 1975, *45,* 446–454.

Alleged rape: an invitational symposium. *J. Reproductive Med.,* 1974, *12,* 133–144.

AMIR, M. The role of the victim in sex offences. In H. L. Resnik & M. E. Wolfgang (Eds.) *Sexual behavior: Social, clinical and legal aspects.* Boston: Little, Brown, 1972.

BART, P. B. Unalienating abortion, demystifying depression, and restoring rape victims. Paper presented at the annual meeting of the American Psychiatric Association, Anaheim, 1975.

BOLTER, S. The psychiatrist's role in therapeutic abortion: The unwitting accomplice. *Amer. J. Psychiat.*, 1962, *119*, 312–318.

BRACKEN, B., PHIL, M., HACHAMOVITCH, M. & GROSSMAN, G. The decision to abort and psychological sequelae. *J. Nerv. Ment. Dis.*, 1974, *158*(2), 154–162.

BREKKE, B. *Abortion in the United States.* New York: Harper and Row-Hoeber, Inc., 1958.

BROWNMILLER, S. *Against our will: Men, women, and rape.* New York: Simon and Schuster, 1975.

BURGESS, A. W. & HOLSTROM, L. L. Crisis and counseling requests of rape victims. *Nursing Research,* 1974, Vol. 23 (3), 196–202.

BURGESS, A. W. & HOLSTROM, L. L. The rape victim in the emergency ward. *J. Nursing,* 1973, *73*, 1740–1745.

CALHOUN, L. G., SELBY, J. W. & WARRING, L. J. Social perception of the victim's causal role in rape: an exploratory examination of four factors. *Human Relations,* 1976, in press.

CASADY, M. Abortion: No lasting emotional scars. *Psychol. Today,* 1974, *8*(6), 148–149.

CHESSLER, P. *Women and madness.* New York: Avon Books, 1972.

CONNELL, N. & WILSON, C. (Eds.) *Rape: The first sourcebook for women.* New York: New American Library, 1974.

ERKBLAD, M. Induced abortion on psychiatric grounds: A followup study of 479 women. *Acta Psychiat. Neurol. Scand.* 1955, Supplements 96–100: 1–239.

FALK, GERHARD J. The public image of the sex offender. *Mental Hygiene,* 1964, *48*, 612–620.

Federal Bureau of Investigation: *Crime in the United States: Uniform crime reports,* 1973, 1974.

FINGERER, M. E. Psychological sequelae of abortion: anxiety and depression. *J. Community Psychol.,* 1973, *1*, 221–225.

FLECK, S. Some psychiatric aspects of abortion. *J. Nerv. Ment. Dis.,* 1970, *151*, 42–50.

FORSSMAN, H. & THUWE, I. One hundred and twenty children born after application for therapeutic abortion refused. *Acta Psychiat. Scand.,* 1966, *42*, 71–88.

Grady Memorial Hospital grant application for discretionary funds for the development of a rape crisis center. Atlanta, 1975.

GUTTMACHER, A. F. Why I favor liberalized abortion. *Reader's Digest,* 1973, 1–5.

HAMILTON, J. A. *Post-partum psychiatric problems.* St. Louis: Mosby, 1962.

HALLECK, S. L. The physician's role in the management of victims of sex offenders. *J. Amer. Med. Assoc.,* 1962, *180*, 273–278.

HARDIN, GARRETT. Abortion versus the right to life. The evil of mandatory motherhood. *Psychol. Today,* 1974, *8*, 42–50.

HAYMAN, C. R., LEWIS, F. R., STEWART, W. F. & GRANT. A public health program for sexually assaulted females. *Public Health Report,* 1967, *82,* 497–504.

KATAN, A. Children who were raped. *Psychoanalytic Study of the Child,* 1973, *28,* 208–244.

KING, H. E., ROTTER, M. J., CALHOUN, L. G. & SELBY, J. W. Perceptions of the rape incident: Views from the rape crisis center. Paper presented at the annual meeting of the Southeastern Psychological Association, in Atlanta, 1975.

KOLSTAD, P. Therapeutic abortion. *Acta Obstet. Gynecol. Scand.,* 1957, *36:* Supplement 6.

KUMMER, J. M. Post-abortion psychiatric illness—A myth? *Amer. J. Psychiat.,* 1963, *119,* 89–93.

McDONALD, J. M. *Rape offenders and their victims.* Springfield, Ill.: C. C. Thomas, 1971.

METZGER, D. It is always the woman who is raped. Paper presented at the annual meeting of the American Psychiatric Association, Anaheim, 1975.

NISWANDER, K. R. & PATTERSON, R. J. Psychological reaction to abortion: Subjective patient responses. *Obstet. Gynecol.,* 1967, *29,* 702–706.

NOTMAN, M. T. & NADELSON, C. C. The rape victim: psychodynamic considerations. Paper presented at the annual meeting of the American Psychiatric Association, Anaheim, 1975.

OSOFSKY, H. J. & OSOFSKY, J. D. *The abortion experience: Psychological and medical impact.* Hagerstown: Harper and Row, 1973.

OSOFSKY, J. D. & OSOFSKY, H. J. The psychological reaction of patients to legalized abortion. *Amer. J. Orthopsychiatry,* 1972, *42,* 48–60.

PECK, A. & MARCUS, H. Psychiatric sequelae of therapeutic intervention of pregnancy. *J. Nerv. Ment. Dis.,* 1966, *143,* 417–425.

PETERS, J. J. Social psychiatric study of victims reporting rape. Paper presented at the annual meeting of the American Psychiatric Association, Anaheim, 1975.

President's Commission on Law Enforcement and Administration of Justice. *The challenge of crime in a free society.* Govt. Printing Office, Washington, D. C. 1967.

ROTTER, M. J. & KING, H. E. Volunteer counselors in a rape crisis center. Paper presented at the annual meeting of the Southeastern Psychological Association, Atlanta, 1975.

SARVIN, B. & RODMAN, H. *The abortion controversy.* New York: Columbia University Press, 1974.

SCHWARTZ, R. A. Abortion on request: The psychiatric implications. In Wallert, D. F. & Butler, J. D. *Abortion, society and the law.* Cleveland: Case Western Reserve Press, 1973.

SIMON, N. M., SENTURIA, A. G. & ROTHMAN, D. Psychiatric illness following therapeutic abortion. *Amer. J. Psychiat.* 1967, *124,* 97–103.

SUTHERLAND, S. & SCHERL, D. J. Patterns of response among victims of rape. *Amer. J. Orthopsychiatry,* 1970, *40,* 503–511.

WALTER, G. Psychologic and emotional consequences of elective abortion: A review. *Obstet. Gynecol.*, 1970, *40*, 503–511.

WILLIAMS, C. C. & WILLIAMS, R. A. Rape: A plea for help in the hospital emergency room. *Nursing Forum,* 1973, *12*, 388–401.

Psychological Impact of Divorce

CHAPTER 7

In Chapter 4, we considered a variety of factors affecting marital discord. Throughout the recorded history of man, divorce has been one solution to marital problems. Certainly, within the United States, many marriages currently end in divorce. The rate for the U.S. is among the highest in the world (Goode, 1956; Kenkel, 1966). Although divorce may be a way of ending an unsatisfactory marriage, it is an event commonly accompanied by problems of its own. Within this chapter, we will look at some of these problems for the adults and their children. In beginning this discussion, it is important to keep in mind some of the correlates of divorce discussed in Chapter 4.

HOW PROMINENT IS DIVORCE?

Movies, television, novels, and short stories depict episodes of divorce as part of their dramatic fare, contributing to the common belief that divorce is on the increase. Research concerning the over-all prevalence of divorce in the United States is basically in agreement with this belief. In the years just after the Civil War, approximately 10,000 people were divorced each year. This average had risen to approximately 100,000 by 1914 and reached a high point of 610,000 in 1946. By 1959, the number of individuals divorced in one year had decreased to approximately 350,000.

From 1959, the rate once again began to rise, reaching approximately 400,000 persons by 1966 (Kenkel, 1966). If we look at the number of divorces each year per 100 marriages, we find that the rates for 1946 through 1949 and 1963 through 1965 are quite similar—10.6 and 10.3 respectively (Carter & Glick, 1970). If we look at the rate of divorce in relation to the total number of marriages, we find that in 1900 8.5 per cent of all marriages ended in divorce; from 1960 to 1972, approximately 25 per cent ended in divorce and in 1972, 28.2 per cent ended in divorce (Lantz & Snyder, 1962; Kenkel, 1966; Udry, 1971).

Over-all, these data would seem to indicate that the rate of divorce has been on the increase, reaching a high point in the period immediately following the Second World War. The change from wartime to peacetime represented considerable social adjustment, which strain seems to be reflected in the divorce rate for the period. With the 1950s, the rate declined and then began to rise again in the early 1960s. In considering this kind of data, several factors should be kept in mind. For instance, from such data it cannot be concluded that people are more dissatisfied with their marriages now. It is quite conceivable that they were just as miserable in the post-Civil War period as they are now. They may merely have been more willing to remain in a miserable relationship. It could be argued that social and cultural values have changed regarding divorce. With strong social prohibitions against divorce, people would be generally less likely to elect this option. As prohibitions diminish, people become more disposed toward divorce as a solution to their marital problems. Thus, the nature or extent of marital problems may remain the same while the accessibility of divorce changes. Certainly, the problems in marriages may have changed over the years; however, the statistics concerning divorce cannot be viewed as proof of it.

THE LEGAL BASIS OF DIVORCE

Marriage is a union regulated by law. Laws prescribe minimum ages for marriage just as they do minimum ages for entering into any other binding contract. A set of procedures are specified, and individuals must obtain a marriage license in order to be married.

Similarly, divorce represents a legal phenomenon. Initiating divorce proceedings might be thought of as asking to break a contract. Various societies at different stages of history have provided a variety of grounds for breaking this marital union. A brief overview of some of the ancient grounds may help place in perspective current laws regulating divorce.

Ancient Laws Concerning Divorce

In general, ancient laws greatly favored the man. Frequently, the man could divorce his wife for no reason, but the wife was rarely allowed even to consider divorce. If a man questioned the fidelity of his wife, he had the right of trial by ordeal; he would take her to their local priest. The priest would sprinkle dust from the sanctuary over holy water, and the woman would be required to drink the mixture. The water was thought to make her barren if she were guilty, and thus she became a dreadful example (Deen, 1963). In the code of Hammurabi in the eighteenth century B.C., a man could divorce his wife by saying to her that she was no longer his wife and paying a small amount of money. If the wife even suggested a divorce, she could be thrown into the river. She could also be thrown into the river if she belittled her husband, was not a careful mistress, or neglected her house. The penalty was also the same for a wife's adultery, only in that situation, the man with whom she was having sexual relations and the wife would be bound together and then thrown into the river (Lichtenberger, 1931).

Some of the Hebrew regulations were not so physically harmful but were nevertheless strict. Rabbi Hillel believed that a man had the right to divorce his wife if she so much as spoiled his dinner (Deen, 1963). According to Rabbi Hillel, if the man grew tired of his wife or preferred another woman, he could divorce her. Rabbi Shama took a different approach indicating that a divorce could only be obtained if one party was guilty of some shameful deed.

Within ancient Christianity, the marital rights of men and women were seen as more equitable. The teachings of Jesus viewed marriage as a lifelong bond, and neither marital partner could end the union lightly (Deen, 1963). In the book of Matthew, Jesus states that adultery is the only legitimate ground for divorce.

Legal Bases in the U.S.

Today, adultery is the single most common legal basis for divorce among the various states. In Texas, however, the adultery must be accompanied by abandonment in order for there to be grounds for divorce (Haussamen & Guitar, 1960). Until 1941, South Carolina had no legal grounds for divorce at all (Baber, 1953). Other grounds commonly included physical or mental cruelty and desertion. Perhaps the divorce law for North Carolina is representative. Divorce can be obtained on the grounds of adultery, natural impotence, insanity (after five years from the onset of the condition), pregnancy at the time of the marriage provided the husband is not the father and did not know of the condition at the time of the marriage, and separation for one year.

The adversary aspect of our legal system has traditionally been applied to divorce. One member is viewed as the wronged party, and the other member is the wrongdoer. The law typically assumes that if the offender is innocent, he will protest the divorce and defend himself. Thus, no protest is viewed as an admission of guilt. In actuality, it seems likely that both members contribute to most cases of divorce; however, legally, both cannot want it because collusion would be involved and the divorce could not be granted (Lantz & Snyder, 1962).

Traditionally, the wife gets the divorce with the husband taking the blame. This arrangement reflects what apparently has been a common belief that the social stigma attached to being divorced is greater for a woman than a man. Similarly, it seems likely that often the marital difficulties leading to the break-up of the couple are not those prescribed by the particular state laws. Consequently, the couple must tailor their complaints to fit the law. Often this process occurs in off-the-record legal negotiations, looking for the least-stigmatizing acceptable reason.

Divorce laws have begun to be changed in a number of states. In general, the changes represent attempts to get away from the notion that one person must be guilty. One of the changes involves the introduction of irreconcilable differences as grounds for divorce. Here it is recognized that a couple may be unable to live together without either one of them being a "bad person." The second change involves the use of separation agreements, whereby divorce may be granted if the couple stops living together for a specified period of time. The third, and perhaps most liberal, change initiated in some states is a procedure referred to as dissolutionment of marriage. In this procedure, both members of the couple sign a formal agreement to dissolve the marriage. Typically, there is a brief waiting period after which the divorce is granted. These changes are relatively recent; however, it is interesting to note that in ancient Rome, divorce could also be obtained through mutual consent (Haussamen & Guitar, 1960).

DIVORCE AS A PSYCHOLOGICAL CRISIS

Psychologists and laymen probably began thinking about divorce as a brief, if stressful, event. Certainly, the legal ruling is handed down a particular day; however, the psychological problems for the individuals seldom begin on that day. It would seem that the marital relationship progressively breaks down over a period of weeks, months, or years. As we discussed in Chapter 4, such marital discord is likely to be troubling for the individuals. At some point, one or both members of the couple decide that the relationship should be ended. Divorce proceedings are initiated. Such proceedings may involve repeated conferences with lawyers trying to work out grounds for the divorce, custody arrangements if children are present, property settlements, and potential alimony payments. In many states, there are extended waiting periods before the divorce is finalized. If children are involved, contact with the ex-spouse may continue through visitation rights with children. All in all, the process may be a long-drawn-out one, forcing the individuals to face the break-up of marriage and work out various practical problems repeatedly. As a consequence, the emotional distress may be provoked repeatedly as the various steps unfold. Thus, in studies of divorced individuals, it may be that psychological changes within the individual existed prior to the actual divorce, perhaps contributing to the divorce. Often, it is impossible to determine whether such psychological changes emerged as the marital break-up became more imminent or whether they represent reactions to the divorce itself.

The Physical and Mental Health of Divorced Individuals

As might be expected from our general discussion of life changes and physical illness in Chapter 8, divorced individuals over-all seem more susceptible to physical ailments than married individuals (Carter & Glick, 1970). It also seems that divorced individuals are more likely to have chronic physical dysfunction and that their activities are more likely to be limited by such a dysfunction than are married persons. Their rate of death is also apparently higher than that for comparable married people (Carter & Glick, 1970). Further, divorced persons seem much more likely to have accidents of various sorts. Their accident rate with motor vehicles, regardless of their race or sex, appears to average about three times as high as that for their married counterparts (Carter & Glick, 1970).

As with physical health, a number of studies suggest that the mental health of divorcees is likely to be poor. Crago (1972) found, in general, lower rates of psychosis among married individuals than among divorced persons. Similarly, divorced persons seem significantly more prevalent in multiple psychiatric hospital admissions than married persons (Rosenblatt, Gross & Chartoff, 1969).

Bernard (1956) described six types of neuroticism that may be observed in women after a divorce: (1) withdrawal into an inner world of daydreams about a potential second marriage which would approach romantic perfection; (2) an attempt to revenge herself against her husband through adopting an exploitative attitude toward all men; (3) women who seek revenge against their ex-spouse through attempting to become independent of all men, rejecting male advances with contempt; (4) women who experience a multitude of sexual relationships without genuine affection; (5) women who retreat into motherhood, devoting themselves exclusively to their children; and (6) women who turn to suicide as the result of divorce. In identifying these neurotic trends, Bernard is probably not suggesting that all women who go through a divorce experience one of these; rather, Bernard is suggesting that among women who would encounter substantial psychological difficulties around divorce, one or more of these trends are likely to be involved. It would also seem reasonable to guess that these trends have their counterparts among men who have experienced divorce. Generally, men are less likely to seek psychological help than women and consequently, we know less about their reactions.

Brisco et al. (1973), in his study of divorce, felt that women were more likely to encounter psychiatric difficulties around divorce than were men. He classified three fourths of the women and two thirds of the men as having a "psychiatric disease." In considering his findings in relation to those of other workers, there seems to be fair agreement that divorced persons are more likely to experience some form of psychological disturbance than married individuals; however, Brisco's specific figures of three fourths for women and two thirds for men seem considerably higher. This difference in magnitude may reflect differences in the definition of psychiatric disease employed by the various investigators.

The findings of Overall (1971) disagree somewhat with those previously summarized. He found no substantial difference in the psychopathology of married individuals and people who had been divorced once. He did find a difference between those who had been married and divorced only once and those individuals who had had many marriages and divorces.

In seeking to understand the psychological effects of divorce, an issue of particular importance is the relationship of divorce and suicide. Although investigations differ in terms of precise figures, there does seem to be agreement in the basic observation that suicide is more likely among divorced individuals than among married persons. Cashion (1970) found that suicide is three to four times higher among divorced persons in general. Carter and Glick (1970) found that divorced white males are five times more likely to commit suicide, and a nonwhite male is twice as likely to commit suicide. The rate for divorced white females is three times higher while the rate for nonwhite divorced females is a little less than twice as high. Interestingly, a study by Pearlman (1970) looked at suicide among wives of submariners where their husbands tended to be away from home for extended periods. Pearlman found that suicide was also high among these wives.

As we discuss in Chapter 11, suicide tends to be associated with depression. As it seems that many divorced individuals experience a significant degree of depression, it may not be surprising that relatively high numbers of divorced persons turn to suicide. In considering the relationship of divorce to various forms of psychological disturbance, it is important to keep in mind that we are dealing with correlations. It consequently is difficult to tell which event caused the other or whether both were caused by some third factor. Thus, it might be that having such psychological problems leads to a divorce as well as that the divorce is the cause of the psychological problems.

If we examine the relationship of divorce to institutionalization, we find that divorced persons are more likely to be placed in a mental hospital, prisons, homes for the aged and needy, and tuberculosis than married persons; however, divorced persons are not as likely to be placed in such institutions as people who have never been married (Carter & Glick, 1970). Such differences in the rate of institutionalization are consistent with the overall findings that the physical and mental health of divorced persons is likely to be poorer than that of married individuals. In addition, this higher rate of institutionalization may indicate that the social resources of the divorced individuals are less than for married people. Thus, it may be that when a divorced person becomes dysfunctional, he has fewer people to provide assistance and consequently turns to institutions for care. On the other hand, a married individual who becomes dysfunctional can more often obtain assistance and support from a spouse and thus is less likely to require institutional assistance.

REACTIONS TO DIVORCE

Within the American culture, marriage has traditionally been viewed as a lifelong commitment. The family is seen as a basic social institution, and much of our lives revolves around family commitments. It is not surprising then that when the family breaks up through divorce considerable stress is involved. Negative emotions are often experienced; old habits must be abandoned and replaced by new ones; social relationships change; and new responsibilities must be met. These factors all go into making divorce a challenging experience for most people.

Perhaps the most common emotions experienced as a reaction to divorce are a sense of hurt over the loss of a spouse and a sense of failure (Pfaff, 1965). Feelings of being unwanted or a sense of rejection may also be important even when the divorce is a product of mutual consent. Lantz and Snyder (1962) suggest that the sense of being rejected may be particularly poignant if one spouse remarries while the other had hoped they could get back together. At times, the divorced individual seems to experience a sense of numbness and dissociation as if not really there (Duvall & Hill, 1960; Waller, 1972).

Some divorced individuals appear to experience a good deal of anger toward their ex-spouses, blaming them for what happened. Such a feeling may lead to a desire to punish the spouse (Goode, 1956). According to a study by Bernard (1956), about half of the divorced persons report feeling indifferent toward their spouse, while about one fourth report feeling unfriendly and one fourth friendly toward their former spouse.

Goode (1956), studying a group of divorced women, attempted to relate characteristics of the individual to the severity of the reaction. He used the term "high trauma" to indicate that the woman had experienced at least three of the following four effects —poor health, poor sleeping, lowered work efficiency, or problems in memory. He found that women with the following characteristics were more likely to experience high trauma—Catholic, residing in a small town or rural area, former husband had a middle-or upper-class occupation, divorce resulted from husband's initiation, particularly if his action was associated with an involvement with another woman, a longer duration of the marriage, more children, and being older. It should be noted that many of these factors were described in Chapter 4 as correlates of divorce. Over-all, it would seem that the less likely the divorce from a statistical point of view, the more likely it will be associated with high trauma.

Economic Changes

With divorce, a single household is divided into two households while the financial resources often remain the same. Consequently, even with a reasonably good income, there is likely to be a decline in the standard of living for everyone (Glasser & Navarre, 1965; Groves, 1941; Hetherington, 1966). According to Pfaff (1965), about three fourths of the women seek employment because the ex-husband's income cannot support two households. As Haussamen and Guitar (1960) note, the women may have to learn for the first time how to earn and manage money, while husbands may have to learn for the first time how to run a house.

Social and Sexual Changes

Our culture is pair-oriented. It terms of social relations, we have such cultural sayings as, "Two is company and three is a crowd." When an individual becomes divorced, he or she often falls into the position of being a single adult. There is likely to be a decline in the number of his friends (Waller, 1967). Goode (1956) estimates that most divorced individuals retain about half of the friends they had when they were married. Certainly, some of this reduction in the number of friends may come from increased responsibilities— contributing to the support of the household, keeping up a home, and having total care of the children.

In addition to increased responsibilities, community attitudes may also contribute to the reduction in social life. Duvall and Hill (1960) suggest that the labeling of someone as divorced sets him or her into a separate class, Lantz and Snyder (1962) suggest that for many people divorce has a sinful connotation because their religious convictions. Further, they suggest that some married people are uncomfortable around divorced individuals because the married persons become more aware that divorce could happen to them.

Hetherington, Cox, and Cox (1975) did a longitudinal study of the effects of divorce. Their study covered the first two years after divorce. They found that during the first year the restriction in social life was most marked for women. During that year, men appear to have a relatively active social life, but in the second year, their social activities decline. The divorced women complained of being locked into a child-centered world, with such complaints being less characteristic of working mothers than nonworking mothers.

INTIMACY

Marriage typically involves an intimate relationship between the marital partners. With divorce, this intimate relationship typically ends. This loss of intimacy can be a difficult feature of the divorce. Some authors have described a rebound phenomenon in which a person, needing love and security, may transfer all of his or her desires almost immediately to a new acquaintance (Waller, 1967; Glasser & Navarre, 1965).

Hetherington, Cox, and Cox (1975) note that heterosexual relations are important with respect to one's view of himself. They found that feelings of competence in heterosexual relations, happiness, and self-esteem were highly correlated in married and divorced individuals. Further, they found a steady increase in these areas for divorced men and women over the two-year period after divorce. This improvement in feelings and attitudes would seem consistent with the findings of Goode (1956) that 76 per cent of divorced men and women are either remarried or steadily dating someone by 26 months after their divorce.

An important part of most intimate heterosexual relationships is sexual contact; for divorced individuals, this aspect of their life must also undergo reorganization. As Goode (1956) observes, women divorcees may be labeled as sexual pushovers because they are viewed as having previously had sexual experiences. Hetherington, Cox, and Cox (1975) found that the reported frequency of sexual intercourse was lower for divorced individuals than married persons at two months after the divorce, higher than married persons one year after the divorce and about the same after two years. They also rated the divorced individuals on the extent to which they had been able to establish an intimate relationship with someone after their divorce. Among those who were rated high on intimacy, reported frequency of sexual intercourse was positively associated with reported happiness and self-esteem, i.e., the more frequent the intercourse, the higher the feelings of happiness and self-esteem. Women expressed particularly negative emotions around casual sexual encounters, often talking about feelings of desperation, depression, and low self-worth after such occurrences.

Thus, it would seem that in many areas divorce involves a breaking of old habits and patterns of behavior and an establishment of new ones (Blair, 1970). Readjustments must be made in terms of economic, social, and sexual spheres. Such changes seem often to be associated with feelings like hurt, a sense of failure, and unhappiness. It seems reasonable to expect that the longer the marriage has gone on, the harder readjustments will be. Fortunately, most people seem able to make such changes over the course of a couple of years.

THE CHILDREN OF DIVORCE

In looking at the effects of divorce, attention must be paid to the children. As the family and household break up, the lives of the children are significantly altered. Most often, the mother receives custody of the children, and they form a single-parent household. The father typically receives visitation rights, allowing him to see his children at specified intervals. These arrangements are typically worked out through a custody hearing in a court of law. Consequently, when examining the effects of divorce on the children involved, we are mostly considering children raised by a mother in the absence of a father. This family constellation can actually result from several causes—divorce or separation, the death of the father, or the occupational demands of the father, to name a few. We will focus our attention on father-absent homes resulting from divorce, drawing comparisons with the others wherever appropriate.

It has been estimated that 10 percent of the children in this country are raised in father-absent homes (Hetherington & Deur, 1971). Children from such homes appear to represent a high-risk group for such social and psychological problems as delinquency and criminal behavior (Peterson & Becker, 1965; Bacon, Child & Barry, 1963; Cohen, 1955; Glasser, 1965). In the case of delinquency, the high risk is associated with broken homes resulting from divorce rather than broken homes resulting from death of a parent (Burt, 1929; McCord, McCord, & Thurber, 1962).

Effects of Divorce on Boys

From a variety of theoretical perspectives, including common sense, it would be expected that the absence of a father would be an important factor in the development of boys. This expectation has been confirmed in numerous studies examining different aspects of development in various populations of boys. Hetherington and Deur (1971) provide a detailed review of these studies involving both boys and girls.

In general, the research indicates that the performance of sex-typed behavior is particularly affected by father absence (Hetherington & Deur, 1971; Lynn & Sorrel, 1959; Boch, 1956; Sears, 1951; Burton & Whiting, 1961). Thus, their behavior appears less "masculine" than boys from intact families. The picture is not entirely clear-cut, however, as Lynn and Sawrey (1959) identified a pattern of compensatory masculinity among eight- and nine-year-old boys, who according to maternal reports tended to show inconsistent extremes of sex-typed behavior. According to Hetherington and Deur (1971), these observations were consistent with the findings of McCord, McCord, and Thurber (1962). They found that boys with absent fathers tended to show extremes of aggressiveness coupled with dependency on adults and homosexual tendencies, both of which are seen as inconsistent with appropriate sex-typed behavior.

In addition, boys from father-absent homes have been described as less self-controlled, more impulsive, and less able to delay immediate gratification (Mischel, 1961). Siegman (1966), studying first-year law and medical students, found that those individuals whose fathers had been absent for at least one year while the subject was between the ages of one to four reported more parental disobedience, more likelihood of inflicting property damage, and drinking than individuals whose fathers had been present during that period of their development. Similarly, in a study of Peace Corps volunteers, Suedfeld (1967) found that volunteers whose fathers had been absent for at least five years before they were 15 years old tended to be among those volunteers who returned to this country early because of adjustment or conduct problems. Finally, in a study of seventh-grade boys, Mischel (1961) compared boys from father-absent homes with boys from father-present homes. The former group were rated by their teachers as more aggressive and less willing to conform to rules. They seemed to evidence less guilt, being unwilling to accept blame for their own behavior.

Father absence has also been found to be associated with the intellectual functioning of children (Deutch & Brown, 1964; Sutton-Smith, Rosenberg, & Landy, 1967). Using various achievement tests, these studies have found that children whose fathers are absent perform below what is expected for their educational level. Carlsmith (1964) cites a considerable body of research indicating that the pattern of cognitive aptitude differs for boys and for girls, with girls showing relatively better verbal ability than boys but boys showing relatively better mathematical ability than girls. This pattern of cognitive functioning appears to change with father absence. Carlsmith (1964) reported that boys from father-absent homes showed a pattern of cognitive performance more comparable to girls than to boys from father-present homes. Hetherington and Deur (1971), reviewing this area of research, note that the patterning of intellectual functioning may be affected by a number of familial influences aside from father absence. Thus, father absence may not represent a specific cause of the change of pattern of intellectual functioning but rather, father absence may merely be one instance of the more general cause, namely, family stress.

Effects of Father Absence on Girls

The absence of fathers has also been found to affect the behavior of daughters (Biller & Weiss, 1970). The most striking effects appear to develop during adolescence when father-absent girls appear to have difficulty in heterosexual relationships (Hetherington & Deur, 1971). There appear to be few, if any, effects of father absence on girls' behavior before adolescence in terms of their "feminine" interests and activities. Although girls over-all are less likely than boys to be identified as delinquent, those girls who are arrested for delinquent behavior are more likely than delinquent boys to come from broken homes. The delinquent conduct of girls is also more likely to involve sexual behavior than boys (Cohen, 1955).

Hetherington (1972) conducted a carefully controlled study of adolescent girls. They compared girls from intact homes with girls from homes broken because of the death of the father and with girls from homes broken because of divorce. They compared these groups on measures of feminine identification, social relationships with boys, and social relationships with females. They found little difference between the three groups of girls in terms of feminine identification or in terms of social relationships with other females; however, a number of significant differences emerged with respect to relationships with males. Adolescent girls from divorced homes reported earlier and more frequent sexual contact with males. They also seemed inappropriately assertive in social situations with males. Finally, they displayed more attention-seeking behavior and initiated more physical contact with males than either of the other two groups of girls. In contrast, adolescent girls from homes broken by the death of the father showed anxiety in heterosexual situations, appearing shy and inhibited. It would seem that the father-absent girls had failed to acquire the necessary judgment and social skills for heterosexual relationships typical of girls their age.

The cognitive functioning of girls from father-absent homes shows similar deficits to that exhibited by boys from father-absent homes. Again, while the specific nature of the intellectual deficit may be unclear, it seems that over-all their intellectual performance is less than expected (Nelson & Maccoby, 1966; Landy, Rosenberg & Sutton-Smith, 1969). Again, as with the boys, it seems that poor cognitive functioning of these girls is associated with general familial stress rather than father absence specifically.

Moderating Influences

The extent to which paternal absence from the home influences child development is influenced by a number of considerations. In general, most studies, as summarized by Hetherington and Deur (1971) indicate that early separation has a greater impact than later separation. This result seems to be the case for both boys (Hetherington, 1966) and girls (Hetherington, 1972). Similarly, the presence of older male siblings appears to reduce the effect of father absence (Hetherington & Deur, 1971). Organizations such as The Big Brother Association have been built on this general notion. These organizations recruit adult male volunteers to establish friendship relationships with boys without fathers. While little research has been done on their effectiveness, they would seem consistent with the general findings previously reviewed.

It seems likely that a major factor influencing the extent to which paternal absence influences child development would be the behavior of the mother. Hetherington & Deur (1971) has argued that in a single-parent home, the behavior of that parent is even more influential in the child's development than the behavior of one parent in an intact home. Some research summarized by Hetherington and Deur (1971) has indicated that father-absent boys with warm, nondeviant mothers show less psychopathology or delinquency than father-absent boys with rejecting or emotionally troubled mothers. Additionally, mothers who valued aggressive and masculine behavior in sons had sons with a more masculine self-concept. A number of other investigations have examined more broadly the relationship between divorced parents and their children. Some of these studies will be considered in the next section.

Divorced Parents and Their Children

As we have noted earlier, divorce involves a breakdown and dissolutionment of the family system. Typically, this breakdown involves a good deal of conflict between the husband and wife, and this conflict is likely to affect the children. As Milgram notes in a conversation with Nathan Ackerman (a leading family theorist) (1972), although divorce involves a termination of the relationship of the spouses, the individuals remain as parents to their children. Thus, for the adults, the children serve as a continuing connection to the previous marital relationship.

A number of clinicians (Milgram, 1972; Harris, 1972) have suggested that children often get embroiled in the conflicts of the divorcing and divorced parents. Harris (1972), who has paid particular attention to the various ways in which children become involved in the conflicts between parents, suggests that the child often serves as a hostage. The child may be used to insure continued contact by one parent with the other parent. Threats of cutting off contact with the child may be used as a means of insuring child support or alimony payments. The parent having custody may hinder contact between the child and the other parent in retaliation for personal grievances. It might be expected that using the child as a hostage in these ways places a good deal of strain on that child.

In a particularly careful and systematic study, Hetherington, Cox, and Cox (1975) examined the interactions of divorced parents with their children. These relationships were studied over the first two years after the divorce. In general, these authors found that the households of divorced mother and divorced father went through a period of considerable disequilibrium during the first year, with reorganization occurring during the second year. Over the two years, divorced fathers showed a gradual decline in contact with their children. Initially, these fathers showed a highly permissive and indulgent attitude toward their children. There was an initial frequent use of praise by these fathers with a gradual decline over the two years. It seems that in the initial year after the divorce, the fathers strove to make their contact with their children as positive as possible.

In contrast with parents in intact families, divorced parents appeared to make fewer demands for self-sufficient, autonomous, or mature behavior from their children. Divorced parents, again in comparison with parents of intact families, seemed less likely to solicit the child's opinion and less likely to use explanations in their communications with their children. In structured play situations, Hetherington, Cox, and Cox (1975) found that divorced parents were less able to control their children's behavior than parents of intact households. This lack of control reached a low point at the end of the first year and then gradually increased. Unlike divorced fathers, divorced mothers seemed to begin by giving many commands, restrictions, and using many negative sanctions. Over the two-year period, they appear to become more effective in controlling their children's behavior as they become less restrictive and use positive sanctions (praise) relatively more frequently.

As might be expected, Hetherington, Cox, and Cox (1975) also found that effectiveness in dealing with children for both married and divorced parents was related to support in child rearing from the spouse and agreement between the spouses concerning the disciplining of the children. When support and agreement in child rearing existed between divorced couples, the disruption in family functioning seemed to be less severe and shorter-lived. They also noted that frequency of contact between father and child was associated with more positive mother-child interactions when there was agreement in child rearing, a positive attitude toward the spouse, and when the father was emotionally mature. On the other hand, when these conditions did not exist, frequency of the father's visits were associated with poorer mother-child relations. Finally, they found that the emotional maturity of the mother was also associated with her adequacy in coping with stresses in her new life, including her relationship with her children.

CONCLUSIONS

In considering the effects of divorce, it seems clear that it constitutes a substantial psychological hazard for all the persons involved. The studies reviewed in this chapter would seem to suggest that the majority of people going through divorce experience some emotional discomfort and turmoil during and immediately following the divorce. For some individuals, there appear to be significant longer-term consequences. Certainly, it seems that divorce can have a significant impact on the development of children, particularly when there is continuing conflict between the parents.

These findings probably should not be taken as evidence that all individuals will suffer profound psychological consequences from divorce, nor should the findings be taken as evidence that divorce represents a bad option for some marital difficulties. These research findings might best be viewed as indicating some of the potential pitfalls and problems which may be encountered with divorce. Further, they present a challenge to clinicians to develop theoretical notions and therapeutic techniques specifically designed to aid divorced persons and the children of divorce. Perhaps, once the decision to seek a divorce has been made, a couple might benefit from seeking professional assistance in working out some of their difficulties in order to achieve the most rational and civilized arrangement.

PROJECTS AND QUESTIONS

1. In small-group discussions, consider how the various effects of divorce might differ for individuals of different ages—20 to 30, 30 to 40, 40 to 50, 60 and over.
2. In what ways do reactions to divorce differ from reactions to the death of a spouse, and in what ways are they similar?
3. How might professional counseling assist the couple seeking a divorce or assist the single person after a divorce?
4. How do you think children of various ages should be told about their parents' divorce?

SUGGESTED READINGS

H. CARTER & P. GLICK, *Marriage and divorce: A social and economic study.* Cambridge: Harvard University Press, 1970.

I. STUART AND L. EDWIN, (Eds.). *Children of separation and divorce.* New York: Grossman Publishers, 1972.

J. GREENHILL. *Some syndromes of love.* New York: Impact Press, 1965, 203–218.

REFERENCES

BABER, R. E. *Marriage and the family,* New York: McGraw-Hill, 1953, 443–529.

BACK, G. R. Father-fantasies and father-typing in father-separated children. *Child Devel.* 1946, *17,* 63–80.

BACON, M. K., CHILD, I. L. & BARRY, H. A cross-cultural study of correlates of crime. *J. Abnorm. Soc. Psychol.* 1963, *66*, 291–300.

BERNARD, J. Marital stability and patterns of status variables. *J. Marriage Family,* 1966, *28(4)*, 421–439.

BERNARD, J. *Remarriage: A study of marriage.* New York: Dryden and Press, 1956.

BILLER, H. B. & WEISS, S. D. The father-daughter relationship and the personality development of the female. *J. Genetic Psychol.,* 1970, *116*, 79–93.

BLAIR, M. Divorce's adjustment and attitudinal changes about life. *Dissertation Abstracts International,* 1970, June, *30(12-A)*, 5541–5542.

BRISCO, C. W., et al. Divorce and psychiatric disease. *Arch. gen. Psychiat.* 1973, *29(1)*, 119–125.

BURT, C. *The young delinquent.* New York: Appleton, 1929.

BURTON, A. Marriage without failure. *Psychol. Reports,* 1973, *32(3)* pt. 2., 1199–1208.

BURTON, R. V. & WHITING, J. W. The absent father and cross-sex identity. *Merrill-Palmer Quarterly,* 1961, *7*, 85–95.

CAPRIO, F. W. Divorce or martyrdom. In J. Greenhill. *Some syndromes of love.* New York: Import Press, 1965, 138–140.

CARLSMITH, L. Effect of early father-absence on scholastic aptitude. *Harvard Educational Review,* 1964, *34*, 3–21.

CARTER, H. & GLICK, P. *Marriage and divorce: A social and economic study.* Cambridge: Harvard University Press, 1970.

CASHION, B. Durkheim's concept of anomie and its relationship to divorce. *Sociology and Social Research,* 1970, *55(1)*, 72–83.

COHEN, A. K. *Delinquent boys: The culture of the gang.* Glencoe, Ill.: The Free Press, 1955.

CRAGO, M. Psychopathology in married couples. *Psychol. Bull.,* 1972, *77(2)*, 114–128.

DEEN, E. *Family living in the Bible.* New York: Harper and Row, 1963.

DEUTCH, M. & BROWN, B. Social influences in Negro-white intelligence differences. *J. Soc. Issues,* 1964, *20*, 24–35.

DILYAN, E. Divorce-depression-drugs. In J. Greenhill. *Some syndromes of love.* New York: Impact Press, 1965, 165–178.

DUVALL, E. & HILL, R. *Being married.* New York: Association Press, 1960, 313–336.

GLASER, D. Social disorganization and delinquent subcultures. In H. C. Quay (Ed.). *Juvenile delinquency.* New York: Van Nostrand, 1965.

GLASSER, P. & NAVARRE, E. Structural problems of the one-parent family. *J. Soc. Issues,* 1965, *21(1)*, 98–109.

GOODE, W. *Women in divorce.* New York: The Free Press, 1956.

GROVES, E. *Marriage.* New York: Henry Holt, 1941.

HARRIS, M. The child as hostage. In I. Stuart & L. Edwin (Eds.). *Children of separation and divorce.* New York: Grossman Publishers, 1972.

HAUSSAMEN, F. & GUITAR, M. A. *The divorce handbook.* New York: Van Rees Press, 1960.

HETHERINGTON, E. M. Effects of paternal absence on sex-typed behaviors in Negro and white pre-adolescent males. *J. Personality and Soc. Psychol.* 1966, *4*, 87–91.

HETHERINGTON, E. M. Effects of father absence on personality development in adolescent daughters. *Devel. Psychol.*, 1972, November, *7(3)*, 313–326.

HETHERINGTON, E. M., COX, M. & COX, R. Beyond father absence—conceptualization of effects of divorce. Paper presented at the meetings of the Society for Research in Child Development at Denver, April, 1975.

HETHERINGTON, E. M. & DEUR, J. L. The effects of father absence on child development. *Young children*, 1971, (March), 233–248.

KENKEL, W. *The family in perspective.* New York: Appleton-Century-Crofts, 1966, 301–337.

LANDY, F., ROSENBERG, B. & SUTTON-SMITH, B. The effect of limited father absence on cognitive development. *Child Devel.*, 1969, *40*, 941–944.

LANTZ, H. & SNYDER, E. *Marriage: An examination of the man-woman relationship.* New York: John Wiley, 1962, 315–334.

LICHTENBERGER, J. P. *Divorce: A social interpretation.* New York: McGraw-Hill, 1931.

LYNN, D. B. & SAWREY, W. L. The effects of father absence on Norwegian boys and girls. *J. Abnorm. soc. Psychol.*, 1959, *59*, 258–262.

MCCORD, J., MCCORD, W. & THURBER, E. Some effects of paternal absence on male children. *J. abnorm. soc. Psychol.*, 1962, *64*, 361–369.

MISCHEL, W. Father absence and delay of gratification. *J. abnorm. soc. Psychol.*, 1961, *63*, 116–124.

MILGRAM, S. The adolescent in relation to his separated yet inseparable parents. In I. Stuart and L. Edwin, (Eds.). *Children of separation and divorce.* New York: 1972, Grossman Publishers.

NELSON, E. A. & MACCOBY, E. E. The relationship between social development and differential abilities on the scholastic aptitude test. *Merrill-Palmer Quarterly*, 1966, *12*, 356–361.

OVERALL, J. Associations between marital history and the nature of manifest psychopathology. *J. abnorm. Psychol.*, 1971, *78(2)*, 213–221.

PEARLMAN, C. Separation reactions of married women. *Amer. J. Psychiat.*, 1970, *126:2(7)*, 946–950.

PETERSON, D. R. & BECKER, W. C. Family interaction and delinquency. In H. C. Quay (Ed.). *Juvenile delinquency.* New York: Van Nostrand, 1965, 63–99.

PFAFF, R. A personal message to parents. In J. Greenhill. *Some syndromes of love.* New York: Impact Press, 1965, 203–218.

ROSENBLATT, S., GROSS, M. & CHARTOFF, S. Marital status and multiple psychiatric admissions for alcoholism. *Quarterly Journal for Studies on Alcohol*, 1969, *30 A(2)*, 445–447.

SEARS, P. S. Doll-play aggression in normal young children: Influence of sex, age sibling status, father's absence. *Psychol. Monographs,* 1951, *65* (6, Whole No. 323).

SIEGMAN, A. W. Father absence during childhood and anti-social behavior. *J. abnorm. soc. Psychol.*, 1966, *71*, 71–74.

SUEDFELD, P. Paternal absence and overseas success of Peace Corps volunteers. *J. Consulting Psychol.*, 1967, *31*, 424–425.

SUTTON-SMITH, B., ROSENBERG, B. & LANDY, F. Father absence effects in families of different sibling compositions. *Child Devel.* 1968, *39*, 1213–1221.

UDRY, J. R. Marital instability by race, sex, education, and occupation using 1960 census data. *Amer. J. Sociology*, 1966, *72(2)*, 203–209.

WALLER, W. *The old love and the new.* Carbondale, Ill.: Southern Illinois University Press, 1967.

Psychological Factors in Physical Illness

CHAPTER 8

Over the course of a normal life span, most people experience episodes of physical illness. At times, the illness lasts for a brief period and is only mildly distressing; but many individuals must face prolonged illness involving more severe consequences, and some individuals encounter physical disabilities that last throughout their lives. Such episodes of illness represent significant events in a person's life, and the present chapter examines the psychological factors associated with such illnesses.

In tackling this problem, we land squarely in an old philosophical debate, the "mind–body problem." Renaissance philosophers like Descartes and Spinoza became absorbed in the difference between the subjective private experience of the mind and the more objective public nature of the physical body. They believed that there were two basic kinds of material in the world, the stuff of physical reality and the stuff of which the mind is made. Descartes believed that these two kinds of material interacted within an individual, each affecting the other. Spinoza, on the other hand, believed that they coexisted in parallel, following the same time course but never directly influencing each other.

Although this controversy represents an old debate, it nevertheless reflects some of the questions raised by people today. How can what you think or feel influence what happens within your body? Throughout our discussion, we will stick to the common-sense assumption that our private subjective experiences as well as the regulation of bodily systems are a function of the central nervous system.

PSYCHOPHYSIOLOGIC DISORDERS

Over the first half of this century, psychiatrists and physicians examined the relationship of psychological factors and physical illness within a rather narrow perspective. Certain diseases were viewed as "psychosomatic" disorders and became part of the official psychiatric classification system. Psychophysiologic disorders, as they are now referred to, are characterized by physical symptoms caused by psychological factors. Usually, these symptoms involve a single organ system, such as the gastrointestinal or the circulatory system, under autonomic nervous system control.

Here we are talking about actual physiological impairment or damage, like ulcers, some forms of asthma, hives, essential hypertension and the like. Very often an individual will go to his family physician with a pain in his stomach. The physician will conduct a medical examination, and if there is no evidence that the pain and corresponding tissue damage in the stomach is caused by a physical disease, he is likely to conclude that the ulcer is the result of psychological problems. Presumably treatment will involve some form of psychotherapy and physical measures aimed at symptomatic relief.

We should note that this approach to psychophysiologic disorders represents a negative diagnosis, that is, if you can rule out physiological causes, then it must be psychologically caused. Such an approach to diagnosing runs at least two risks. First, our knowledge about the physiological processes involved or our techniques for measuring such processes may not be good enough. The disorder may have a physiological cause that we just cannot detect at present. Second, the negative diagnosis (if not a, then b) minimizes the possibility that the two factors might be working together to produce the disorder.

In the early 1950s, investigators began to broaden their perspective. Stressful life situations, as well as internal emotional conflicts, began to be studied in relation to physical symptoms

(Silverman, 1968). Researchers began to find that such psychosocial factors were associated with the onset and intensification of a wide variety of physical disorders, including many which had not been thought of as psychophysiologic conditions. Over the past two decades, such findings have led to a drastic change in our approach to psychological factors in physical illness. Physical diseases across the board began to be thought of in a multifactorial way—with physical, emotional, and social influences all playing a role in the onset, course, and treatment of physical disorders. The remainder of this chapter will consider some of the psychosocial factors associated with each aspect—onset, course, and treatment —of physical disorders.

ONSET OF ILLNESS

Over the past two decades considerable research attention has been devoted to the psychological and social factors associated with the onset of disease. Researchers working in this area have either looked at stressful situations in relation to particular kinds of disorders such as diabetes mellitus (Hinkle, Evans & Wolf, 1951) or leukemia (Green, 1958) or in relation to illness as a whole. Throughout most of the work, the general notion is that stressful situations can facilitate physical causes of disease.

Madison and Viola (1968) and Parks, Benjamin, and Fitzgerald (1969), viewing the death of a spouse as a stressful event, examined the incidents of physical illness in widows and widowers during the first year of their bereavement. They found that these individuals did indeed show an increase in physical illnesses when compared with similar individuals who had not just lost a spouse.

Sheldon and Hooper (1969) found ill health to be associated with marital-problems adjustment. Similarly, Mutter and Schleifer (1968) observed that families with physically ill children tended to be more disorganized and to have undergone more significant life changes than families with healthy children. Parens, McConville, and Kaplan (1966) report an increase in ill health among student nurses who had recently experienced a difficult separation from their home and family.

It would seem that loss of a close person through death, departure, and other significant life changes, as well as discontent in close relationships, may be associated with the onset of illness. Schmale (1958) studied a series of individuals admitted to a general hospital. He tape-recorded interviews with each of these persons and concluded that in many instances feelings of hopelessness and helplessness from actual or threatened psychological loss preceded any clinical manifestation of disease. On the other hand, Imboden, Canter, and Cluff (1963) did a carefully controlled study of adults and found no evidence that separation (loss of a close interpersonal relationship) was a specific precondition for disease. Hinkle et al. (1958), in investigating Chinese students studying in the U.S., point to the importance of the way in which the individual interprets such events. They divided the students into those who frequently experienced episodes of physical illness and those who did not. He noted that although the two groups did not differ appreciably in the actual number of separation experiences, the frequently ill group tended to view their lives as more conflict-laden and reacted with greater psychological as well as somatic dysfunctions than did the seldom-ill group. Similarly, Rahe (1958) found that individuals who were sick at the time of his study reported more significant life changes than did individuals who were not ill at that time.

Rahe (1968) has attempted to unify and quantify the idea of life change in relation to the onset of physical illness. He constructed a list of various kinds of life changes, such as moving from one town to another, changing jobs, getting divorced, and the death of a close person, and had people rate each of these items on how much change tended to be involved with each. He referred to scores on the scale as life-change units (LCU). With this instrument, he has looked at the onset of physical illness in several populations. In a study of sailors, Rahe found a significant relationship between LCU totals and the number of physical illnesses. Individuals having higher LCU scores also tended to have more illnesses. Similar relationships have been found for students entering officer training school between preschool LCU totals and the number of physical illnesses reported at six weeks, four months, and one year following the beginning of their training (Cline, cited in Rahe 1972). Finally, Wagner (cited in Rahe, 1972), found that the number of days missed from practice or games because of injury was associated with pre-season LCU totals for college football players.

Other investigators have examined psychological factors associated with the onset of particular diseases, and again psychological loss and separation appear prominent. It has been found to be associated with such diseases as tuberculosis (Kissen, 1956), various forms of cancer (Bacon, Renneker & Cutler 1952; Green, 1958), rheumatoid arthritis (Ludwig, 1954), ulcerative colitis (Engels, 1955), infectious hepatitis (Pappers & Handy 1956), and functional uterine bleeding (Heiman, 1956).

At times, a somewhat broader definition of life stress has been employed in studying the onset of worsening of particular diseases. For instance, Ripley and Wolff (1950) have found that the development and intensification of symptoms in glaucoma (an eye disease) were related in time to life stresses. Holmes and Wolff (1952) have found that some patients with a backache syndrome were reacting to security-threatening situations accompanied by feelings of anxiety, hostility, or guilt. Holmes, Treuting, and Wolff (1951) noted that conflict and anxiety could increase the severity of symptoms of rhinitis and other sensitive mucous membrane responses that might already be present.

Many studies have been concerned with the relationship of disturbances of the heart and stressful situations. Duncan, Stevenson, and Ripley (1950) examined a number of individuals suffering paroxysmal arhythmia (disturbances in the rhythm of the heartbeat), half of whom had some structural heart disease. Among these patients, it was found that cardiac irregularities tended to occur during periods of emotional stress. They also noted several common personality traits in these patients, although they did not compare the personality characteristics of these patients with non-cardiac patients. The commonly occurring traits among the cardiac patients studied included unexpressed hostility, compulsion, undue ambition, and longstanding anxiety. The notion of a personality constellation serving as a predisposing factor for cardiac disturbances has received widespread attention (Jenkins 1971), but at present, this issue is still highly controversial.

Other investigators have looked at cardiac dysfunctions in terms of the life-change units developed by Rahe and his colleagues. Aarajarvi (cited in Rahe, 1972), in an epidemiological study in

Finland, observed that the incidence of coronary heart disease is much higher among eastern Finns than western Finns. He also noted that the LCU totals for the eastern Finns tended to be twice as high as that for the western Finns. Similarly, a research group in Stockholm (cited in Rahe 1972) found that the LCU totals (according to surviving relatives) was much higher for people who died from a heart attack than the LCU totals for individuals who survived such an episode.

Taken as a whole, it would seem that the research concerning psychological factors in the initiation of disease has established some connections between such events. Both when considering illness generally and when considering various specific diseases, *life changes such as the death of a close person, loss of a job, divorce, and the like should be regarded as potential contributors to the disease process.* Many questions remain, however. The mechanism by which such stressful events affect the body to facilitate disease is a wide-open question. Regardless of the specific processes involved, it seems clear from what we currently know that any comprehensive understanding of disease will require taking such psychological and social factors into account.

PSYCHOLOGICAL FACTORS ASSOCIATED WITH THE COURSE OF ILLNESS

In this section, our interest shifts to the kinds of psychological changes that develop as a disease runs its course. Physical illness itself is seen as a potential problem requiring adjustments on the part of the individual.

The psychological consequences of physical illness or injury have been of considerable interest to hospital medical staffs while the person is still in the hospital (Kahana & Bibring, 1964). Psychologists, psychiatrists, social workers, and rehabilitation counselors have tried to help patients deal with the stress of illness and injury. As there is an enormous variety of illness and injury, the kinds of limitations imposed by these problems vary, for example, inability to walk, inability to breathe easily, inability to see, and the like. There are also wide variations in the degree of impairment involved, e.g., a slight limp, needing a crutch, needing a leg brace, not being able to stand at all; and there is variation in how long it is likely to last, e.g., a few hours, weeks, months, years, or for the rest of the person's life. This variety is reflected in the available research. Investigations have covered areas such as emotional factors associated with heart disease (Kits Van Heijungen & Trevrniet, 1966; Bastiaans, 1968; Hackett & Weisman, 1969), personal and social adjustment of diabetic adults and children (Koski, 1969; Leeman, 1970), personality factors in various respiratory diseases including lung cancer and obstructive lung diseases (Decencio, Leshner, & Leshner, 1968). Although all these areas have received some research attention, few have been investigated in depth; and much of the research is based on the clinical impression of practitioners working with particular kinds of patients in particular settings. Many of the findings are tentative, still needing additional research for verification.

Verwoerdt (1972) has suggested categories of factors for thinking about psychological responses to physical illness. These include characteristics of the illness, characteristics of the individual, and characteristics of the situation. In terms of the characteristics of the illness, time factors have been shown to be important in influencing the psychological reactions of individuals.

Time Factors

Beigler (1957) has found that patients with slowly progressing malignancies were less anxious, in general, than patients with rapidly progressing malignancies. It would seem that for the patients with the slow-growing malignancy, the prospect of death is more remote and there is more opportunity for the individual to find ways of coping with the resulting anxiety than there is for patients with fast-growing malignancy. Lazarus and Opton (1966) have summarized work showing that the intensity of the anxiety response increased as a stressful event drew closer in time, and they have shown that the intensity of the anxiety diminishes with the operation of various kinds of coping mechanisms.

Consistent with these ideas, investigators have developed a time measure referred to as *distance to death*. Here, the time interval involved is between when an illness is observed in a patient and when that patient dies. One investigation using this approach (Verwoerdt & Elmore, 1967) examined 30 patients thought to have a fatal illness. After one year, 22 had died, with a median distance to death of 2 months from the beginning of the study. Those who died in less than 2 months consistently had been described as more hopeless and less future-oriented at the time of the initial assessment than patients who died from 2 to 9 months after that initial assessment.

A final aspect of the time factor concerns how long the disease process lasts. Certainly we would expect longer-lasting diseases to be more stressful for the individual than brief diseases. One investigation (Dovenmuehle & Verwoerdt, 1962), studying cardiac patients, found that individuals with mild and severe cardiac diseases showed an equivalent degree of depression early in the disease process. As the course of the illness continued over several years, the patients with mild cardiac disease began to show a decline in depression, but for the severe cardiac patients, the depressive symptoms continued throughout.

The Organ Affected

A second important feature of the disease would appear to be the organ affected. Certainly, some organ systems such as the heart are more essential for life than are others such as the skeleton or the muscles, and it seems reasonable to expect that illness involving very important systems would be more stressful than would be disease of other organ systems of less importance. In addition, however, Fisher and Cleveland (1968) have suggested that individuals form a body concept, that is, an image of what their body is like. They suggest that this image incorporates not only the objective features of their physique but also the significance of these features for their personality functioning. Thus, the body concept of a football player might emphasize shoulder musculature. Cassell (1972) suggests that some illnesses affect the way in which afflicted bodily regions are perceived, and such perceptions wil depend in part on the preexisting body concept.

One organ system should be singled out for special consideration. Injury or illness directly involving the central nervous system will likely involve some psychological changes. With impairment to other organ systems, psychological changes, like depression or anxiety, represent secondary changes based on the meaning of the impairment for the individual. In the case of damage to the central nervous system, the accompanying psychological changes are primary in that they are directly due to the injury or illness. What kinds of changes are involved depend on what portion of the central nervous system is disrupted, but typically the changes include perceptual defects, language disturbances, memory impairment, and perhaps over-all intellectual ability. Aside from these changes, there may also be the same kind of secondary changes observed with disruption of other organ systems. Finally, another complicating factor is that at times fevers, metabolic disturbances, and other conditions involving a generalized disturbance are also likely to affect the central nervous system. Such episodes typically represent short-term brain dysfunction and may be characterized by cloudy or confused thoughts and perceptions.

Personal Factors

Other investigators have emphasized the meaning or significance of particular illness as determined by the personality as well as social and ethnic background of each individual. For instance, Verwoerdt (1972) suggests the illness or injury that detracts from personal attractiveness is more distressing for women than for men. On the other hand, illness or injury that leads to helplessness or threatens ability to perform active instrumental tasks may be more stressful for men than for women. Such theorizing seems consistent with observations concerning differences in sex-role stereotypes of men and women.

The speculation is also consistent with the idea implicit in the work of many authors that an illness is psychologically stressful for an individual to the extent that the illness prevents a highly valued activity or threatens to damage or remove any highly valued personal quality (Shontz, 1972). For example, a physical disease that leads to baldness might be quite distressful for someone who valued the attractiveness of his hair while the same illness might be much less distressing for someone who did not value his hair particularly. Similarly, for someone who derives a lot of gratification from athletics, an illness leading to muscular weakness in the legs might be quite stressful although the same illness might be much less troublesome for a more sedentary individual.

In considering the various factors which go into an individual's trying to live with an illness, most of the features we have just talked about are also quite pertinent, as it would seem that the greater the psychological distress the more pressure exists for active coping measures. Further, Shontz (1972) points out that coping is most needed during the early stages of a significant illness or immediately following the onset of a significant disability. At such times, the situation is unclear and unpredictable for the individual, and both of these attributes contribute to anxiety. For the most part, however, investigators concerned with coping measures have looked for various methods of coping employed by individuals.

Lipowsky (1970) suggests that the way individuals cope with illness depends on their cognitive style, i.e., the way in which they think and perceive. For instance, he suggests that some people tend to be "minimizers"—treating serious and unwanted information lightly, being selectively inattentive to some information, and refusing to accept the implications of disagreeable information about illness. On the other hand, Lipowsky describes a contrasting cognitive style referred to as "vigilant focusing." This latter style is characterized by a sharply focused attention to detail, careful planning and orderliness, and a questioning of the intentions of others. When such individuals are seriously ill, Lipowsky suggests that they become highly interested in what is happening, particularly in terms of treatment plans. They will want meticulous explanations of medical tests and procedures, and they become even more upset and uneasy when treatment departs from what is expected.

Along with the cognitive style differences, Lipowsky describes three prominent kinds of *behavioral reactions* to illness. These include what he calls "tackling," "capitulating," or "avoiding." "Tackling" refers to behavior aimed at overcoming the direct and indirect limitations imposed by the illness. "Capitulating" refers to passive dependence on caretakers for assistance and represents a giving-up. "Avoiding" behavior refers to actions designed to keep the illness and its implications at a distance, e. g., forgetting medical appointments, avoiding taking medicines, and the like.

Such clinical observations are a good source of hypotheses, or guesses, but they need confirmation with carefully controlled methods of study. Such confirmation is particularly important when considering the idea of differences in modes of reaction based on different personality types. The usefulness of the concept of personality types has been questioned by the work of Mischel (1969).

SOCIAL REACTIONS ASSOCIATED WITH PHYSICAL ILLNESS

In addition to the psychological changes within the individual, being ill also affects the person's social relationships. It seems that what is expected of an individual by others changes when that individual is viewed as ill. Parsons (1958), a sociological theorist, has taken a leading role in describing what kinds of changes in social expectations occur with illness. He formulated the idea of a *sick role*, i.e., a standard set of social expectations that go into effect whenever an individual is sick.

As Twaddle (1972) summarizes these social expectations, there are four. (1) Exemption from normal role responsibilities. For instance, the child who is sick is excused from going to school, the mother who is ill is excused from her normal household duties, and the ill father is allowed to stay home in bed rather than go to work. (2) The sick individual is not seen as responsible for his condition because, presumably, he cannot get well by a deliberate decision or act of will. The sick person is seen as an innocent victim of some disease process over which he has no control. Consequently, he must be taken care of by others. (3) Being ill is thought of as an undesirable state, carrying with it the obligation to want to get well. This element represents an expectation by others that the sick person should want to get well. (4) The final element of the sick role is the obligation of the sick person to seek technically competent help, usually a physician, and cooperate with the help in getting over the illness. This obligation, of course, is in proportion to the severity of the illness. Thus, with both the third and fourth elements, the individual is expected by those around him to want to get better and take action toward that end.

As Twaddle (1972) points out, there have been several criticisms of the idea of the sick role. Such criticisms have primarily been concerned with when it is applicable. For instance, it has been argued that when stigmatized illnesses are involved, the ill person may be held as responsible for the onset of the condition if not for the course of the disorder. Gordon (1966) has found that in illnesses resulting in longstanding disability exemptions from obligations occur for a while, but after a period, the obligations are redefined on the basis of the existing capacities of the ill person, and meeting these revised obligations is then expected.

It has also been suggested that expectations of the sick individual vary with the type of illness and the social standing of the individual. Mechanic (1962) has offered a somewhat broader concept referred to as illness behavior. He suggests that sick persons may behave in a variety of ways depending on various aspects of their social environment. In this broader concept, Mechanic is saying that the way in which symptoms are perceived, evaluated, and acted upon will depend on a variety of factors including previous personal experience with illness, norms and values of the particular social group, and the expected rewards and punishments from the individual's social group.

Effects on the Family

Perhaps the social group of most importance in an individual's life is the family. Families tend to be close-knit groups where changes in one member affect the family as a whole. Consequently, it might be expected that significant illness in one of the family members will have implications for the entire family. Parsons and Fox (1960) have suggested that illness is a difficult problem for American families because they are relatively small and isolated units. Unlike other cultures where extended family relationships include grandparents, aunts, uncles, and cousins who play a substantial and continuing role, American family units tend to be made up of only parents and their children. There are fewer familial resources for coping with significant illness, and help is sought from institutions.

Katz (1969), studying the wives of a group of diabetic men, found marital conflict to be common. He suggests that such conflict in these cases represented incompatibility of the wife's needs with the dependency imposed by the diabetes on their husbands. He also noted that impotence, often observed in diabetic males, presented particular sexual problems for their wives.

Fink (1968) studied a group of disabled wives. He found that disability, in itself, was not a predictor of marital satisfaction. He suggested that many of the motherly and wifely functions could continue to be carried out despite considerable disability. Such a conclusion is consistent with the theoretical analysis of both Speigel (1960) and Anthony and Koupornik (1973). These authors suggested that illness in a parent will be particularly disruptive for family life when it interferes with the performance of role assignments. For instance, when illness or disability of the father keeps him from working, there is likely to be a decline in the family's standard of living and perhaps a decline in the social standing within the community. Both changes are likely to alter family life.

Anthony (1972), basing his work on a series of case studies of families with psychiatrically or physically ill parents, described three types of family reactions to illness. The *first* type he refers to as a growth response characterized by the family pooling resources and working out the most constructive solution through open discussion and debate. The *second* type of response is described as a breakdown and then rally. The breakdown phase may be characterized by a constriction of outside family contacts, extreme care in avoiding future hazards, and a general confusion in communication among family members. Through some process not clearly identified, the family may be able to gain some perspective on what is happening and begin to make positive changes. Family members may begin to empathize and sympathize with the ill member and reintegrate social contacts and begin functioning in a constructive way to solve the problems presented by the illness. In the *third* form of family reaction, these processes do not seem to occur, and the family encounters more and more difficulty functioning.

Olsen (1970) suggests the following characteristics of families who cope well with crises: (1) clear separation of generations, (2) flexibility within and between roles, (3) direct and consistent communication among family members, and (4) tolerance of individuals within the family.

Illness in Children

Illness in children presents particular difficulties for them and their families. Many investigators have examined a wide variety of psychological and social factors associated with many illnesses in children. Several themes seem consistent across different childhood illnesses. First, an illness of almost any kind seems to impose limitations on the activity of the child either in terms of the physical capacities of the child as is the case in congenital heart disease or in terms of treatment demands as in the case of juvenile diabetes. Such limitations are imposed by the parents, encouraging dependence of the child on the parents (Anthony, 1972; Gonrevitch, 1973; Rausch de Traubenberg, 1972). Such imposed dependence seems likely to interfere with the normal development of independence and self-reliance of the growing child.

Illness would certainly seem to be a stressful event for the child, and a number of investigators have examined the emotional consequences for the child himself. Cytryn, Moore, and Robinson (1973) studied a group of 29 children, 15 boys and 14 girls, having cystic fibrosis. (Cystic fibrosis is an inherited disease affecting primarily the respiratory system.) The authors rated each of these children in terms of emotional adjustment on a four-point scale. Twelve of the children were seen as well-adjusted, showing some acceptance of their illness and age-appropriate behavior. Four children were rated as severely disturbed, and they were characterized as hostile toward the examiner. Their relationships with their mothers seemed to be infantile and clinging. Generally these children seemed to show situationally inappropriate aggressive behavior and a high degree of anxiety and poor social adjustment. The remaining 13 children fell in between these two extremes in terms of emotional and social adjustment. Cytryn et al, noted that among the more disturbed children, boys outnumbered girls 2 to 1.

Similar emotional difficulties have been described in the case of heart disorders by Rausch de Traubenberg (1973), in the case of kidney disorders by Raimbault (1973), and in the case of juvenile diabetes by Zeidal (1973). Zeidal (1973) in his study of juvenile diabetics found that approximately one third of 80 patients examined were referred for psychiatric consultation because of gross emotional maladjustment, familial difficulties, or difficulties in maintaining their diet. He felt that on closer examination, most of the the two thirds of the patients who had not been referred also showed some emotional conflicts involving their illness. A particular problem among these juvenile diabetics was the discrepancy between the therapeutic requirements, e.g., daily urine examination, controlled diet, and intake of insulin, and their subjective feelings of well-being. Unlike most other childhood illnesses, most of the time diabetic children feel well, and consequently the therapeutic regimen makes little sense to them.

Most of the major illnesses in children represent a very realistic stress for the family. With cystic fibrosis, heart disease, and kidney dysfunction, medical treatment may span many years, with repeated hospitalizations. Leiken and Hassakis (1973) report several cases of families having a child with cystic fibrosis where the parents had seldom, if ever, gotten away from their children for any time at all. Certainly with such children, a great deal of responsibility is placed on the parents for the child's well-being.

For many parents, the most difficult period is just before or just after they are informed of the diagnosis and the likely outcome of the disease. Before the diagnosis is given, ambiguity concerning the entire situation is greatest (Cytryn et al., 1973). Parents, at least for children with cystic fibrosis, are aware that the child is quite ill but at a loss as to the nature of the disorder.

On the other hand, when the diagnosis carries grave implications, the parents may find it difficult to accept this information. They may show disbelief, seeking reassurance in numerous medical opinions. In the case of leukemia where death is highly likely, Conrevitch (1973) has observed an anticipatory mourning among family members. When the outcome is less certain, as in cystic fibrosis, anticipatory mourning is not as likely; however, Cytryn et al. (1973) and Leiken and Hassikas (1973) have found that parents have a hard time talking about the possibility of the child's death with the child or with themselves. Interestingly, these investigators have observed a relatively high likelihood of pregnancy in mothers of children who are dying. It would seem that the new child represents a replacement for the dying child.

Ill children, as well as their parents, typically seek explanations for their illness. The explanations developed by the children, of course, depend on their stage of cognitive development. With fairly young children, the explanations are likely to reflect magical thinking, believing that their condition is the result of what they have done or thought or because they are bad. At times, the explanations of their parents follow similar lines. One or both parents often feel guilty for their child's illness, as if they had done something to cause the condition. Such situations may also lead to recriminations of one parent by the other. Leiken and Hassikas (1973) describe one case where a wife accused the husband of being responsible for their child's cystic fibrosis because she had had two normal children by a previous marriage. Such events reflect the extent to which illness can present difficulties for the entire family.

PSYCHOLOGICAL FACTORS ASSOCIATED WITH TREATMENT

The Decision to Seek Medical Help

In considering psychological factors in the treatment of illness, the first step involves the decision to seek medical assistance. At first glance, this decision would seem to represent a simple event. Whenever a person is ill, he goes to the doctor. Unfortunately, it is not so simple. Zola (1972) summarizes a number of studies indicating that many illness episodes in individuals go without medical treatment. The illnesses in question range from minor disturbances to major illnesses like diabetes. Thus, it would seem that more than the presence of illness is involved in seeking medical help. The decision to seek medical aid has been correlated to socioeconomic status as well as ethnic differences. For a discussion of such studies the reader is referred to Vaco (1972).

Barker (1953) viewed the decision to seek medical help as a complex conflict involving five separate factors. These included the severity of the symptom, the anticipation of return to health through treatment, the person's view of himself as a healthy individual not needing medical care, the person's recognition that a trip to the physician may disclose illnesses, and the negative aspects of diagnosis and treatment such as cost. Shontz (1972) tested this model by constructing a number of paragraph descriptions of a case. In these descriptions, he varied the strength of these five factors and asked a group of undergraduates to indicate whether they thought the person would be likely to seek medical aid. His findings were consistent with the model showing that when the symptom was severe, when the person was strongly anticipating a return to health, when the person strongly believed in himself as a healthy individual, when the fear of discovering additional illness was low, and when the other costs of seeking such help were low, the undergraduates felt the person would be very likely to seek aid. As these factors diminished, they felt the person would become increasingly less likely to seek such assistance.

In addition to these factors "within" the individual, help-seeking is also influenced by the individual social environment. Several authors have referred to a lay referral and consultative system (Twaddle, 1972; Zola, 1972). This concept reflects the tendencies of individuals to seek the advice of other laymen concerning their physical state. Such an interpersonal network might well aid the individual in deciding whether a physical condition deserved professional medical treatment or whether it might be helped through home remedies.

The Doctor–Patient Relationship

Medical diagnosis and treatment virtually always occur within the context of the interpersonal relationship between the physician and the patient. The nature and quality of this relationship, therefore, take on particular importance. One feature of the doctor-patient relationship that has received particular attention is the amount of information transmitted from the physician to the patient. Studies have shown that patients tend to be more dissatisfied with the amount of information they receive from their physician concerning their illness than any other feature of their medical care (Duff & Hollingshead, 1968; Skipper & Leonard, 1965). As Waitzkin and Stockle (1972) point out, communication of information about disease influences patient care in several ways. It increases the accuracy of medical histories provided by patients. It increases the patient's compliance with treatment programs, and it improves the patient's psychological and physiological responses to treatment.

Several investigations have found that many individuals are reluctant to ask questions of their physician. This reluctance appears particularly marked among skilled and unskilled workers as compared with professional individuals (Cartwright, 1964; Pratt, Seligmann & Reader, 1957, and Korsh, Gozzi & Francis, 1968). In addition, Cartwright (1964), by interviewing patients recently discharged from a hospital, found that professionals tended to ask more direct questions of their physicians and nurses than did the skilled and unskilled workers. The latter group tended to get less information over-all. Several explanations have been offered for these differences in asking questions of doctors. Waitzkin and Stoeckle (1972) emphasize the differences in the way language is used among the various social classes. Cartwright (1964) points to a combination of several ingredients: doctors do not expect members of the working class to ask questions and consequently do not encourage questions; ignorance concerning the meaning of technical terms on the part of the skilled and unskilled workers; the awe with which physicians are viewed; and the degree of social distance between the upper-class physician and working-class patient.

Waitzkin and Stoeckle (1972) have argued that physicians withhold information from patients, thus maintaining uncertainty within the patient. They suggest that physicians actively maintain uncertainty in their patients as a means of keeping or enhancing their power over patients. They review several studies which support this general notion; although we cannot consider it an established fact, it is an interesting notion.

PSYCHOLOGICAL FACTORS ASSOCIATED WITH RECOVERY

As pointed out previously, psychological factors play a significant role in the onset of disease. Consequently, it seems likely that
such factors may also influence the course of illness as well as
response to treatment. In modern medicine, there is a wide range
of therapeutic procedures and techniques. Many of these have
been studied in relation to the psychological reaction of the individual, and throughout the remainder of this chapter, we will
examine this area.

One set of researchers (Imboden, Canter & Cluff, 1959)
examined a group of 24 persons suffering from acute brucellosis
(a generalized infection characterized by remittent fever and
malaise, and contracted through contact with infected domestic
animals). Eight of these patients were symptom-free after a short
period, while the remaining 16 continued to experience symptoms
after one year. There was no significant difference between these
two groups on their initial medical evaluation. However, from
psychiatric interviews, it appeared that all of the 16 who had not
recovered had experienced some relatively gross traumatic event or
circumstance during their early lives while this was true for only
2 of the 8 recovered individuals. Similarly, difficult life situations
were found to exist at the time of the onset of the disease or within
one year prior to onset in all of the 16 who had not recovered
and in none of the individuals who had recovered. Psychological
tests at the time the illness began revealed that the recovered group
was significantly less depressed than the nonrecovered group at
that time.

Similar findings were obtained in a study of Asiatic influenza
(Imboden, Canter & Cluff, 1961). Those who showed relatively
rapid recovery had experienced fewer psychological difficulties
and were less depressed than those who took longer to recover.
Reviewing these findings, Imboden (1972) suggests that symptoms
of tension and depression characteristic of psychological distress
become intermingled and the symptoms associated with acute
infections, thus obscuring the end of the physical disorder. He
suggests that this intermingling allows the patient to attribute his
subjective feelings to the physical illness rather than his psychological problems.

Imboden (1972) suggests that psychological factors may have a more direct influence on recovery. He cites several studies showing psychological factors to be important in the recovery from tuberculosis. For instance, Calden, Dupertius, and Hokanson (1960) found slow recoverers from TB were more depressed, socially withdrawn, and preoccupied with themselves when compared with fast recoverers. Holmes (1961) observed that TB patients with generally fewer psychological assets had a greater probability of treatment failure. In a subsequent section, dealing with surgery, we will find that similar emotional factors significantly influence recovery from surgery.

Hospitalization

Being hospitalized has come to be an event experienced by most individuals within our society. Today, most people are born in a hospital and very many die in them as well. Hospitalization is something typically encountered at difficult times in our lives, with significant illnesses or injuries. Television has capitalized on this fact, having many medical shows with dramatic events taking place within the hospital setting. Social scientists have begun to recognize that hospitalization often represents a threatening. situation for individuals (Kornfeld, 1972) and that hospitalization involves at least a temporary disruption of the individual's life style.

The typical hospital procedures, having patients remain in their beds and play only a passive role in their treatment, would seem to reinforce the sick role of the patient. This orientation would seem to enhance feelings of helplessness and depression on the part of the patient. Thus, typical hospital procedures might be seen as enhancing the detrimental psychological state of the patient. This interpretation would seem consistent with the observations of Klagsbrun as summarized by Kornfeld (1972). Klagsbrun, a psychiatrist, served as a consultant on a cancer ward. When he began his work, morale on the ward was generally low. The physicians were distant with their patients, leaving the nurses to handle the emotional reactions of the patients. The nurses found this a difficult position, and the turnover rate for nurses was relatively high.

Klagsbrun worked with the nurses, helping them in their role as emotional supporters. A communal dining room was established because many of the patients did not require total bed rest. The patients began taking over some of the routine chores on the ward and generally playing a more active role in their treatment and the operation of the unit. With these changes, morale improved markedly. The turnover rate among the nurses dropped noticeably, and the attitudes of the patients improved.

Much attention has been focused on the psychological impairment associated with being placed in specialized units within the hospital. In particular, tank respirators (Mendelson, 1958), recovery rooms for open-heart surgery (Lazarus & Hagens, 1968), and cardiac care units (Parker & Hodge, 1967) have been viewed as psychologically stressful. These researchers have observed that a significant number of patients in these environments experience an acute psychiatric syndrome. Prominent features in these reactions appear to involve a delirious state in which the individual becomes quite confused and disoriented. There is also likely to be visual, auditory, or tactile hallucinations. This reaction appears to be terminated by returning the patient to a more normal hospital environment. As summarized by Kornfeld (1972), this psychiatric reaction seems to result from sensory deprivation or monotony and sleep deprivation associated with the procedures typical in these specialized units. The open-heart recovery room and the cardiac-care unit both involve constant monitoring of the patient by sophisticated electronic equipment. Overhead lights tend to remain on, and nurses and house officers make frequent checks of the patient. Further, there is always the possibility of a cardiac arrest among any of the several patients within the room, with the accompanying scurry of activity by the staff.

Surgery

For many people, surgery is the most distressing form of medical treatment. The anxiety-provoking nature of surgery has been well documented by numerous studies (Auerback, 1973; Johnson & Leventhal, 1971; Speilberger, Wadsworth, Auerback, Dunn, & Taulbee, 1973).

Many reasons have been offered for this pre-surgery anxiety including the threat to life itself, loss of important bodily parts or functions, the danger of chronic invalidism, post-operative pain (Rosen, 1952), not knowing what to expect, the fear of not being told the truth, and fear of losing control under anesthesis (Carmenoli, cited in Wu, 1973).

Several investigators have sought to identify factors which influence the severity of the pre-surgery anxiety. Auerback (1973) found that individuals who were chronically more anxious reacted with greater distress and anxiety prior to surgery than individuals who were typically more relaxed and calm. Lucente and Flech (1972), studying 408 surgical patients, found anxiety level related to the kind of hospital, with anxiety highest among patients in a university hospital and anxiety lowest among patients in a small community hospital, with anxiety intermediate among patients in city hospitals. They also found that the anxiety levels experienced by pre-surgery patients decreased with age.

Graham and Conley (1971), in their study of 70 surgical patients, failed to find this decrease with age; however, they did find that women tended to report greater anxiety in relation to surgery than men. Wu (1973) suggests that the degree of distress associated with surgery, in part, may be determined by the importance placed on the organ or function threatened. He suggests that this importance is in terms of the individual's valuing of a sex role or occupational role. If the organ or function is crucial to a highly valued role, then distress around the surgery will be greater. Although he provides no direct empirical support for this idea, it would seem consistent with some of the ideas previously described concerning the degree of distress associated with particular illnesses.

Recovery from Surgery

As anxiety before surgery is a well established fact, many investigators have sought to discover whether anxiety affects an individual's recovery from surgery. Concerning this question, the picture is somewhat ambiguous. Certainly, with respect to routine surgery, numerous investigators have found anxiety not to be related to recovery or the experiencing of pain (Rothberg, 1966; Cohen & Lazarus, 1973; Wolfer & Davis, 1970; Martinez, 1973).

When open-heart surgery is considered, Kimball (1969) found that those patients experiencing significant pre-operative anxiety or depression had a greater chance of not surviving the surgery and a greater risk of death after the surgery than those showing less pre-operative anxiety or depression. Hendricks, Mackenzie, and Almond (1969) found that most of their 110 open-heart surgery cases experienced problems of depression, anger, personal discord, or unusual and sometimes bizzarre feelings. Jeglyewski (1973) found similar results when amputation of a limb was involved. He reported that many patients experienced sensations from the amputated limb (referred to as the phantom-limb phenomenon) and experienced anxiety, depression, and hostility.

As noted previously in this chapter, the communication of specific information about the illness can have beneficial effects for treatment. This effect has been documented in two studies involving recovery from surgery. Schmitt and Woodridge (1973) compared the recovery of two groups of men undergoing surgery. One group received the typical medical treatment and information pre-operatively. The second group of men participated in a small-group discussion concerning their feelings and questions about surgery. This latter group of men showed less tension and anxiety. They took a more active role in their post-operative treatment, and they went home sooner than the men receiving the typical treatment. Egbert, Battit, Welch, and Bartlett (1964) obtained comparable results. In their study, the anesthetist talked to the patient the night before surgery. The patient was given information about where it would likely hurt, for how long, and that the pain was a normal reaction to the surgery. They were also told that relaxation and deep breathing would help diminish the pain. A control group of patients were not given this information. On the day of the surgery, there was no difference between the two groups; however, over the next four days, the group receiving the additional information required only half as much medication for pain. Further, they seemed more comfortable and their physical and emotional condition appeared better than the group not receiving the additional information. Finally, members of the group receiving the additional information tended to be discharged sooner than those of the other group.

Cohen and Lazarus (1973) examined recovery from surgery in relation to the coping style of the individual. It will be recalled from our earlier discussion, that individuals appear to differ in the way in which they typically react. Lipowsky (1970) has distinguished between minimizing and vigilance as coping styles. Cohen and Lazarus in their study compared recovery from surgery for these individuals showing these two coping styles. They found that the vigilant style seemed to be associated with slower recovery.

CONCLUSION

In considering the findings reported in this chapter, it seems clear that psychological factors influence physical illnesses in terms of the onset, course, and treatment of the disorders. In general, it seems that these psychological variables do not serve as necessary or sufficient causes of any of the phenomena related to physical illness. The emotional, cognitive, and behavioral events serve as contributing elements, that is, they may facilitate or hinder the development of an illness; lengthen or perhaps shorten the course of the disorder; and enhance or diminish the effectiveness of treatment programs.

In terms of medical practice, the present findings would seem to have several implications. On the one hand, it would seem that physicians need to be trained in the identification of such psychological contributors in particular cases. Further, it would seem advisable to provide physicians with some training in how to work with patients whose physical illness is significantly affected by psychological factors. The findings reported in the present chapter would also seem to support the growing practice of having psychologists and psychiatrists working with patients in general hospitals and other medical facilities. Finally, it would seem important to provide counselors working in all settings with information relating to psychological factors in physical illness. Counselors equipped with such information might be better able to serve a preventative function, perhaps reducing the likelihood that individuals experiencing psychological troubles will develop a physical illness as well.

PROJECTS AND QUESTIONS

1. Based on what you know of yourself, consider which form of physical disease or disability would be most distressing for you and why.
2. In small-group discussions, consider what specific kinds of life changes would have to occur with being deaf, blind, or crippled or having a serious heart condition.
3. In reviewing your own life and particularly the episodes of physical illness, how often were such episodes associated with emotional distress or life changes?
4. In a small-group discussion, consider what factors go into your decision to seek medical assistance or follow medical instructions.

SUGGESTED READINGS

Popular Sources

P. B. KUNHARDT, JR. *My father's house.* New York: Random House, 1970.
R. RUSSELL. *To catch an angel: Adventures in the world I cannot see.* New York: Vanguard, 1962.

Advanced Sources

Z. V. LIPOWSKI, (ed.). Psychosocial aspects of physical illness. *Advances in Psychosomatic Medicine*, Vol. 8, Basel, Switzerland: S. Karger AG, 1972.
MATTHEW DEBUSKEY, (Ed.). *The chronically ill child and his family.* Springfield, Ill.: Charles C. Thomas, 1970.

REFERENCES

ANTHONY, E. J. The mutative impact of serious mental and physical illness in a parent on family life. In E. J. Anthony & C. Koupernik (Eds.). *The child in his family.* Vol. 1. New York: John Wiley & Sons, 1970.
ANTHONY, E. J. & KOUPERNIK, C. *The child in his family*, Vol. 2. New York: John Wiley & Sons, 1973.

AUERBACK, S. M. Trait-state anxiety and adjustment to surgery. *J. Consulting and Clinical Psychol.*, 1973, *40*.

BACON, C. L., RENNEKER, R., CUTLER, M. A. A psychosomatic survey of cancer of the breast. *Psychosom. Med.*, 1952, *14*.

BARKER, R. G., WRIGHT, B. A., MERGERSON, L. & GONICK, M. R. *Adjustment to physical handicap and illness: A survey of the social psychology of physique and disability.* Second edition, bull. 55. New York: Social Science Research Council, 1953.

BASTIAANS, J. Psychoanalytic investigations on the psychic aspects of acute myocardial infarction. *Psychother. Psychosom.*, 1968, *16*.

BEIGLER, J. S. Anxiety as an aid in the prognostication of impending death. *Arch. Neurol. Psychiat.*, Chicago, 1957, *77*.

CALDEN, G., DUPERTIUS, C. W., HOKANSON, J. E. & LEWIS, WM. C. Psychosomatic factors in the rate of recovery from tuberculosis. *Psychosom. Med.*, 1960, *22*.

CARTWRIGHT, A. *Human relations and hospital care.* London: Routledge and Kegan Paul, 1964.

CASSELL, W. A. Individual differences in somatic perception: A projective method of investigation. In Lipowski, Z. J. & Hanover, N. H. (Eds.). *Psychosocial aspects of physical illness.* Switzerland: Karger and Basel, 1972.

COHEN, F. & LAZARUS, R. Active coping processes, coping disposition, and recovery from surgery. *Psychosom. Med.*, 1973, *35*.

CYTRYN, L., MOORE, P. V. P., & ROBINSON, M. E. Psychological adjustment of children with cystic fibrosis. In Anthony, E. J. & Koupernik, C. (Eds.). *The child in his family.* Vol. 2. Toronto, Canada: John Wiley & Sons, Inc., 1973.

DECENCIO, D. V. LESHNER, M. & LESHNER, B. Personality characteristics of patients with chronic obstructive pulmonary emphysema. *Arch. Phys. Med.*, 1968, *49*.

DOVENMUEHLE, R. H. & VERWOERDT, A. Physical illness and depressive symptomatology. I. Incidence of depressive symptoms in hospitalized cardiac patients. *J. Amer. Geriat. Soc.*, 1962, *10*.

DUFF, R. S. & HOLLINGSHEAD, A. B. *Sickness and society.* New York: Harper and Row, 1968.

DUNCAN, C. H., STEVENSON, I. P. & RIPLEY, H. S. Life situations, emotions and paroxysmal auricular arrhythmias. *Psychosom. Med.*, 1950, *12*.

EGBERT, J. D., BATTIT, G. E., WELCH, C. E., & BARTLETT, M. K. Reduction of postoperative pain by encouragement and instruction of patients. *New Eng. J. Med.*, 1964, *270*.

ENGEL, G. L. Studies of ulcerative colitis. III. The nature of the psychologic processes. *Amer. J. Med.*, 1955, *19*.

FINK, S., et al. Physical disability and problems in marriage. *J. Marriage Family*, 1968, *30*.

FISHER, S. & CLEVELAND, S. E. *Body image and personality.* New York: Dover Publications, 1968.

FRENCH, T. M. & ALEXANDER, F. Psychogenic factors in bronchial asthma. *Psychosom. Med. Monogr.*, 1941, *4*, No. 1.

GORDON, G. *Role theory and illness.* New Haven: College and University Press, 1966.

GOUREVITCH, M. A survey of family reactions to disease and death in a family member. In: Anthony, E. V. & Koupernik, C. *The child in his family.* Vol. 2. John Wiley & Sons, New York, 1973.

GRAHAM, L. E. & CONLEY, E. M. Evaluation of anxiety and fear in adult surgical patients. *Nursing Research,* 1971, *20.*

GREENE, W. A., JR. Psychological factors and reticuloendothelial disease. I. Preliminary observations on a group of males with lymphomas and leukemias. *Psychosom. Med.,* 1958, *20.*

HACKETT, T. F. & WEISMAN, A. D. Denial as a factor in patients with heart disease and cancer. *Ann. N. Y. Acad. Sci.,* 1969, *164.*

HEIMAN, M. The role of stress situations and psychological factors in functional uterine bleeding. *J. Mount Sinai Hosp.,* N.Y., 1956, *23.*

HENRICKS, T. F., MACKENZIE, J. W., & ALMOND, C. H. Psychological adjustment and acute response to open heart surgery. *J. Nerv. Ment. Dis.,* 1969, *148.*

HINKLE, L. E., JR., EVANS, F. M. & WOLF, S. Studies in diabetes mellitus: III. Life history of three persons with labile diabetes, and relation of significant experiences in their lives to the onset and course of the disease. *Psychosom. Med.,* 1951a, *13.*

HINKLE, L. E. JR., EVANS, F. M. & WOLF, S. Studies in diabetes mellitus: IV. Life history of three persons with relatively mild, stable diabetes and relation of significant experiences in their lives to the onset and course of the disease. *Psychosom. Med.,* 1951b. *13.*

HINKLE, L. E., JR., CHRISTENSON, W. N., KANE, F. D., OSTFELD, A., THETFORD, W. H. & WOLFF, H. G. An investigation of the relation between life experience personality characteristics, and general susceptibility to illness. *Psychosom. Med.,* 1958, *20.*

HOLMES, T. H., JOFFEE, J. R., KETCHAN, J. W. & SHEEHY, T. F. Experimental study of prognosis. *J. Psychosom. Res.,* 1961, *5.*

HOLMES, T. H., TREUTING, T. & WOLFF, H. G. Life situations, emotions, and nasal disease: Evidence on summative effects exhibited in patients with hay "fever." *Psychosom. Med.,* 1951, *13.*

HOLMES, T. H. & WOLFF, H. G. Life situations, emotions, and backache. *Psychosom. Med.,* 1952, *14.*

IMBODEN, J. B. Psychosocial determinants of recovery. In Lipowski, Z. J. & Hanover, N. H. (Eds.). *Psychosocial aspects of physical illness.* Switzerland: Karger and Basel, 1972.

IMBODEN, J. B., CANTER, A. & CLUFF, L. E. Convalescence from influenza. *Arch. Intern. Med., 108:* 393, 1961.

IMBODEN, J. B., CANTER, A. & CLUFF, L. E. Brucellosis. III. Psychologic aspects of delayed convalescence. *Arch. Intern. Med.* 103:406, 1959.

IMBODEN, J. B., CANTER, A. & CLUFF, L. Separation experiences and health records in a group of normal adults. *Psychosom. Med.,* 1963, *25.*

JAW, E. G. (Ed.). *Patients, physicians and illness.* New York: The Free Press, 1972.

JEGLYEWSKI, J. Target: Outside world. *Amer. J. Nursing,* 1973, *73.*

JENKINS, G. D. Psychologic and social precursors of coronary disease. *New England J. Med.* 1971, *284,* 244–327.

JOHNSON, J. E. & LEVENTHAL, H. Contribution of emotional and instrumental response processes in adaptation to surgery. *J. Personality and Social Psychol.*, 1971, *20*.

KATZ, A. M. Wives of diabetic men. *Bull. Menninger Clin.*, 1969, *33*.

KIMBALL, C. P. Psychological responses to the experience of open heart surgery. *Amer. J. Psychiat.*, 1969, *126*.

KISSEN, D. M. Specific psychological factors in pulmonary tuberculosis. *Health Bulletin.* Issued by the Chief Medical Officer of the Department of Health for Scotland, 1956, *14*.

KITS VAN HEIJINGEN, H. & TREURNIET, N. Psychodynamic factors in acute myocardial infarction. *Int. J. Psycho-Anal.*, 1966, *47*.

KORNFELD, D. S. The hospital environment: Its impact on the patient. In Lipowski, S. J. & Hanover, N. H. (Eds.). *Psychosocial aspects of physical illness.* Switzerland: Karger and Basel, 1972.

KORSCH, B. M., GOZZI, E. K. & FRANCIS, V. Gaps in doctor-patient communication: Doctor-patient interaction and patient satisfaction. *Pediatrics,* 1968, *42*.

KOSKI, M. L. The coping processes in childhood diabetes. *Acta paediat. scand.,* 1969, *198*.

LAZARUS, H. R., & HAGENS, J. H. Prevention of psychosis following open-heart surgery. *Amer. J. Psychiat.*, 1968, *124*.

LAZARUS, R. S..& OPTON, E. M. The study of psychological stress: A summary of theoretical formulations and experimental findings. In: Spielberger, C. D. (Ed.). *Anxiety and behavior.* New York: Academic Press, 1966.

LEEMAN, C. P. Dependency, anger, and denial in pregnant diabetic women: A group approach. *Psychiat. Quart.,* 1970, *44*.

LEIKEN, S. J. & HASSAKIS, P. Psychological study of parents of children with cystic fibrosis. In Anthony, E. J. & Koupernik, C. (Eds.). *The child in his family.* Vol. 2. Toronto, Canada: John Wiley & Sons, Inc., 1973.

LIPOWSKY, Z. J. Physical illness, the individual, and the coping process. *Psychiat. Med. I,* 1970.

LUCENTE, F. E. & FLECK, S. A study of hospitalization anxiety in 408 medical surgical patients. *Psychosom. Med.,* 1972, *34*.

LUDWIG, A. O. Rheumatoid arthritis. In E. Wittkower & R. A. Cleghorn, (Eds.). *Recent developments in psychosomatic medicine.* Philadelphia: Lippincott, 1954.

MADDISON, D. & VIOLA, A. The health of widows in the year following bereavement. *J. Psychosom. Res.,* 1968, *12*.

MARTINEZ, V. A. Pain and anxiety in surgical patients (doctoral dissertation, Florida State University, 1973). *Dissertation Abstracts International,* 1973, *33*.

MECHANIC, D. The concept of illness behavior. *J. Chron. Dis.,* 1962, *15*.

MENDELSOHN, J., SOLOMON, P. & LINDEMAN, E. Hallucinations of poliomyelitis patients during treatment in a respirator. *J. Nerv. Ment. Dis.* 1958, *126*.

MISCHEL, W. Continuity and change in personality. *Amer. Psychol.,* 1969, 24, 1012-1018.

MUTTER, A. Z. & SCHLEIFER, M. J. The role of psychological and social factors in the onset of somatic illness in children. *Psychosom. Med.*, 1966, *28*.

OLSEN, H. The impact of serious illness on the family system. *Med.* 1970, *47*.

PAPPER, S. & HANDY, J. Observations in a "control" group of patients in psychosomatic investigation. *New Eng. J. Med.*, 1956, *255*.

PARENS, H., MCCONVILLE, B. J. & KAPLAN, S. M. The prediction of frequency of illness from the response to separation. A preliminary study and replication attempt. *Psychosom. Med.*, 1966, *28*.

PARKER, D. L. & HODGE, J. R. Delirium in a coronary care unit. *J. Amer. Med. Assoc.*, 1967, *201*.

PARKES, C. M., BENJAMIN, B. & FITZGERALD, R. G. Broken heart. A statistical study of increased mortality among widowers. *Brit Med. J.*, 1969, 1.

PARSONS, T. *Definitions of health and illness in the light of American values and social structure; in JACO patients, physicians and illness.* New York: Free Press, 1958.

PARSONS, T. & FOX R. C. *Illness, therapy and the modern urban American family. Modern introduction to the family.* Glencoe, Ill.: Free Press, 1960.

PRATT, L., SELIGMANN, A. & READER, G. Physicians' views on the level of medical information among patients. *Amer. J. Public Health, 47,* 1957.

RAHE, R. H. Subjects' recent life changes and their near-future illness suscepti-bility. In Lipowski, Z. J. & Hanover, N. W. (Eds.). *Psychosocial aspects of physical illness.* Switzerland: Karger and Basel, 1972.

RAIMBAULT, G. Psychological problems in the chronic nephropathies of child-hood. In Anthony, E. J. & Koupernik, C. (Eds.). *The child in his family.* Vol. 2. Toronto, Canada: John Wiley & Sons, Inc., 1973.

RAUSCH DE TRAUBENBERG, N. Psychological aspects of congenital heart disease in the child. In Anthony, E. J. & Koupernik, C. (Eds.). *The child in his family.* Vol. 2. Toronto, Canada: John Wiley & Sons, Inc., 1973.

REISER, M. F., BRUST, A. A. & FERRIS, E. B. Life situations, emotions, and the course of patients with arterial hypertension. *Psychosom. Med.*, 1951a, *13*.

RIPLEY, H. S. & WOLFF, H. G. Life situations, emotions, and glaucoma. *Psychosom. Med.*, 1950, *12*.

ROSEN, V. H. Psychiatric problems in general surgery. In L. Bellack (Ed.). *Psychology of physical illness.* New York: Grune & Stratton, 1952.

ROTHBERG, J. S. Dependence and anxiety in male patients following surgery: An investigation of the relationship between dependence, anxiety, and physical manifestations of recovery following surgery in male patients (doctoral disser-tation, University of Utah, 1966). *Dissertation Abstracts*, 1966, *27*.

SCHMALE, A. H., JR. Relationship of separation and depression to disease: I. A report on a hospitalized medical population. *Psychosom. Med.*, 1958, *20*.

SCHMITT, F. E. & WOOLDRIDGE, R. J. Psychological preparation of surgical patients. *Nursing Research*, 1973, *22*.

SHELDON, A. & HOOPER, D. An inquiry into health and ill health adjustment in early marriage. *J. Psychosom. Res.*, 1969, *13*.

SHONTZ, F. C. The personal meanings of illness. In Lipowski, Z. J. & Hanover, N. H. (Eds.). *Psychosocial aspects of physical illness*. Switzerland: Karger and Basel, 1972.

SKIPPER, J. K. & LEONARD, R. C. (Eds.). *Social interaction and patient care*. Philadelphia: Lippincott, 1965.

SPEIGEL, J. P. The resolution of role conflict within the family. In N. W. Bell and E. F. Vogel (Eds.). *A modern introduction to the family*. Glencoe: Free Press, 1960.

SPIELBERGER, C. D., WADSWORTH, A. P., AUERBACK, S. M., DUNN, T. M. & TAULBEE, E. S. Emotional reactions to surgery. *J. Consulting and Clinical Psychol.*, 1973, *40*, 33–38.

TWADDLE, A. C. The concepts of the sick role and illness behavior. In Lipowski, Z. J. & Hanover, N. H. (Eds.). *Psychosocial aspects of physical illness*. Switzerland: Karger and Basel, 1972.

VERWOERDT, A. Psychopathological responses to the stress of physical illness. In Lipowski, Z. J. & Hanover, N. H. (Eds.). *Psychosocial aspects of physical illness*. Switzerland: Karger and Basel, 1972.

VERWOERDT, A. & ELMORE, J. C. Psychological reaction in fatal illness. I. The prospect of impending death. *J. Amer. Geriat. Soc.*, 1967, 15, 9–19.

WAGNER, N. Personal Communication.

WAITZKIN, H. & STOECKLE, J. D. The communication of information about illness. Clinical, sociological, and methodological considerations. In Lipowski, Z. J. and Hanover, N. H. (Eds.). *Psychosocial aspects of physical illness*. Switzerland: Karger and Basel, 1972.

WOLFER, J. A. & DAVIS, C. E. Assessment of surgical patients' preoperative emotional condition and postoperative welfare. *Nursing Research*, 1970, *19*.

WU, R. *Behavior and illness*. Englewood Cliffs, New Jersey: Prentice-Hall, 1973.

ZEIDAL, A. Problems of emotional adjustment in juvenile diabetes. In Anthony, E. J. & Koupernik, C. (Eds.). *The child in his family*. Vol. 2. Toronto, Canada: John Wiley & Sons, Inc., 1973.

ZOLA, I. K. Studying the decision to see a doctor. Review, critique, corrective. In Lipowski, Z. J. & Hanover, N. H. (Eds.). *Psychosocial aspects of physical illness*. Switzerland: Karger and Basel, 1972.

Aging and Retirement

CHAPTER 9

Benjamin Franklin once remarked in a letter that nothing in this world is certain but death and taxes. With the dramatic increase in the life expectancy of Americans in the last 75 years, it might be possible for us to add that nothing is certain but death, taxes, and growing old.

Old age can bring with it a great variety of events and life changes which can be sources of stress for the individual growing older. Previously learned ways of dealing with everyday problems may not be suited for dealing with the potential problems caused by growing old. As we grow older we experience physical changes, intellectual changes, changes in our sexual behavior, and changes in occupational status. In this chapter we will look at the changes and possible consequences of the critical life problem of growing old.

The life expectancy for males in the United States is approximately 70 to 72 years, and the life expectancy of females is approximately 75 to 77 years (Botwinick, 1973; U.S. Department of Health, Education, and Welfare, 1971). About one out of every 10 Americans is over 65 years old and of these roughly 60 per cent are females and 40 per cent are males. Most persons over 65 are not actively employed, and in general, after age 65 the older the individual is the lower the likelihood that he/she will be gainfully employed. Close to 22 million Americans are over 65. Although it is strictly an arbitrary choice, it is persons over 65 who will be referred to as old in this chapter. It should be recognized, however, that this definition of the word "old" is in no way a universal one; it is one used simply for clarity of communication.

Regardless of how we define it here, however, the terms "old," "old person," "elderly", and the like tend to be associated with certain attitudes. In general, attitudes toward "old people" tend to be somewhat negative (Altrocchi & Eisdorfer, 1962; Botwinick, 1973; Blau, 1973; Riley & Fener, 1968). The old person tends to be regarded as less competent, different, unable to learn, and as hav-ing a variety of other undesirable qualities and characteristics.

Although available data suggest that attitudes toward old people tend to be generally negative, there is some indication that under certain conditions the expressed attitudes will not necessarily be negative towards the old (Colbert, Kalish, & Chang, 1973). For example, when asked to rate old people in general as compared to young people in general, one group of subjects did in fact rate old people more negatively; however, the same group of individuals did not rate a *specific* old person more negatively than a specific young person (Weinberger & Millham, 1975). In spite of these more optimistic findings, the over-all picture seems to be one in which being old is not seen as a desirable state and "old persons" tend to be perceived somewhat negatively.

In this chapter, it is our intent to examine some of the aspects of growing old. We will examine four areas of change and potential problems in growing old, as follows: (1) physical functions and changes in old age, (2) intellectual changes in old age, (3) sexual functioning in old age, and (4) retirement and its potential con-sequences.

PHYSICAL FUNCTIONS AND CHANGES IN OLD AGE

The investigation of physical aging has included an immense variety of factors from the microbiological to the human body as a whole. In this section we will look briefly at some general physical changes associated with aging, and we will focus on changes in the senses.

Human beings tend to go through a wide variety of potential

physical changes as they grow old. There is increased probability of loss of teeth, the skin becomes wrinkled and less resilient, and changes in bone arrangement tend to produce small amounts of shrinkage in height (Liang, 1973; Rossman, 1971; Young, 1971). There tends to be less bodily hair in some areas, while in other areas of the body hair growth may occur. The hair on the scalp becomes thinner and gray (Rossman, 1971). There is a general tendency to become slower in responding to stimulation from the environment, with an increase in the time it takes to react (Botwinick, 1973; Palmore, 1970). Finally, although most old persons are in good health, the probability of physical illness and death increases (Verwoerdt, 1973). These are only some of the more easily observable changes which can occur as individuals age, but this list illustrates well the physical changes which can happen to us as we grow older.

It is in the area of sensing and perceiving the world, however, that perhaps the more dramatic changes occur. Although psychologists indicate that human beings probably have more than five senses, perhaps many more, the focus here will be on the traditional five senses, vision, hearing, taste, touch, and smell. The reason for this restriction is not only a desire for simplicity, but also because the data available tend to be restricted primarily to these senses.

The popular notion that old people tend to experience greater problems with their *eyesight* as they grow older is confirmed by the available information. As human beings grow older there tends to be a reduction in visual acuity, i.e., in the ability to see and discriminate fine detail. This reduction in visual acuity has been reported in a variety of research data and by authorities in the field of aging (Anderson & Palmore, 1974; Botwinick, 1973; Goldman, 1971; Liang, 1973). Although decline in visual acuity is perhaps the most readily observable change in vision, other changes in the vision of old persons can also occur, such as a reduction in the capacity of the eye to adapt to the dark and a greater need for more light in order to see. There is some possibility that the ability to discriminate certain shades of color may also be affected (Botwinick, 1973).

Along with vision, *hearing* is the other sensory modality that has received the greatest amount of research effort. Not unexpectedly, the research on the relation of aging to hearing ability indicates that hearing ability also has a tendency to decline in old age. An interesting fact, however, is that hearing impairment with old age tends to be much more characteristic with high-pitched sounds than with lower tones (Eisdorfer & Wilkie, 1974; Goldman, 1971). Another interesting fact is that this greater hearing loss for higher-pitched sounds is more characteristic of men than of women.

As human beings grow old, there tends to be a loss of *taste buds*. As older persons we have fewer taste buds than when we were younger (Goldman, 1971). Whether or not this reduction in taste buds is reflected in a reduction in the sensation of taste is still somewhat unclear. This reduction in taste buds is certainly in agreement with the idea that the sensation of taste does in fact become less intense with age (Barrett, 1972; Kimmel, 1974). This presumed change in taste sensations with old age, however, still needs further study.

The relation of aging to the sensations of *touch and smell* has received, perhaps, the least attention of all. Therefore, what happens with our sense of touch and our sense of smell as we grow old still needs to be studied in greater detail. What the available evidence suggests is that both touch and smell tend to become less sensitive in old age (Botwinick, 1973; Goldman, 1971).

To summarize, there is a good bit of evidence that the sensitivity of both vision and hearing tend to be reduced in old age. Although data are much less plentiful for the sense of taste, the sense of touch, and the sense of smell, the available evidence gives some indication that the sensitivity of these senses also declines with old age.

It is certainly not news to say that individual human beings differ from each other. It is important to remember this idea in the present context, because individuals differ in how they change with age as well. The physical changes we have briefly discussed, and other changes with age to be discussed, refer to how people are affected by age *on the average*. That simply means that when we observe groups of persons as they grow older, certain average changes are observed. What must be remembered is that those "average" changes are not necessarily going to happen to all people who get old. These summaries of what the research findings suggest only tell us what happens in general; they do not tell what is going to happen to a specific old person.

INTELLECTUAL FUNCTIONS AND CHANGES IN OLD AGE

Many different types of tasks have been used to study intellectual functioning and intellectual changes in old age. In this section we will look only at two specific areas, memory and scores on intelligence tests.

Memory

This subcategory of intellectual functioning has itself been investigated with the use of a wide variety of specific tests and memory tasks. Individuals have been studied as they try to memorize lists of numbers, word pairs, word lists, and so on. Not only have the tasks themselves varied, but the way in which memory is assessed has also varied, through free recall, recognition, selecting the correct choice from several alternatives, and others. While recognizing the complexity of this area of research, distinctions between different memory tasks or different ways of assessing memory will not be made. We address ourselves to the more general question, how does age affect the ability to remember in general?

In general, there tends to be agreement in the available evidence, indicating that on the average old persons tend not to do as well on memory tasks as younger persons (Barrett, 1972; Botwinick, 1973; Kimmel, 1974; Smith, 1975). For example, Drachman and Leavitt (1972) compared the performance of a group of older persons with the performance of a group of young people on a series of memory tasks. Although the older group was not worse than the younger group on all tasks, the results indicated that the older group had significantly more difficulty remembering than did the younger group. The results of this study tend to be representative of the findings regarding the performance of groups of older persons on memory tasks. Although there are tasks on which older persons perform just as well as younger persons, on the whole groups of older persons tend to perform more poorly on memory tasks than groups of younger persons.

However, data do indicate that old persons can remember a surprising amount of material from their distant past including, for example, many of the names and faces of their high school friends (Bahrick, Bahrick & Wittlinger, 1975). Psychologists are still in disagreement over whether old persons have more trouble remembering things from the immediate past (for example, a list of words just learned) than they do remembering things from the more distant past (for example, names and faces from a college yearbook). Keeping in mind that this issue is still being investigated, we will venture the suggestion that old persons appear to have more problems with remembering things from the immediate past than with remembering things from the more distant past. The reasons for this may involve amount of practice, importance of the material, or any of a number of other factors.

In summary, then, the available evidence suggests that old age may in fact be associated with an increase in problems with memory. The increased probability of memory impairment does not necessarily occur with every kind of memory task, and perhaps more importantly it should be emphasized that there are many persons who retain a perfectly sound memory regardless of age. The available data simply suggest that as a group old persons tend to do more poorly on memory tasks than younger persons.

Scores on Intelligence Tests

Tests of intelligence have received much attention lately, particularly from persons who feel that the content of tests is often biased in favor of middle-class, younger, white persons. We will not deal with the issue of the potential bias in intelligence tests, but it is important to remember that such a challenge to these tests exists. For this reason, we purposefully focus on the test *scores* themselves, rather than on the concept of intelligence. The assumption is that the tests do in fact measure some form of intellectual ability, but the exact nature of what the tests measure will not concern us here. With that word of caution and disclaimer let us turn to the test scores of older persons.

Individual tests of intelligence traditionally include a group of items which can be called "verbal" items and a group of items which can be called "visual-motor" items. The *verbal* items include such tasks as word definitions, arithmetic problems, and explaining the meaning of proverbs. The *visual-motor* items include such tasks as arranging colored blocks into a particular pattern, putting a puzzle together, and stringing beads on a string.

The distinction between these two broad categories of intelligence test items is important in the study of what happens to intelligence test scores in old age. The distinction is important, because scores on verbal and visual motor tests apparently are not affected in the same way by old age. In general, the available data suggest that while test scores on the visual-motor items do show some decline as human beings grow older, test scores on the verbal types of test items tend to show little or no decline with age (Botwinick, 1973; Baltes & Schaie, 1974; Jarvik, 1973; Kinsbourne, 1974). Contrary to the popular belief, the test performance of old persons as a group does not go down on tests composed of verbal items; however, performance on tests composed of visual-motor items does tend to show some decrease with age.

As good psychologists, now that we have made the simple generalization about the intelligence test scores of groups of persons as they grow old, we must introduce some qualifications. On the whole, the statements made above about the change in verbal and visual-motor tests as people grow older are in fact in agreement with most of the currently available evidence. However, several factors that may affect the observed change in intelligence test scores as groups of individuals grow older *must temper the degree to which findings about test scores can be generalized.* For example, among the factors which may affect the test scores observed in old persons are general health (Jarvik, 1973), blood pressure (Wilkie & Eisdorfer, 1971), nearness of the date of death (Riegel & Riegel, 1972; Wilkie & Eisdorfer, 1974), and presence of acute illnesses (Wilkie & Eisdorfer, 1974).

A series of relatively recent studies have suggested that the intelligence test scores of groups of old persons may be related to the length of time between the test and the occurrence of death. The specific relationship still is not clear, but there are data suggesting that lowered scores on intelligence tests are associated with the occurrence of death within five years (Baltes & Schaie, 1974; Reimanis & Green, 1971; Riegel & Riegel, 1972). Although a very interesting group of studies offer support for the relationship between death and decline in intelligence-test scores, the exact nature of that relationship is still unclear. As with many findings about human behavior the studies show some contradictory results (for example, compare Reimanis & Green, 1971, with Wilkie & Eisdorfer, 1974).

In summary, research evidence suggests that old people as a group show some decline on visual-motor intelligence-test scores, but as a rule verbal test scores tend to remain relatively stable into old age. It must be emphasized that many factors can affect the tests scores and can affect the presence or absence of decline in intelligence test scores with old age. One of the more intriguing lines of investigation has attempted to tie intelligence test scores to the imminence of death, and research on this issue is still in progress.

Sexual Functioning in Old Age: Good News

Although the common stereotype of the "old person" suggests that older persons are not interested in sex (or if they are they are dirty old people), sexual activity and interest are not discontinued in old age. Available data clearly indicate that the ability to have sex and to enjoy it are *not* lost in later years (Newman & Nichols, 1970; Verwoerdt, 1973).

With the coming of old age there does seem to be a reduction in the *frequency* of sexual activity and perhaps some decrease in sexual interest (Verwoerdt, Pfeifer & Wang, 1970; Newman & Nichols, 1970). Whether or not it declines, sexual interest very clearly persists into old age. With the coming of old age, however, there are certain physical changes which affect the sexual systems of the human body. Let us look briefly at some of the physical changes which old age is likely to produce in men and women.

Masters and Johnson (1966, 1970) have provided valuable data on a variety of physical changes which older males and females are likely to experience. Let us turn our attention first to physical changes occurring in older men.

Older men tend to experience a *slowing* in the rate at which a full erection is developed, but the ability to have erections is maintained. Once an erection is achieved it may be possible for the older man to maintain that erection without ejaculation for extended periods of time. The need to experience ejaculation may become reduced for aging males. When ejaculation does occur the force of the ejaculation tends to be reduced and the volume of seminal fluid ejaculated is reduced. After ejaculation loss of the erection of the penis tends to become faster as males grow older, and the time before another erection can be produced tends to become longer.

As with the older males Masters and Johnson (1966, 1970) have provided information on a wide variety of changes which can occur in the aging female. Among the changes observed in women as they grow old are thinning of the walls of the vagina along with a reduction in the length and width of the vagina. Lubrication of the vagina in sexual excitement becomes slower, and the vagina loses some of its ability to expand.

For both men and women there are many changes with age other than those we have chosen to list. What seems to be common to the changes in sexual functioning of both men and women with age is that *responses occur more slowly and with less vigor.* Beyond this slowing and reduction in the strength of physiological responses, the data indicate that *such physical changes do not reduce the ability of either males or females to experience orgasm and sexual pleasure and release in old age.*

One of the suggestions made by authorities on sexual functioning is that in a sense "practice makes perfect." One of the factors that appears to be reliably associated with the maintenance of good sexual capacity into old age is regularity of sexual activity. The specific nature of the obtained sexual release is unimportant, as long as the sexual activity is regular. It must be emphasized that available data are for the most part correlational, i.e., persons who do have patterns of regular activity in earlier years also tend to have higher levels of sexual capacity in old age; whether this is in fact a causal relationship is still not clear. At the very least, however, regular sexual activity in early and middle adulthood in no way reduces sexual capacity in old age. With that word of caution about the nature of the available data, we will agree with the suggestion that regular sexual activity may in fact be one potential way for maintaining sexual capacity into old age (Rubin, 1968).

RETIREMENT

In thinking about the potential difficulties and problems in living created by growing older, it is perhaps retirement which is identified as the worst aspect of all. Retirement has rated relatively high on lists of events seen as stressful (Holmes & Rahe, 1967). From a sociological perspective the suggestion has been made that old persons tend to lose status and respect when they are no longer employed (Rosow, 1971). On the other hand, many of us may see retirement as a time of leisure when we can freely pursue hobbies, interests, and other activities that cannot be pursued because of the continual demands of regular employment. In this section of the chapter we turn our attention to the question, *what does the available evidence suggest about the psychological consequences of retirement?*

Psychological Consequences of Retirement

Not unexpectedly, the available information suggests that there can be some negative psychological consequences of retirement. Riley and Foner (1968) concluded that older persons who are still working give themselves higher ratings of over-all satisfaction with life than old persons who are no longer working.

Back and Guptill (1966) asked a group of retired persons and a group of nonretired persons to give ratings of the word "myself." The assumption is that such ratings can provide some information about how an individual sees and rates himself, giving some indication of his feelings of self-esteem, feelings of usefulness, and the like. The results indicated that in fact retired persons did rate themselves somewhat differently than nonretired persons. Retired persons rated themselves as less useful and somewhat less active than nonretired persons.[1]

In a study of workers and retirement Streib and Schneider (1971) were able to obtain a wide variety of information from a rather large group of subjects who were workers in the United States. As part of the investigation, the participants were asked to answer a wide variety of questions and among those were questions asking how useful the respondent felt. Streib and Schneider (1971) reported that in the year after retirement there was an increase in the number of persons who expressed feelings of *uselessness*. Approximately 25 per cent of the persons who had retired reported feeling useless. Of this group of persons expressing feelings of uselessness, only about one fourth attributed their feeling useless to their stopping work!

As with other critical life problems, the effects of retirement also depends on many factors. In one study, for example, higher-status retired persons reported missing their jobs *less* than retired persons of lower socioeconomic status, and the higher-status group had a higher level of morale in general (Simpson, Back & McKinney, 1966a). Individual characteristics or "personality styles" have also been reported to affect adjustment to retirement (Reichard, Livson & Peterson, 1968). Another factor which seems to have an effect on many aspects of old age also tends to affect adjustment to retirement, and that is health. Individuals in good health report better satisfaction with their lives than individuals in poor health. Finally, although common sense suggests that the more you like your job the less you will like retirement, available data tend to contradict this notion. The relation between liking work and not liking retirement is very small, if it exists at all (Goudy, Powers & Keith, 1975).

Although retirement is clearly a period which can produce feelings of uselessness and inactivity for some individuals, negative changes may *not* be the rule for individuals who retire. Old persons

[1]We should point out that studies which simply compare a group of workers with a group of retirees cannot be regarded as conclusive, because the groups may differ in ways other than retirement status alone (for example, health or income).

do not typically change their basic interests and activities after retirement (Simpson, 1973). Furthermore, the *ratings of over-all life satisfaction given by persons who retire may not go down at all* (Streib & Schneider, 1971).

The potential stress and difficulty caused by retirement should not be ignored because there will be some individuals for whom retirement is a very difficult problem. On the other hand, indications are that individuals who have not yet retired tend to overestimate the adverse influence of retirement on their lives. In other words, it seems that workers who have not yet retired may see retirement as significantly more stressful than it actually is (Streib & Schneider, 1971).

Because of the potential unpleasant consequences of retirement for some persons and because of some of the misconceptions about retirement, the question has been raised about whether anything can be done to prepare individuals for a more successful retirement.

Pre-Retirement Planning

Retirement is almost inevitable at some point of old age, but indications are that most adult workers do not have definite plans for retirement. Although pre-retirement programs are increasing in number, these programs are still not widespread in American companies (Riley & Foner, 1968). The suggestion has frequently been made that planning should be done by all persons well before the actual time for retirement occurs (Granick & Friedman, 1973).

Barrett (1972) has suggested that problems associated with retirement could be avoided through *careful planning before retirement*. Available evidence very tentatively supports the idea that being exposed to information about retirement may in fact be related to missing work less, especially for persons whose attitude toward retirement was somewhat positive before retirement (Simpson, Back & McKinney, 1966b). As Eisdorfer (1972) has pointed out, however, the value of pre-retirement planning still requires further investigation. Whether or not the evidence will eventually give strong support to the usefulness of pre-retirement planning, it seems reasonable that such planning would be a good idea.

In planning for retirement there are several areas which should be considered (Barrett, 1972; Hunter, 1973). *Income* is perhaps the area of planning which most of us might think of first. Determining the level of retirement income we will have under particular pension plans, knowing the predicted buying power of the money we will have available, and making a tentative budget for retirement are some ways of planning for one's retirement income.

Living arrangements after retirement should also be considered. Do you plan to live alone in your own house or apartment? Do you plan to live close to certain members of your family, or is a retirement community in a different area of the country a way of living that appeals to you? These and other considerations may make the decisions about where and with whom to live easier when retirement comes.

Use of leisure time is also an area which should be given serious thought. With the reduction of time spent in work-related activities, retired persons can find that there is much free time available to them. Consideration must be given to how the great amounts of free time are to be spent. What hobbies might be pleasant in retirement? If some form of work is desired, what requirements will you need to meet in order to qualify for it? The possibility of volunteering your time can also be a meaningful way of using the leisure time of retirement.

Although closely tied to other areas of pre-retirement planning, some consideration might profitably be given to the *interpersonal relationships* you will have after retirement. If there are particular friends or members of the family who are important to you, then this consideration may have an impact on some of the decisions made about living arrangements and use of leisure time. The need to realize that the relationship with children may need to be altered in some respects, with a greater openness to accepting help under some circumstances, should be considered in pre-retirement planning.

Retirement brings with it changes in a wide variety of areas. Some form of systematic planning for these changes would seem to be desirable, with planning beginning several years before retirement is either planned or forced by circumstances. We have briefly touched on some of the questions to consider in planning your retirement.

CONCLUSIONS

In this chapter we have examined old age and some of the evidence about changes associated with the aging process. Although some changes in memory and in some forms of intelligence test scores tend to occur with old age, it is perhaps the physical changes that are more obvious and more readily apparent. Changes in physical appearance and physical functioning are noted in a wide variety of the structures of the human body.

The sexual systems of the human body also tend to undergo some changes with age. In general there is a reduction in the speed and intensity of the physical responses of the body. However, contrary to the common myth, both males and females continue to have sexual feelings into old age. The ability to experience sexual pleasure also continues into old age.

Retirement, in our society, is perhaps the most predictable and expected event associated with growing old. As we have seen, some persons may in fact experience some feelings of uselessness and low morale; but it must be remembered that there can be a tendency for workers not yet retired to overestimate the bad consequences of retirement. Retirement turns out to be less unpleasant than many workers assume. Although many factors will determine the effects of retirement on any particular individual, the available evidence suggests that retirement may not necessarily be an unpleasant experience at all. It has been suggested by some students of aging that most of the problems of retirement can be avoided by careful planning in the years that come before retirement.

Some changes are inevitable in old age, especially physical changes. The argument has been recently made that many psychological changes that occur in old age may *not* be inevitable, but can be avoided through changes in the environment of old persons (Labouvie-Vief, Hoyer, Baltes, & Baltes, 1974). Whether or not most changes observed in old age are inevitable is still to be decided by further research. It is clear that if health remains good then old age will be a time in which good things can happen. *The notion that old age is a time of inevitalbe mental deterioration, sexual dysfunction and disinterest, and loss of self-respect is wrong.* It is a stage of life which can present problems for some, but for most persons it is simply a new life stage, with new joys and sorrows. It is where physical and mental inactivity exist that old age can become a time of deterioration (Jarvik, 1975).

PROJECTS AND QUESTIONS

1. Present the following words on paper to each person, individually or in small groups, and have each individual give a written list of *four* associations to each word. Discuss your responses.

> senility
> retirement
> old people
> aging
> 85th birthday

2. Here are two short descriptions of two different individuals. Read the descriptions carefully and then write a short paragraph giving your impression of each person.

    Case A: Mrs. W is a 75-year-old woman who lives alone. Her income is $300.00 a month. She has a small dog and a cat. She enjoys reading, horseback riding, and meeting other people. She dates regularly and enjoys an active sex life.

    Case B: Miss W is a 25-year-old woman who lives alone. Her income is $300.00 a month. She has a small dog and a cat. She enjoys reading, horseback riding, and meeting other people. She dates regularly and enjoys an active sex life.

    After writing separate reactions to each case description, compare the two. Were they different? How? Do you have different expectations of the two persons based on their ages? How did the expectations differ?

3. In small groups discuss how you would like your life to be when you are 80. Considering such things as income, companionship, sex, and housing. Try to reach consensus in the group on the ideal situation for you at 80 years of age.

4. Plan your retirement. Decide on the age at which you want to retire, what you want to do after you retire, and how you will spend your leisure time, and give careful consideration to what you must do to reach the goals you set for your old age.

SUGGESTED READINGS

Popular Sources

R. EDER. The English do old best of all. *Esquire,* 1975 (April), *83* (4), 174ff. An entertaining journalistic account of old people in Great Britain.

M. LAHEY. Aging's gift: Freedom. *New Catholic World*, 1973 (July), *216*, 166–170. An optimistic look at the positive aspects of growing old.

M. HELLIE-HUYCK. *Growing Older.* Englewood Cliffs, N.J.: Prentice-Hall, 1974.

N. M. LOBSENZ. Sex and the senior citizen. *Reader's Digest,* 1973 (April), *104*, 74–78. A brief discussion of the sexuality of older persons, focusing on recent research findings.

Advanced Sources

J. BOTWINICK. *Aging and behavior.* New York: Sprinzer, 1973. Research based discussion of various aspects of human aging.

D. C. KIMMEL. *Adulthood and aging.* New York: Wiley, 1974. A readable undergraduate-level text that covers a broader spectrum than old age alone.

E. PALMORE. (Ed.). *Normal Aging I and II.* Durham, N. C.: Duke Univ. Press, 1970 and 1974. Compilations of articles published on aging, based on work done by researchers associated with Duke University.

REFERENCES

ANDERSON, B. & PALMORE, E. Longitudinal evaluation of ocular function. In E. Palmore (Ed.). *Normal Aging II.* Durham, N.C.: Duke Univ. Press, 1974.

ALTROCCHI, J. & EISDORFER, C. Comparisons of attitudes toward old people, mental illness, and other concepts. In C. Tibbitts & W. Donahue (Eds.). *Social and psychological aspects of aging.* New York: Columbia Univ. Press, 1962.

BACK, K. W. & GUPTILL, C. S. Retirement and self-ratings. In I. H. Simpson & J. C. McKinney (Eds.). *Social aspects of aging.* Durham, N.C.: Duke Univ. Press, 1966.

BAHRICK, H. P., BAHRICK, P. O. & WITTLINGER, R. P. Those unforgettable high-school days. *Psychol. Today,* June, 1975, 50–56.

BALTES, P. B. & SCHAIE, K. W. The myth of the twilight year. *Psychol. Today,* March, 1974, 35–40.

BARRETT, J. H. *Gerontological psychology.* Springfield: C. C. Thomas, 1972.

BLAU, Z. S. *Old age in a changing society.* New York: New Viewpoints, 1973.

BOTWINICK, J. *Aging and behavior.* New York: Sprinzer, 1973.

COLBERT, J. N., KALISH, R. A. & CHANZ, P. Two psychological portals of entry for disadvantaged groups. *Rehabilitation Literature,* 1973, *34*, 194–202.

DRACHMAN, D. A. & LEAVITT, J. Memory impairment in the aged: Storage vs. retrieval deficit. *J. Exp. Psychol.* 1972, *93*, 302–308.

EISDORFER, C. Adaptation to loss of work. In F. C. Carp (Ed.). *Retirement.* New York: Behavioral Publications, 1972.

EISDORFER, C. & M. P. LAWTON (Eds.). *The psychology of adult development and aging.* Washington, D.C.: American Psychological Assoc., 1973.

EISDORFER, C. & WILKIE, F. Intellectual changes. In E. Palmore (Ed.). *Normal Aging II.* Durham, N.C.: Duke Univ. Press, 1974.

GOLDMAN, R. Decline in organ functioning with aging. In I. Rossman (Ed.). *Clinical geriatrics.* Philadelphia: Lippincott, 1971, pp. 19–48.

GOUDY, W. J., POWERS, E. A. & KEITH, P. Work and retirement. *J. of Gerontology,* 1975, *30,* 193–198.

GRANICK, S. & FRIEDMAN, A. S. Educational experience and the maintenance of intellectual functioning by the aged: An overview. In L. F. Jarvik, et al. (Eds.). *Intellectual functioning in adults.* Springer: New York, 1973.

HOLMES, T. H. & RAHE, R. H. The social readjustment rating scale. *J. Psychosom. Res.,* 1967, *11,* 213–218.

HUNTER, W. W. Preretirement education programs. In R. R. Boyd & C. G. Oakes (Eds.). *Foundations of practical gerontology.* Second edition. Columbia, S.C.: University of S.C. Press, 1973.

HUYCK, M. H. *Growing older.* Englewood Cliffs, N.J.: Prentice-Hall, 1974.

JACKSON, D. W. Relationship of residence, education, and socialization to cognitive tasks in normal people of advanced old age. *Psychol. Reports,* 1974, *35,* 423–426.

JARVIK, L. F. Discussion: Patterns of intellectual functioning in the later years. In L. F. Jarvik, C. Eisdorfer & J. E. Blum (Eds.). *Intellectual functioning in adults.* Springer: New York, 1973.

JARVIK, L. F. Thoughts on the psychobiology of aging. *Amer. Psychol.,* 1975, *30,* 576–583.

KIMMEL, D. C. *Adulthood and aging.* New York: Wiley, 1974.

KINSBOURNE, M. Cognitive deficit and the aging brain: A behavioral analysis. *Internat. J. Aging Hum. Devel.,* 1974, *5,* 41–49.

LABOUVIE-VIEF, G., HOYER, W. J., BALTES, M. M. & BALTES, P. B. Operant analysis of intellectual behavior in old age. *Hum. Devel.,* 1974, *17,* 259–272.

MASTERS, W. H. & JOHNSON, V. E. *Human sexual response.* Boston: Little, Brown, 1966.

MASTERS, W. H. & JOHNSON, V. E. *Human sexual inadequacy.* Boston: Little, Brown, 1970.

NEWMAN, G. & NICHOLS, C. R. Sexual activities and attitudes in older persons. In E. Palmore (Ed.). *Normal aging.* Durham, N.C.: Duke Univ. Press, 1970.

PALMORE, E. (Ed.). *Normal aging.* Durham, N.C.: Duke Univ. Press, 1970.

REICHARD, S., LIVSON, F. & PETERSEN, P. G. Adjustment to retirement. In B.C. Neugarten (Ed.). *Middle age and aging.* Chicago: Univ. of Chicago Press, 1968.

REIMANIS, G. & GREEN, R. F. Imminence of death and intellectual decrement in aging. *Develop. Psychol.,* 1971, *5,* 270–272.

RIEGEL, K. F. & RIEGEL, R. M. Development, drop and death. *Develop. Psychol.* 1972, *6,* 306–319.

RILEY, M. W. & FONER, A. *Aging and society.* Vol. 1. New York: Russell Sage, 1968.

ROSOW, I. Retirement leisure and social class. In F. G. Scott & R. M. Brewer (Eds.). *Perspectives in aging I.* Corvallis, Oregon: Continuing Education, 1971.

ROSSMAN, I. The anatomy of aging. In I. Rossman (Ed.). *Clinical geriatrics.* Philadelphia: Lippincott, 1971, pp. 3–18.

RUBIN, I. Sex and the aging man and woman. In C. E. Vincent (Ed.). *Human sexuality in medical education and practice.* Springfield, Ill.: C. C. Thomas, 1968.

SHEPPARD, H. L. The potential role of behavioral science in the solution of the "older worker problem." *Amer. Behav. Scient.,* 1970, *14,* 71–80.

SIMPSON, I. H. Problems of the aging in work and retirement. In R. R. Boyd & C. G. Oakes (Eds.). *Foundations of practical gerontology.* Second edition. Columbia, S.C.: Univ. of S.C. Press, 1973.

SIMPSON, I. H., BACK, K. W. & MCKINNEY, J. C. Attributes of work, involvement in society, and self-evaluation in retirement. In I. H. Simpson & J. C. McKinney (Eds.). *Social aspects of aging.* Durham, N.C.: Duke Univ. Press, 1966a.

SIMPSON, I. H., BACK, K. W. & MCKINNEY, J. C. Exposure to information, preparation for, and self-evaluation in retirement. In I. H. Simpson & J. C. McKinney (Eds.). *Social aspects of aging.* Durham, N.C.: Duke Univ. Press, 1966b.

SIMPSON, I. H., BACK, K. W. & MCKINNEY, J. C. Orientation toward work and retirement, and self-evaluation in retirement. In I. H. Simpson & J. C. McKinney (Eds.). *Social aspects of aging.* Durham, N.C.: Duke Univ. Press, 1966c.

SMITH, A. D. Aging and interference with memory. *J. geront.,* 1975, *30,* 319–325.

STREIB, G. F. & SCHNEIDER, S. J. *Retirement in American society.* Ithaca: Cornell Press, 1971.

U.S. Department of Health, Education & Welfare. Facts on aging. In F. G. Scott & R. M. Brewer (Eds.). *Perspectives on Aging I.* Corvallis, Oregon: Continuing Education, 1971.

VERWOERDT, A. Biological characteristics of the elderly. In R. R. Boyd & C. G. Oakes (Eds.). *Foundations of practical gerontology.* Second edition. Columbia, S. C.: University of S. C. Press, 1973.

VERWOERDT, A., PFEIFFER, E. & WANG, H. Sexual behavior in senescence. In E. Palmore (Ed.). *Normal aging.* Durham, N. C.: Duke Univ. Press, 1970.

WEINBERGER, L. E. & MILLHAM, J. A. Multi-dimensional, multiple method analysis of attitudes toward the elderly. *J. Geront.* 1975, *30,* 343–348.

WILKIE, F. & EISDORFER, C. Intelligence and blood pressure in the aged. *Science,* 1971, *172,* 959–962.

WILKIE, F. & EISDORFER, C. Terminal changes in intelligence. In E. Palmore (Ed.). *Normal aging II.* Durham, N. C.: Duke Univ. Press, 1974.

YOUNG, A. W. Skin disease. In I. Rossman (Ed.). *Clinical geriatrics.* Philadelphia: Lippincott, 1971, pp. 203–218.

Dying and Grieving

CHAPTER 10

Death is a concept most people find both frightening and depressing. La Rouchefoucauld, a seventeenth-century writer, expressed this very succinctly in his comment, "One can no more look steadily at death than at the sun." Geoffrey Gorer, an English anthropologist, makes the analogy that death is as unmentionable a subject to us today as sex was to the Victorians.

This inability or unwillingness to look at a phenomenon we will all experience seems especially true of the Western culture in the past century. In the nineteenth century, when the concept of an "afterlife" or place where one would be united with lost loved ones was strongly believed, death was accepted, if only as a bridge to another life. Still the concept of death as an end or termination was avoided. The twentieth century has seen a weakening in the concept of life after death, and in religion in general for that matter (Wahl, 1965). Thus the inability to rely on the idea of a future life appears to have resulted in a decreased ability of people to discuss or even contemplate death and dying. We do not speak of a person as having died, but rather as having "passed away" or "departed." Because of this denial and active avoidance of the one certainty in life, most of us are ill-equipped to deal with the death of a friend or loved one, to say nothing of our own.

In addition to the increase in discomfort about death provided by the loss of religion, other factors have also accentuated this problem. Modern man, unlike his earlier predecessors, has learned that he is more successful utilizing his brain than his physical strength. Using these intellectual abilities, man has come to alter and control his environment to a degree not previously even imagined. He is able to move across continents and oceans in a matter of hours, to eradicate diseases such as smallpox and diphtheria in most countries, to implant artificial organs that satisfactorily replace their damaged or diseased natural counterparts, and to conquer pain to a major extent. Man is the unchallenged center of this planet, and he has even begun to explore new ones. He is successful in overcoming almost any problem to which he applies himself over time, with one exception—death. He can postpone dying, as exemplified by the increasing life span that can be expected of the average person, but death remains a totally democratic certainty at some point.

Not only has our success in technology led us to be unfamiliar with failure, thus increasing our anxiety in regard to death, but it has made the process of dying less familiar and hence more frightening to modern man. No longer do people die in their own homes surrounded and supported by the people they love. Instead, modern dying is a public event attended by many strangers and unfamiliar to most people except medical professionals. People now usually die in an institution, most typically a hospital. Here children are often not allowed to visit dying relatives. All must alter their interactions with the dying person to conform to the regulations of the particular institution whose focus is to prolong life rather than assist with dying. Not only do hospital regulations prevent interaction between family and the dying patient, but the failure on the part of many physicians to communicate the nearness of death inhibits communication between the dying person and significant others. A conspiracy of silence often occurs whereby everyone attempts to shield the dying patient, but typically these attempts only result in the isolation and abandonment of the dying person (Glaser & Strauss, 1965; Feifel, 1965).

Feifel (1963), studying 60 dying patients, found that "77–89 percent of patients want to be told about their impending death and prefer honest, plain talk from physicians and family about the seriousness of their illness" (p. 18). Most physicians, however, are in favor of not telling (77 to 89 per cent). The reasons for most physicians' reluctance to communicate to a patient that he is dying are unclear; however, several tentative explanations have been posited. Feifel (1963) reports a study which found that physicians were more afraid of their own deaths than were any of the control groups.

Medical training itself may be very influential, as two of the guidelines given to medical students regarding communication about death have been to not tell patients things which might induce psychopathology and to never allow hope to die before the patient (Aronson, 1959).

Saul and Kass (1969) used the S-R Inventory of Anxiousness to evaluate the anxiety of freshman students in a medical school before and after their first year of training. They found that the two most threatening situations for entering freshmen were discussing his fatal illness with a dying patient and telling a relative that a patient had died. After one year in medical school these situations were still the two most threatening, with higher anxiety scores than originally. This study suggests that perhaps medical schools should direct some training to those situations which doctors must continually encounter, especially because current training appears to increase rather than alleviate students' anxiety about these situations.

This failure in communication is not the rule, however, and some patients are told of their impending death. In this case nurses and physicians may view the dying patient with culturally influenced, specialized views. We expect patients to be dying, yet happy. In the hospital setting, if they are not "noble" or do not "put up a brave front," they are often secluded. Also the dying patient's expression of the most natural of responses to his own death, anger, may effectively close off communication with those professionals who surround him (Quint, 1967; Kübler-Ross, 1969).

GRIEF

For the grieving family, the mobility that has afforded man so many opportunities has resulted in some significant losses. Specifically, the support provided the family members by the extended family and/or community and the comfort of traditional rituals have been removed. The loss of the extended family has resulted in such a profound attachment to members of the immediate family that readjustment following a death is extremely difficult.

> Whereas we stress the sense of loss and recognize the need for replacement, basically the culture creates the conditions in which the deceased is irreplaceable because he cannot ever really be duplicated. . . . In this way the bereaved person has no alternative cultural solution to the problem of replacement (Volkart, p. 214).

Traditions and rituals have also been abandoned by many modern Americans. Along with mobility has come a less prescribed way of living. There has been a decrease in the practice of attending and even of providing the traditional funeral, which serves so many psychological and social functions.

As late as 1963 investigators found that "death is a taboo subject in the United States, surrounded by disapproval and shame" (Feifel, 1963, p. 17). But the publication in 1969 of *On Death and Dying* by Elizabeth Kübler-Ross received much public acclaim and appears to have signaled the willingness of many people to deal with the subject. Granted, most of these people are mental health or medical professionals, but it represents a beginning. More recently, Stewart Alsop, the articulate and famous journalist, has provided a personal account of receiving a terminal diagnosis. His book, *Stay of Execution*, and the many editorials and articles written by and about him have possible given the American public a more intimate knowledge about dying than they would ever have obtained on their own from immediate experience.

The Stages of a Grief Reaction

In conjunction with the recent interest in gaining an awareness of death and the dying process comes the desire to cope better with the stages of the grief reaction that follows the death of a close friend or relative. Grief and bereavement can be described as a period in which an individual or family unit is under severe emotional and psychological stress because of the loss of a loved one. The grief reaction is similar to almost any reaction to a crisis in that it is characterized by shock and disbelief.

In the *initial stage,* after becoming aware of the death of a friend or loved one, the grieving person emotionally denies the loss. The person may be immobile, numb, and dazed. The feelings reported during this time are "numbness," feeling dazed, or feeling "frozen." Following this initial refusal to accept or comprehend the reality of death, the mourner typically returns to routine daily activities. However, on close observation one is immediately struck by the mechanical or automatic fashion in which they are done. It is usual at this point for the grieving person to accept the loss intellectually and to begin initiating many appropriate activities. However, this massive effort at intellectualization of the loss and denial of the overwhelming feelings of grief and despair cannot be maintained continually. Thus there are periods of time in which the mourner experiences these feelings acutely and his anguish is apparent. This first stage appears to be one in which the mourner protects himself psychologically and emotionally by simply refusing to think about the loss he has just experienced and the devastating feelings that have resulted.

The *second stage* is one in which the mourner slowly develops an awareness not only of the reality of the death, but of the effect it will have on the lives of the survivors. It begins within minutes to hours after the death. There is much overlap between the stages, and people typically do not complete one stage before moving into another. In the "developing awareness" stage the grieving person often experiences much somatic distress (Engel, 1964). He complains of a painful emptiness in the chest, a tightness in the throat, a shortness of breath, and a lack of strength. The symptoms often increase after someone mentions the deceased or offers sympathy, which may lead to attempts to avoid this physical and mental distress by refusing visits from friends and deliberately avoiding any references to or thoughts about the deceased.

The environment of the mourner becomes very frustrating and very empty because it no longer includes the loved person, and the mourner may become very angry. This anger is often directed toward the physicians or nurses caring for the patient at the time of the death or perhaps another family member, or even directed inward. Lindemann (1944) describes the case of a young man who was obsessed by guilt because he had been unable to save his wife during the Coconut Grove fire. When he had tried to pull her out he had fainted and was pushed out by the crowd. He had lived while she had died. He stated, "I should have saved her, or I should have died too." Although reactions of this type are not very common, they do occur, and the mourners may attempt to hurt or punish themselves in some way. A more common picture is that the mourner lashes out at others and may worry about small omissions or arguments that occurred in the past. Although it usually occurs later, the mourner may feel much anger toward the deceased for dying and leaving the mourner alone. Unless recognized as natural, these feelings may cause the mourner intense guilt and may hinder the grief process. The intense anger felt in this situation is bewildering to many grief-stricken persons, and they may feel very guilty for lashing out at others. Support and understanding are needed so that the situation does not become overwhelming.

Crying is also very typical of this phase, as the most intense feelings of anguish are experienced and expressed during this time. This is one occasion in which our culture accepts the tears of adult males without prejudice. The wish and need to cry seems to be prevalent in spite of family expectations or cultural patterns. Lindemann (1944) states that crying fills an important function in the work of mourning. An inability to cry, as distinguished from crying when alone or not crying because the deceased is not seriously missed, may be indicative of the mourner's mixed feelings about the deceased or of the mourner's feelings of guilt about the deceased.

For most mourners an inability to cry is not experienced, however, and crying serves many important functions. It serves to acknowledge the loss and to communicate to others the grief that is felt and the need for assistance or help. Thus, much support and help are offered to the mourner during this stage of the grief reaction.

The *third stage* is restitution, the work of mourning, and it may be initiated by the various rites and rituals associated with the funeral. The family members and close friends come together to share in their loss and to recognize and support those who are the most upset. This is a time of unity, and the overt anger present in stage two is not evident. The funeral itself serves many useful purposes. It acknowledges the death publicly, and the reality of the death can no longer be denied. At the same time it provides a public acknowledgement of the loss of the mourner and allows and supports the expression of grief by all the mourners. The mourners can share their feelings and obtain much support for them. Just as important is the message to the survivors that they remain a part of the community and that they have not been forgotten; thus the mourners' place in the community is recognized by means of the funeral.

Resolving the loss of the deceased is the *fourth stage* of the grief process, and it is a more individual process than the previous stages. The mourner becomes aware of an incompleteness due to the loss of the person with whom he had a relationship, but he is not yet ready to accept a new object of love. Often a passive but extremely dependent relationship develops with the family and friends. This often allows the mourner to think most of the time about the deceased. The feelings of loss are initially the major concern, but this later changes to thoughts of the deceased person. This process is slow and gradual, probably because of sadness involved, but slowly through the sharing of memories and experiences, the mourner erects an image of the deceased almost devoid of negative and undesirable features.

This process of idealization is the *fifth stage* of the grief reaction. It requires that the mourner not allow himself to experience any negative or hostile feelings toward the deceased nor to remember any of his faults. This in turn heightens the guilt concerning any inconsiderate past actions of the mourner toward the deceased. In some, this is not only guilt but fear concerning remembered hostilities toward the deceased. There may also be a preoccupation with feelings of responsibility for the death or with not having fulfilled one's role during the dying process.

Through this process of idealization the mourner establishes an image of the deceased that is used along with various mementos to remember the positive aspects of the lost relationship. Thus, the mourner can periodically relive some of the happy times of the past. In addition the mourner may begin to imitate and identify with the deceased person, as may be evidenced through certain mannerisms associated with the deceased or in the mourner's verbalizing the desire to be like the lost person (Engel, 1964).

This fifth stage typically requires many months but as time passes a noticeable decrease in the mourner's preoccupation with the deceased will be noticed. The mourner typically expresses the desire to "carry on for him" or "be what mother wanted me to be." Finally the mourner can tolerate unpleasant as well as pleasant memories of the dead person without being overwhelmed with guilt.

A turning to other relationships also occurs. Concern with the grief of other members of the family allows the mourner to help another person. This very helpful process allows family members to facilitate the grieving process for each other. Another example is the interest shown by families of dying patients in other families of patients on the ward. This is a common occurrence in hospitals and is recognized by the hospital staff as a way in which the families come to terms with their impending loss as well as a way in which they can continue to invest in the living. Typically the mourners become less and less involved with other mourners and begin to form relationships with others.

Length of Grief Reaction

The time required for resolution of the loss varies a great deal, and there is no definitive time period that can be considered normal. In the past, three to six months was considered average by most professionals (Lindemann, 1944); however, this rule has not been found to be true (Clayton, Desmaris & Winokur, 1968; Hendin, 1974). Grieving may last a year or more, and it may never be completely resolved. It is the progress or the manner in which the person grieves rather than the length of time the person grieves that is of importance. Even after the mourner has apparently resolved the loss and has begun to form new relationships, enjoying activities without feeling guilt, many things may continue to trigger grief. For example, a wedding anniversary or the deceased's birthday may continue to be upsetting to a widow for a number of years (Clayton, Halikas & Maurree, 1972).

Anticipatory Mourning

Grief reactions are typically shorter and less intense when death occurs in an older person and has been expected. Under these circumstances the work of mourning is often shortened because part of the grieving process has occurred before the death, in anticipatory grief or mourning. In this situation the person begins to grieve for the loss upon learning of a terminal illness or when a person enters the last phase of a long illness. When anticipatory mourning has occurred, the shock phase is often eliminated because of the gradual acceptance that has occurred during the illness. This does not mean, however, that the mourner will not experience acute grief at the time of death (Lindemann, 1944; Kutscher, 1973).

Relationship of the Deceased to the Mourner

The importance of the deceased to the mourner is critical: the more important the role of the deceased in the mourner's life, the more difficult the mourning process becomes. It has been a contention of many physicians that grief is a significant cause of sickness and death, and many studies have demonstrated very high rates of morbidity and mortality among bereaved adults of all ages. Rees and Lutkins (1967) found that during the first year of bereavement nearly 5 per cent of their experimental group, close relatives of 371 people who died over a six-year period, also died. In a control group the death rate was less than 1 per cent. The death rate among widows and widowers was 12 per cent as compared to 1.2 per cent of their counterparts in the control group. Finally, if a spouse or child died suddenly outside of the home in a hospital, the death rate of the mourners was five times as high. Thus the loss of a spouse or child appears to be capable of triggering many significant problems both emotional and physical.

Death Be Not Proud, a book by John Gunther, is a moving account of how his family dealt with their adolescent son John's illness and death. The helplessness and frustration that parents feel in knowing of the many joys of life that their child will not experience becomes clear in a very personal manner. It is important to note, however, that the behavior of Johnny and the Gunthers was atypical in that the experience is more positive than in most families.

The loss of an adolescent or child is very disruptive for a family, and the process of mourning is more difficult and extended than usual. Even in those cases where the child has died of a terminal illness and some anticipatory mourning has occurred, the process of mourning is often protracted, probably because of the strain already placed on the family by the illness-hospital bills and the isolation of the mother and child from the family being two of the most obvious causes. These families often become isolated from the community, too, as the emotional and physical strain is tremendous. Other children in the family may feel ignored and resent their sick sibling and the attention he is receiving. Behavioral problems often occur in the siblings, causing a further strain on the family. The death of the sick child may then precipitate an inordinate amount of guilt in the siblings as well as the parents, and the family members are often so overwhelmed that they are unable to be supportive to each other (Easson, 1972; Greene & King, 1974; Heffron, Bommelaere & Masters, 1973).

The loss of a parent or other significant figure for a child can have very profound effects. In some cases developmental disturbances can occur as a result of the loss. The severity of the disturbance is the result of many factors: the stage of psychological development achieved by the child (age is, of course, a factor), the length of separation, the way in which the loss was handled, and the availability of other nurturant persons, those close to the child and with whom substitute attachments can be formed. The child, like the adult, goes through a mourning process, and the importance of intervention following the death of a parent cannot be minimized. The child is limited in his defenses, has less experience with losses, and less ability to deal with trauma (Clark, 1974; Schowalter, 1974).

For the child three to five years of age, death is not viewed as a final process. It is a departure, a temporary absence, so that his reactions take the form of separation anxiety or the fear of abandonment. The child six to ten years of age is just beginning to grasp the concept of death, but it is poorly understood. His intellectual ability to formulate a concept of death is not complete, and he does not clearly understand its finality. The child over ten typically has the cognitive ability to understand the concept of death (Nagy, 1965; Spinetta, Rigler & Karon, 1973).

The loss of a parent engenders much fear in the child, as he may begin to fear abandonment by the surviving parent. The fear is often accentuated by the loss of emotional support from the remaining parent caused by the adult's own grief. Thus it is important that other nurturing adults be available. In addition, the child's fears that he will be abandoned should be recognized and assurances given that he will be cared for (Clark, 1972).

It is also common for a child four to six years of age to fear that he may have caused the dead parent to die because of his anger toward the parent. Thus a child may remember being angry at the deceased parent and having wished that the parent would die and may feel that he killed the parent by his wish (Wahl, 1965). This is called "magical thinking" and is very prevalent in children of this age.

Finally, the anger typical of grief with adults is also characteristic of the child. If not expressed toward the dead parent, it may be expressed toward the remaining parent or other children at school or nursery. The encouragement of expressions of the anger as well as the sadness felt by the child is considered crucial by experts. The child needs to feel comfortable in expressing these feelings and should be given the knowledge that the dead parent, who cannot return, did not want to leave.

The child's experience with other losses such as a pet dog or fish can be very helpful toward aiding him in this situation. The loss of a loved pet followed by an explanation that the pet will not return and a burial is a good preparation (Schowalter, 1974).

THE FUNERAL

The funeral is an important rite of passage, and in every culture people surround burial with ritual. Although ostensibly for the dead, the funeral benefits the living. It is personal in focus and societal in consequence. After a death certain things are done in every society, regardless of the level of its complexity. No matter how unprepared or helpless any individual may be following the death of a particular person, the group always has a plan of action in the event of death. The corpse must be disposed of; the bereaved must be helped to reorient themselves; and the whole group must have a way of readjusting after the loss of a member (Mandelbaum, 1965; Hendin, 1974).

Although the particular emphasis of the funeral will vary depending upon the values of the culture, certain activities appear across cultures. The gathering of the family, friends, or members of the tribe gives a public acknowledgement to the death. In addition, those closest to the deceased learn that the loss is a common one. The most upset of the mourners are allowed to express their grief openly, but limits are placed on the extent of their expression. These limits, whether formal or informal, allow the mourners to grieve while providing security through these limits and the support given by other mourners. Not only is immediate support given the grief-stricken family, but the funeral also serves to acknowledge their continuing to have a place within the social structure of the society. Thus the family is assured that the loss of one of its members does not mean the loss of friends (Mandelbaum, 1965).

Children's attendance at funerals varies a great deal, and there are no set guidelines in this area. In most cases the child under eight or nine will only be more upset and confused by the funeral. The feelings of the child should, however, be given consideration and he should not be kept from attending if he so chooses. If the adults in his family are so grief-stricken that they cannot be available to support the child, a close friend of the family should sit with the child. It may also be helpful to let the child know that he may change his mind if he chooses. Seating the child where he may leave during the service provides this opportunity. Care should also be taken to adequately prepare the child by explaining what will happen during the funeral services (Schowalter, 1974).

The decrease in close community ties because of the increased mobility of society has taken away much of the support offered by the funeral. Many times funerals are attended only by family members and a few friends, thus there are few people in attendance who are not experiencing acute grief, and the support received by the mourners is minimal. Furthermore, the lack of familiarity with funerals and grieving people leaves most people ill-equipped to be of assistance when the death of a family member or friend occurs.

ASSISTANCE TO THE MOURNER

It is not uncommon for friends of the mourner to withdraw from him, just as they might from the dying person. The obvious sadness and pain of the mourner overwhelm them, and they do not know how to handle their own anxiety. They may also find themselves at a loss for words and may avoid the subject of the deceased. Of course, this is often said to be done for the sake of the mourner, but the mourner needs to talk about the deceased, as one vehicle for grieving. It is very beneficial for the grief-stricken person to remember and talk about the dead person, which will allow the loss to be experienced in a supportive situation. The emotions that will be expressed are often upsetting to friends, and their avoidance of the topic may be to avoid upsetting themselves. They cannot realistically avoid upsetting the mourners as they are already upset. There is also much literature to suggest that the mourner who is able to express his emotions will have a better resolution of his loss (Lindemann, 1944; Hendin, 1974).

The extent of the discussion should be determined by the person who has experienced the loss. Thus indications that the subject is too painful or has been dealt with long enough should be respected. Well-meaning attempts to make someone deal with their loss will only be detrimental.

Sadness and pain are not the only emotions associated with grief. As previously mentioned, guilt, for no other reason than being the survivor, may occur (Pine, 1971). The guilt may also be a result of anger toward the deceased. It is often helpful for the bereaved to know that this anger is normal and that it is permissible to express it. One young woman who felt angry at her mother for dying and leaving her became even more acutely depressed when someone close to her concurred with her feeling that her anger was immature. She, like many other mourners, was relieved when she later learned that her anger was normal and that it did not signify immaturity or a lack of love on her part.

Anger is always a part of grief, although it may be directed at a variety of people. The physician or nurse who cared for the dying person is often a target. Relatives often feel that they "killed" the loved one or allowed the death to occur. God or his representatives may also be blamed. It is important to be prepared for such outbursts when dealing with mourners and not to reject the person because of it. The anger can best be understood as a reflection of the mourner's frustration at being unable to prevent the death of a loved one (Engel, 1964). The patient, gentle reassurance that everyone, including the mourner, did all that was possible in caring for the dead person will help the mourner in dealing with his guilt (Quint, 1967).

Loneliness and abandonment are frequently felt by the bereaved, and these feelings can be terribly frightening, especially for a spouse of many years. Not only in the days following the funeral, but in the weeks that follow, it is important that relatives and friends be available. The nature of bereavement makes it difficult for the grieving person to ask for help, much less to have the energy to seek it out. For this reason, availability is not enough. Small gifts or food are tangible expressions of caring. Invitations to dinner or a movie are also important and should not be dropped if initially refused. This type of support and reincorporation into life are helpful and may be needed for a period of months.

For some people the loss of a loved one is so upsetting that they need professional assistance in dealing with this crisis. One of the most accepted signs of a pathological grief reaction is the failure to cry or express grief about the death. The absence of visible grief is a signal that something is very wrong and that the person may be unable to resolve this loss without skillful intervention.

Another indication of a pathological grief reaction is the inability to function socially for an extended period of time. Thus, if a person cannot work, never goes out, or begins drinking heavily, intervention is needed. It is normal for an individual to withdraw initially, to stop eating and sleeping, and even to have suicidal thoughts. It is the extent or duration of these reactions that are indications of severe problems. The expression of the wish to die is common, but if the mourner begins talking a great deal about suicide, professional help should be sought immediately.

PROJECTS AND QUESTIONS

1. Groups of 6-8 individuals may be formed to explore the feelings and attitudes of each member toward death and grief. The following topics could be utilized:

   a. Each member could discuss any deaths that he or she might have been aware of during his childhood. Does his or her knowledge of the grief process make the actions of the people involved more understandable?

   b. A discussion centered around the familiarity of the group members with funerals.
      1. Have they ever attended a funeral?
      2. Were they ever refrained from attending a funeral?
      3. What were their reactions to the funeral?
      4. Were they ever forced to attend a funeral?
      5. Does the group agree with the contention that funerals are beneficial to the mourners?

   c. A discussion around supporting the bereaved.
      1. What source of support does each member think might be most helpful to him or her?
      2. How has each member been of support to friends or family in the past?
      3. What specifically would each member do upon learning of the death of the parent of a good friend?

2. As an individual or group project, one or more individuals may wish to contact a priest or rabbi or minister and ask him to discuss the funeral rites of each religion. Differences among the religions could be noted and reasons for these differences might be asked of the resource person. Personal feelings about death and the purpose of the funeral might also be topics. Individual talks with clergymen with a report on each interview would be interesting, or clergymen might be asked to speak at an informal forum where each might respond to questions from the group.

3. One or more individuals might want to visit several funeral homes in the community after reading *The American Way of Death* by Jessica Mitford. This book describes the commercial aspects of the funeral business and the manner in which the bereaved are often taken advantage of. The visits can be useful in evaluating each funeral home in terms of its response to the bereaved. How do they provide emotional support to families?

SUGGESTED READINGS

Popular Press

E. KÜBLER-ROSS in *Death: The Final Stage of Growth.* Englewood Cliffs, N.J.: Prentice-Hall, 1974.

E. KÜBLER-ROSS. *Questions and answers on death and dying.* New York: Collier Books, 1974. Question-and-answer format in which the author deals with specific issues on a wide variety of death-related topics. Uncomplicated and understandable.

S. MORRISON. Dying. *Scientific American,* Sept. 1973, 54–60. Discussion of the conditions under which Americans die and a discussion of issues regarding prolongation of life.

E. S. SHNEIDMAN. The enemy. *Psychology Today,* Aug. 1970, 37–41ff. Discussion of death, with focus on the author's idea that individuals contribute in varying degrees to their own death.

Advanced Sources

R. KASTENBAUM, & R. AISENBERG. *The psychology of death.* New York: Springer, 1972. A scholarly presentation on various aspects of death, including an overview of many of the studies previously conducted in this area.

C. M. PARKES. *Bereavement: Studies of grief in adult life.* New York: International University Press, 1972. Author presents views on the grief process, focusing on his interviews and observations of a group of individuals whose spouses had died.

H. M. RUITENBEEK, (Ed.). *The interpretation of death.* New York: J. Aronson, 1973. Several authors, representing various viewpoints from last several years, discuss various aspects of death and dying.

REFERENCES

ALSOP, S. *Stay of execution.* Philadelphia: J. B. Lippincott Co., 1973.

ARONSON, G. Treatment of the dying patient. *The meaning of death.* Feifel, H. (Ed.). New York: McGraw-Hill, 1965.

CLARK, M. B. A therapeutic approach to treating a grieving 2 1/2-year-old. *J. Amer. Acad. Child Psychiat.,* 1972, *11(4),* 704–711.

CLAYTON, P, DESMARIS, L. & WINOKUR, G. A study of normal bereavement. *Amer. J. Psychiat.,* 1968, *125(2),* 168–178.

CLAYTON, P. J., HALIKAS, J. A. & MAURREE, W. L. The depression of widowhood. *Brit. J. Psychiat.,* 1972, *126(554),* 71–77

EASSON, W. M. The family of the dying child. *Pediatric Clinics of North America,* 1972, *19(4),* 1157–1165.

ENGEL, GEORGE L. Grief and grieving. *Amer. J. Nursing,* 1964, *69(9),* 93–98.

FARBERON, N. (Ed.). *Taboo topics.* New York: Atherton Press, 1963.

FEIFEL, HERMAN (Ed.). *The meaning of death.* New York: McGraw-Hill, 1965.

GREENE, T., & KING, H. E. Behavioral problems in the leukemic child. Paper presented at National Conference for Pediatric Nurses, Atlanta, November, 1974.

GLASER, B. G. & STRAUSS, A. *Awareness of dying.* Chicago: Aldine Publishing Co., 1965.

GUNTHER, J. *Death be not proud.* New York: Modern Library, 1953.

HEFFRON, W. A., BOMMELAERE, K. & MASTERS, R. Group discussions with the parents of leukemic children. *Pediatrics,* 1973, *52(6),* 831–841.

HENDIN, D. *Death as a fact of life.* New York: Warner Paperback Library, 1974.

KING, H. E. Communication, message, recipient: a model of interpersonal communication. Unpublished manuscript, University of Georgia, 1971.

KING, H. E. The effects of expected emotionality of the recipient on the communication of bad news. Paper presented at Southeastern Psychological Association, April, 1973.

KING, H. E. & GREENE, T. Emotional reactions of children to a terminal illness. In preparation.

KÜBLER-ROSS, E. *On death and dying.* New York: The Macmillan Co., 1969.

KÜBLER-ROSS, E. On death and dying. *J. Amer. Med. Assoc.,* 1972, *221(2),* 174–179.

KUTSCHEE, A. H. Anticipatory grief, death, and bereavement: A continuum. In Edith Wyschogrod (ed.). *The phenomenon of death* New York: Harper Coloquin Books, 1973.

LINDEMANN, E. Symptomatology and management of acute grief. *Amer. J. Psychiat.,* 1944, *101,* 141–148.

MANDELBAUM, D. G. Social uses of funeral rites. In H. Feifel (Ed.). *The meaning of death.* New York: McGraw-Hill, 1965.

MILTON, G. W. The care of the dying. *Med. J. Australia,* 1972, *2,* 177–182.

MITFORD, J. *The American way of death.* New York: Fawcett-World, 1969.

NAGY, M. H. The child's view of death. In H. Feifel (Ed.). *The meaning of death.* New York: McGraw-Hill, 1965.

OHEN, D. What to tell cancer patients: a study of medical attitudes. *J. Amer. Med. Assoc.,* 1961, *175,* 1120–1128.

PEARSON, L. (Ed.). *Death and dying: current issues in the treatment of the dying person.* Cleveland: Case Western Reserve, 1969.

PINE, V. R. Grief work and dirty work: the aftermath of an aircrash. Unpublished manuscript, Dartmouth College, 1971.

PINE, V. R. Institutionalized communication about dying and death. Unpublished manuscript, Dartmouth College, 1971.

PINE, V. R. The sociology of death. *American Funeral Director,* 1969, *92,* 29–30.

QUINT, J. G. *The nurse and the dying patient.* New York: Macmillan, 1967.

REES, W. D. & LUTKINS, S. G. Mortality of bereavement. *Brit. Med. J.,* 1967.

SAUL, E. V. & KASS, T. S. Study of anticipated anxiety in a medical school setting. *J. Med. Educ.,* 1969, *44,* 526.

SCHOWALTER, J. Childhood mourning: do children and funerals mix? Paper presented at Emory University School of Medicine, 1974.

Spinetta, J. J., Rigler, D. & Karon, M. Anxiety in the dying child. *Pediatrics*, 1973, *52*, 841–845.

Wahl, C. N. The fear of death. In H. Feifel (Ed.). *The meaning of death*. New York: McGraw-Hill, 1965.

West, D. The psychology of death in geriatrics. *J. Amer. Geriat. Soc.*, 1972, *20(7)*, 340–342.

Wyschogrod, E. (Ed.). *The phenomenon of death.* New York: Harper Coloquin Books, 1973.

The Critical Problem of Suicide

CHAPTER 11

THE PROBLEM

Available data suggest that in the United States suicide is probably one of the top ten causes of death (Hafen & Faux, 1972; World Health Organization, 1968). Because many actual suicides may not be ruled as self-destructive deaths by medical examiners, it is possible that the rate of death by suicide may actually be higher than official statistics suggest. Self-report data suggest that a significant percentage of teen-aged individuals and young adults have thought about suicide at some point in their lives. Thirty to 40 per cent of college students indicate having thought about committing suicide, and over 50 per cent of teen-agers and young adults indicate having had some experience with suicidal behavior in others (Craig & Setner, 1972; Leonard & Flinn, 1972; Murray, 1973). Although suicide is not a crisis that will inevitably be encountered by all persons in our society, the problem of suicide is serious enough so that each of us should have some information about the extent of the problem and about possible strategies for coping with suicidal behavior when it occurs.

Who commits suicide? Self-destructive behavior cuts across all economic, social, and ethnic barriers. There is no group which is immune to suicidal ideation and behavior. However, available data suggest that suicide rates may be different for different types of individuals.

Age

In general, the rate of suicide tends to be higher in older groups. In the United States and in many areas of the world, older persons, especially the aged, tend to be significantly higher suicide risks (Kramer, Pollack, Redick & Locke, 1972; Schneidman, Farberow & Litman, 1970; World Health Organization, 1968). The greater risk of suicide with old age tends to be particularly the case with white males (Kramer et al., 1972). The greater potential of suicide in aged persons should not suggest that young people do not commit suicide. Recent years have seen a dramatic and alarming increase in the suicide rate for teen-agers and young adults (Frederick & Resnik, 1971: Kramer et al., 1972). There are also some data to suggest that the suicide rates for college and university students may be significantly higher than for nonstudents of comparable age (World Health Organization, 1968).

Sex

Both males and females commit suicide. However, the death rate by suicide is higher for males than for females. On the other hand, the rate of *attempted* suicide is higher for females than it is for males (Lester, 1969; Westenkow, 1972). In the United States males are more likely than females to be suicide committers, whereas females are more likely than males to be suicide attempters.

Ethnic Group

Although statistics sometimes conflict regarding suicide rates for different ethnic groups in the United States, available evidence indicates that on the average the death rate by suicide for blacks appears to be lower than the suicide rate for whites (Kramer et al., 1972; Westenkow, 1972). However, there are some recent indications that in the 18-30 age range the suicide rate for young blacks may actually be higher than the rate for other ethnic groups in the United States (Frederick & Resnik, 1971; Seiden, 1971).

American Indians have higher rates of suicide than the national average, and on some reservations the rate of self-destructive behavior is several times greater than the rate for the population as a whole (Kramer et al., 1972; Resnik & Zizmary, 1971).

Marital Status

In general the suicide rates tend to be lower for individuals who are married than for individuals who are not (Kramer et al., 1972; Shneidman et al., 1970; Westenkow, 1972). The rates of self-destructive behavior for divorced and widowed individuals tend to be significantly higher than the rates for married persons (Bock & Webber, 1972; Kramer et al., 1972; World Health Organization, 1968). Finally, the rate for single persons tends to be somewhere between the rate for married persons and the rate for divorced or widowed individuals.

Method

What self-destructive methods are selected by persons who attempt or commit suicide? The methods employed seem to vary significantly for different countries. For example, poisoning seems to be the most frequent method in Brazil, whereas in the British Isles one of the most frequent methods is death by domestic gas (World Health Organization, 1968). In the United States, however, firearms are used as the means of inflicting injury more frequently than any other method. American males and females exhibit differences in the method most often used in suicidal behavior. The most frequently used method for males is some form of firearm, followed in frequency by hanging, gas fumes, and poison. For females the most frequently used methods are poisoning and gases, followed in frequency by the use of firearms and hanging (Hafen

& Faux; 1972; Kramer et al., 1972; Shneidman et al., 1970; World Health Organization, 1968).

CLUES TO SUICIDAL BEHAVIOR

Most experts on suicidal behavior argue that a significant majority of people who commit suicide communicate their self-destructive intent to other individuals in their environment. The available evidence supports this assertion, and it would seem that most individuals do in fact communicate their suicidal intent before actually attempting or committing suicide (Rudestam, 1971; Shneidman et al., 1970; Wahlquist & Pack, 1972). The question arises as to exactly what kinds of clues potentially self-destructive persons might give of their intent to commit suicide. Theory and research in suicide have suggested several possible clues of self-destructive intent (Hafen & Faux, 1972; Lester, 1972; Rudestam, 1971; Shneidman et al., 1970).

Verbal Clues

An individual contemplating or actually planning a suicidal act may communicate this intention verbally in a very *direct* manner. Most of these direct communications will probably be made to relatives or close friends (Rudestam, 1971). Statements such as "I am going to kill myself," or "My parents will be a lot better off after I am dead," are examples of very direct verbal clues to potential suicide. Verbal clues to suicide may also be given in an *indirect* way. Indirect verbal clues are less obvious, and the verbal statements often have a "suicidal double-meaning." Statements such as "This is the last time I will ever see such a beautiful sunset," or "What is it like to die from an overdose of sleeping pills?" may imply potential suicidal behavior, but on the other hand, the statements could very well have a perfectly harmless meaning. Indirect clues are more difficult to evaluate than direct clues, but the presence of such indirect verbal clues should signal the observer to look for the presence of other possible clues to suicidal behavior.

Nonverbal, Behavioral Clues

Suicidal clues can be given not only through verbal communication but also through overt behavior. *Direct* behavioral clues to suicide are perhaps the least ambiguous of all. Self-destructive actions and suicide attempts offer clear indications of the potential of actual self-destruction. Even if fatal consequences are clearly impossible, life-threatening actions should be regarded as clues to potential suicide. *Indirect* behavioral clues to suicide may also be given. As with indirect verbal clues, indirect behavioral clues to suicide may be quite ambiguous, having a harmless alternative explanation. Indirect behavioral clues to suicide are behaviors that suggest a preparation for death. Preparation for going away, putting affairs in order, and preparations for one's death and funeral can be regarded as potential clues to suicide. For example, purchasing a casket for oneself is an example of an indirect behavioral clue to suicide. In a Midwestern town, a middle-aged male purchased a casket for himself and later on the same day committed suicide by shooting himself with a pistol. The purchasing of the casket was an indirect behavioral clue to suicidal behavior.

There are further clues to potential suicidal behavior that may be useful in the interpretation of ambiguous verbal and nonverbal indicants of suicidal behavior. The interpretation of indirect clues in the context of other clues to suicidal behavior may become a less ambiguous task.

Situational Clues

Nonprofessionals see situational stress as an important factor in causing suicide (Selby & Calhoun, 1975), and the presence of situational stresses on an individual are in fact another clue to potential suicidal behavior (Shneidman, 1970). When the situation in which

the individual finds himself involves great stress to him, then the potential for suicide is probably increased. The death of a spouse, financial ruin, disfigurement, and painful physical problems are examples of severe situational stresses. It must be remembered that whereas there are situational factors that would be very stressful to most individuals in our society, certain situational factors may be stressful to the particular individual in question but would not be perceived as particularly stressful to most other persons. For example, the death of a pet cat might not be regarded as an overwhelming stress by most adult individuals; however, the death of a pet cat could feasibly constitute an extremely stressful occurrence for an elderly widow who has little social interaction with other persons. Hence, there may be obvious situational clues to suicidal danger, but situational clues may also exist that are not apparent from a brief examination of the situation. The presence of severe stress in a situation should be regarded as a clue to potential suicidal behavior.

Warning Signals

Up to this point three categories of possible clues to potential suicide have been examined: verbal clues, nonverbal clues, and situational clues. Whenever these indications of suicidal potential are present, there are several "warning signals" that suggest that the suicidal danger should be viewed with particular seriousness. (1) *Depression*. Individuals who are depressed indicate feeling hopeless, helpless, and without control over the things that happen to them (Beck, 1967; Calhoun, Cheney & Dawes, 1974; Melges & Bowlby, 1969). The rate of suicide for individuals who are clinically depressed is much higher than the national average (Paykel & Dienett, 1971). Hence, depression should be regarded as a danger signal in individuals who exhibit other suicidal clues (Shneidman et al., 1970). (2) *Disorientation*. When an individual is experiencing hallucinations and/or delusions, when he is confused and unsure about "reality" as we see it, the danger of suicide is probably greatly increased. When an individual is "acting crazy" or, in the words of the professionals, when an individual is exhibiting

psychotic behavior, the presence of suicidal clues should be regarded with the utmost seriousness. (3) *Panic Reactions.* Individuals in a state of strong, blind panic may present strong suicidal potential. Although probably relatively rare, panic reactions when suicidal clues exist should also be regarded as providing additional warning of suicidal potential. (4) *Presence of a suicidal plan.* When the individual provides clues of suicidal intent and in addition has a specific plan for his self-destruction, the suicidal potential should probably be regarded as very serious. If the individual has already formulated a plan, observers should probably assume that the risk of actual suicidal behavior is very high.

This discussion of suicidal clues may lead some individuals to suspect suicidal intentions in all of their friends, relatives, and acquaintances because some of the clues may be observed relatively frequently. It is clear that not all individuals who are under stress, not all individuals who are clinically depressed, and so on will either commit or attempt suicide. Each particular clue must be evaluated within the context in which it occurs, and the present outline will serve only as a basic frame of reference to evaluate suicidal danger. The question that is often asked, however, is "What do you do when the clues are there?" The appropriate response will, of course, differ with the specific situation. An appropriate response might involve tactfully asking how things are going, it might involve consultation with a professional, or in extreme cases it might involve direct intervention by law-enforcement personnel.

It is clear that we cannot live assuming suicidal intentions by everyone all of the time. However, suicide is a fact of life, and individuals should be prepared to confront potential suicidal situations when clues to suicidal behavior are noted. As Shneidman has suggested, "We may feel chagrined if we turn in a false alarm, but we would feel very much worse if we were too timid to pull the switch that might have prevented a real tragedy" (Shneidman, 1970, p. 439).

The clues given here in no way will permit the prediction of all individuals who commit suicide. It is not an infallible list, and it should not be regarded as such. This brief description of suicidal

clues should be seen as a fallible frame of reference that may be of utility when used wisely and skeptically.

THE CRISIS CENTER APPROACH
TO DIRECT SUICIDE PREVENTION

Psychologists frequently have a strong aversion to making statements about how certain problem behaviors should be handled, because each individual condition is unique and no universal set of guidelines applies in all cases. Therefore, the reader is cautioned to regard this discussion on suicide prevention procedures as a guideline that may be useful, but the discussion should not be regarded as an infallible manual on how to interact with suicidal persons.

Experience and research in the area of suicide prevention have suggested a series of steps that crisis center workers have found to be useful in contacts with persons expressing self-destructive intentions (Lamb, 1970; Murray, 1972; Shneidman, Farberow & Litman, 1970). Specific procedures vary from center to center, but in general, workers dealing with suicidal individuals are encouraged to keep the following steps in mind when talking to suicidal individuals: (1) Establish a relationship and obtain information; (2) clarify existing focal problems; (3) evaluate the suicidal danger; (4) assess the individual's resources; and (5) decide on a course of action.

Establish a Relationship and Obtain Information

Library shelves are full of books describing the appropriate manner in which an interviewer should behave in order to establish a good relationship with another person. Furthermore, as is the case with many skills, actual observation and work with real people is probably necessary for most individuals to develop the interpersonal skills necessary for working well with suicidal individuals. However, a common theme runs through much of the material on suicide prevention, and it can probably be summarized as follows: be patient, be understanding, be *empathetic*. The interpersonal behaviors described as empathetic have received much attention in the area of counseling and psychotherapy. Being empathetic does not mean that the individual confronted with a suicidal person must feel the hopelessness, depression, or anger that the suicidal person may be experiencing; empathy means that the individual should be able to understand what the other individual is feeling, to be able to see what the world looks like from the other person's eyes. In other words, to be able to "walk a mile in his shoes" and know what it feels like. The suicide worker, then, tries to be empathetic with the suicidal individual, trying to understand his feelings, his behaviors, and his perspectives.

The worker in a suicide prevention center is also encouraged to obtain relevant information. What information is relevant will vary with the specific situation: It may include age, sex, information about specific problem situations that may have served as a trigger for suicidal behaviors, specific stresses which the individual is currently undergoing, degree to which the suicide plan has already been implemented, and even the person's name and address if immediate medical help is necessary. Although specific questions merely to satisfy the curiosity of the worker should be avoided, obtaining information useful in dealing with the suicidal crisis is very appropriate. In most situations, information about the presence of the suicidal clues just listed can help in evaluating the danger of actual self-destructive behavior.

Clarification of Existing Focal Problems

Suicidal persons are very often confused. The suicidal individual may have some difficulty thinking clearly about the problems that have led him (or her) to see suicide as a reasonable alternative. Furthermore, in many cases where a person is suicidal, the act of suicide is seen as a solution to a certain problem which is of central, major importance to the individual. The worker is encouraged to help the suicidal individual clarify the severity of the problem, the exact nature of the problem(s), and the like. The worker helps the individual clarify the problem by asking specific questions, by occasionally offering tentative hypotheses about certain things, and by constantly checking the accuracy of his perceptions of the suicidal person's problem.

Evaluation of Suicidal Danger

The list of suicidal clues already discussed offers the suicide crisis worker a list of signs that signal the degree of danger that the individual will actually commit suicide. During all parts of the worker's contact with the suicidal individual, constant information processing as to the actual danger of self-destructive actions should occur. The evaluation of suicidal danger can be of crucial importance in deciding on an appropriate course of action.

Assess the Individual's Resources

The word *resources* appears often in literature about all kinds of crises, including suicide. Resources in this context refers to individual competencies, other people, places, or things that can help the individual with his current difficulty. For the suicidal individual, the list of potential resources is long and includes some of the following: nuclear family, relatives, religious organizations, clergymen, teachers, police, and community mental health centers. The list could go on and on, but the important point is that the worker is encouraged to obtain specific data about the resources available to the particular suicidal individual. The strengths of the suicidal individual himself are also considered resources, and the worker formulates some hypotheses about the specific abilities, competencies, and emotional resources that the suicidal individual demonstrates, as well as areas in which the suicidal individual demonstrates some weakness. Although even untrained persons probably can assess most resources adequately, the assessment of what might be called "personality" strengths and weaknesses probably cannot be adequately done by persons without practical experience in suicide prevention work.

Decide on a Course of Action

The suicide prevention worker, in conference with the suicidal individual, decides on the most appropriate action for the suicidal individual to take. The point at which a decision for immediate action occurs may be after a few short minutes, or in some cases it may take a few hours. It must be remembered that the decision about a course of action should be reached *together* with the caller, rather than the worker presenting the suicidal person with a prescription of what must be done. Many, if not most of the courses of action decided upon in suicide prevention involve the mobilization of the resources to which the individual has access. These run the gamut of those resources the worker has assessed. The specific role played by the resources utilized varies and can include staying with the individual during the night so that the suicidal person has someone with whom to talk, sedating medication given at the emergency room of a hospital, appointments at a psychology clinic for immediate help with distressing depressive feelings, and so on.

The focus of the crisis-center approach to suicide prevention is upon dealing effectively with the immediate suicidal feelings and then to refer the individual to other resources where help for other problems can be found. In many instances the crisis center will help the individual deal with the immediate self-destructive impulse but will refer the individual to other resources for help in working on longer-lasting suicidal feelings. In many ways, the crisis-center approach to suicide can be conceptualized as a "buck-passing" system, where the goal is to help the individual with the self-destructive feelings and behaviors which now threaten his life; when the immediate danger of self-destruction is past, the "buck is passed" by having the individual draw on resources available to him.

Community Resources

The outline just given describes briefly the approach that workers in a crisis center might utilize in helping suicidal persons.

The persons who first encounter suicidal individuals, however, may very well not be the trained professionals and paraprofessionals of a suicide prevention center. The first persons to encounter suicidal feelings and behaviors may very well be individuals who have no training at all in suicide prevention. What should they do? The outline may well serve as a possible frame of reference for interacting with persons who express suicidal feelings. The major difference, however, probably occurs in the decision about a course of action. Nonprofessionals who help suicidal persons decide on a course of action are able to contact the professionals and the paraprofessionals who have been trained in suicide prevention. In most communities in the United States several resources are available with personnel specifically trained in helping suicidal individuals.

Suicide prevention centers may be the best resource to draw upon in helping a suicidal friend, relative, or acquaintance. A direct call or visit to a suicide prevention center may be a very good course of action for most persons who express suicidal feelings. The specific names vary from location to location: hot-line, emergency service, suicide prevention center, and crisis service are some of the most frequently used names. The telephone operator can usually provide the number of such a center when the caller is unable to locate the number himself.

Local mental health facilities are another possible source of help. Although they may not have separate numbers listed as "hot-line" or such, many community mental health facilities maintain personnel who are available on call, 24 hours a day.

Finally, mental health professionals in private practice may be of assistance. Professional clinical psychologists and psychiatrists usually have some experience with suicidal persons. The drawback here is that contacts during odd hours are difficult, and the expense is probably greater than for a public agency.

Up to this point in the discussion we have focused on the situation where an individual gives evidence that he feels suicidal, but where actual life-threatening behavior has not occurred in the immediate past. The issue of what to do when an individual has already engaged in a suicidal action involves something of an ethical dilemma. Although talking to an individual in the hope that his professed goal of self-destruction will be relinquished involves no physical coercion, what are we to do when an individual's own self-destruction is imminent or when an individual has already done severe intentional physical harm to himself? In this situation, the only way in which self-destruction can be prevented may be to contact law enforcement or other personnel who will physically restrain the individual from self-destruction or who will take an individual for medical aid, in spite of the individual's desire for suicide.

An Afterthought

Although this information is of help in understanding the phenomena of suicidal behavior, and the guidelines offered provide a framework for dealing with suicidal persons, it is probably useful to remember that it is impossible for you to prevent all suicide attempts by an individual who is strongly self-destructive. It is very possible that intervention at crucial points and referral to appropriate resources may in fact save that individual's life. Individuals who obtain information on suicidal behavior and suicide prevention may assume that they are now equipped to prevent suicide whenever suicidal feelings are expressed; that is probably an incorrect assumption. Although much can be done to reduce the probability that an individual will actually kill himself, the individual himself is the one who ultimately decides. When an individual expresses suicidal thoughts, it would seem reasonable that those who care for the preservation of human life should intervene, to the extent that it is possible; however, when an individual does destroy himself, the responsibility for taking his own life would seem ultimately to be his own (Murray, 1972).

THE AFTERMATH OF SUICIDE

The survivors of an individual's suicide have undergone not only the death of a friend, relative, or acquaintance, but in addition the survivors must cope with the stress of knowing that the death was self-inflicted. Death is a severe crisis for the survivors in any situation, and suicidal death is probably an even more severe crisis. The survivors of the suicide of a family member experience a variety of distressing reactions (Cain, 1972; Pretzel, 1972; Scholz, 1971), and some of these will now be examined.

Survey data suggest that the public believes that the survivors of a relative's suicide would feel shame (Ginsburg, 1971). The available data do in fact suggest that unfortunately the survivors of a suicidal death do in fact experience embarrassment and shame about the death (Cain, 1972; Pretzel, 1972). As Shneidman (1970, p. 153) has suggested, "the suicide puts his skeleton in the survivor's psychological closets. No other kind of death in our society creates such lasting emotional scars as does suicide."

The survivors may also experience guilt. The survivors may blame themselves for many things about the suicidal act and for many things about the dead individual. The survivors may feel that the suicide could have been prevented if only they had paid more attention, if only they had listened, if only they had done the right thing.

Denial is also observed in survivors of a family member's suicidal death. Denial here refers to the failure to accept the reality of certain things or the failure to perceive certain things. An example may help clarify this reaction. A 13-year-old boy committed suicide by hanging himself. The boy's father refused to accept the reality of his son's suicidal death, and in spite of incontrovertible evidence to the contrary insisted that "foul play" was involved in his son's death (Whitis, 1972).

Feelings of hostility may also occur. Sometimes the angry behavior observed may be directed toward the suicide, but often the angry behavior is exhibited toward other persons in the individual's current environment. For example, the clergyman may be verbally assaulted for performing a very poor burial service or the police may be chastised for conducting such an incompetent and obviously useless investigation of the death.

Finally, as with any death, great feelings of depression and sadness may also be experienced.

Friends and Acquaintances

When a friend or an acquaintance dies, the survivors often feel concerned about how to relate to the remaining family members. This feeling of inadequacy over what to do is probably very much greater when the death is a suicide. Perhaps because of this feeling of inadequacy in relating to the surviving family members, the friends of the family may try to avoid any interaction with them. Our social system tends to produce much supportive behavior when a family member dies: gifts of food, flowers, visits to express sympathy. However, when the death is by suicide the surviving family may receive significantly less of the shared grief and emotional support that would have occurred had the death not been a suicide (Cain, 1972; Pretzel, 1972).

What can you do when the death was a suicide? There are some things which may help in dealing with the surviving family members of a friend's suicide. First, is the maintenance of the usual and expected social contacts with the survivors. What would be done had the individual died of causes other than suicide? Follow whatever guidelines you consider appropriate for your social group. Second, when interacting with the family, it may be helpful both to the visitor and to the surviving family members to talk about the individual's *death* rather than about his *suicide*. In other words, when it is appropriate to discuss the individual who has died, steer away from discussing the self-destructive act itself and focus on the fact that the individual has in fact died. Third, if resources have not been mobilized already, help the surviving family to do so. The surviving family is undergoing severe stress, and the mobilization of resources that may help the survivors deal with this stress can prove useful. Usually, when the family is connected in some way with a religious organization, a clergyman may be contacted. Other family members may also need to be contacted. Any resource that will be helpful to the family in dealing with the current situation should be remembered. Finally, it has been suggested (Pretzel, 1972; Resnik, 1972) that a visit to the survivors by a trained counselor as soon after the death as possible can prove useful in helping the survivors cope with the situation. However, as most localities do not have counselors associated with local agencies who róutinely engage in such visits, the clergyman who has training and experience with death and bereavement may be the one résource person whom the family will accept and who is available in most communities in this country. Suicide prevention centers and local mental health agencies may have such personnel, but the probabilities of finding personnel trained specifically in dealing with the aftermath of suicide are probably low.

In summary, when a friend commits suicide, the best yardstick to use is probably to focus on the fact that the individual has died, and then ask yourself, "What is appropriate and helpful to the survivors, when a family member has died?"

A Final Note

The goal of the present chapter has been to provide some information on the problem of suicide, some of the possible clues to suicidal behavior, a summary of a crisis-center approach to suicidal persons, and an indication of the aftermath of an individual's suicide. Although some practical suggestions have been included in this chapter, it is not without some hesitancy that we have done so. As clinicians we are aware of the infinite variety of distressed human reactions, and it is not possible to turn readers of a discussion of suicide into expert professionals. However, the information summarized here may provide a useful frame of reference for dealing with the crisis of suicide if it is ever directly encountered.

To avoid too much abstraction we have purposefully chosen not to discuss theoretical elaborations on the causes of suicidal behavior. Readers interested in such a discussion may wish to consult Durkheim (1951), Frederick and Resnik (1971), and Litman (1970).

PROJECTS AND QUESTIONS

1. For the discussion of the following issues, groups of 6 to 8 individuals may be formed. The task of the group is to examine feelings, arguments, and opinions which are relevant to the following questions:

a. If an individual is actually going to kill himself, should that person be physically restrained from self-destruction?

b. What do you say to a friend whose brother recently committed suicide?

c. What are some of the reasons for the fact that males tend to commit suicide more frequently than females, but females attempt suicide more often?

d. Other than direct preventive methods (suicide prevention centers, intervention by law enforcement personnel, and so on), what are some steps that can be taken to reduce suicidal deaths in the United States?

2. If a suicide prevention center or a crisis center exists in your community, one or more individuals may wish to contact one of the supervisors of the service and ask some questions about experiences with the service. It may be possible to arrange a visit to the center to make extended observations of its functioning. These individuals may want to present a report on their experiences.

3. Under the direction of the instructor or supervisor, individuals volunteer to participate in different role-playing situations in which one (or more) individuals deal with a suicidal crisis role-played by another volunteer. The individual playing the potentially suicidal person elaborates the role suggested by selecting randomly one item from each of the categories listed:

Age: a. 18 b. 35 c. 57 d. 74

Sex: a. Male b. Female

Focal Problems:

a. None apparent

b. Recent death of a close family member

c. Catastrophic loss of financial nature

d. Severe physical disease

Warning Signals:

a. None apparent

b. Severe depression

c. Confusion and disorientation

Resources:

a. Family, clergyman, close friends

b. No family, 3 or 4 close friends

c. Stranger in city, no immediate resources apparent

d. Suicide prevention center, family, close friends

The individual playing the role of the suicidal person should be the only individual who is aware of the role he is playing ahead of time. After each individual situation has been played, the observers and the participants discuss how the situation was handled, with particular attention being devoted to what was done well. The discussion should occur under the direction of the appropriate instructor or supervisor.

4. In localities where crisis centers exist, many of them offer opportunities for volunteer work. A selection process usually occurs, because many centers have more volunteers than they can utilize. In most cases it will require a significant amount of time and energy, but the opportunities for learning can be great.

SUGGESTED READINGS

Popular Press

H. EPSTEIN. A sin or a right? *New York Times Magazine*, September 8, 1974, 91–94. Brief discussion of suicide, some statistics and some possible causes.

Upsurge in suicides and ways to prevent them. *U. S. News and World Report*, July 1, 1974, 41–42. Brief, slightly oversimplified discussion of current data on suicidal behavior in the U.S.

L. WAINWRIGHT. The man in the middle. *Life*, July 21, 1972, 55–56. Portrait of the suicide of Paul Cabell, the assistant principal of a racially troubled Flint, Michigan, high school.

Advanced Sources

A. C. CAIN (Ed.). *Survivors of suicide*. Springfield, Ill.: C. Thomas, 1972. Clinical discussions of various aspects of the aftermath of suicide. Most discussions tend to emphasize the psychoanalytic perspective.

P. W. PRETZEL. *Understanding and counseling the suicidal person*. Nashville: Abingdon Press, 1972. An uncomplicated presentation for clergymen and counselors. Informative discussions of various issues confronting those working with suicidal persons.

E. S. SHNEIDMAN, N. L. FARBEROW & R. E. LITMAN (Eds.). *The psychology of suicide*. New York: Science House, 1970. A major source on suicidal behavior. A collection of articles and research reports on various aspects of suicidal behavior.

REFERENCES

BOCK, E. W. & WEBBER, I. L. Suicide among the elderly: Isolating widowhood and mitigating alternatives. *J. Marriage Family,* 1972, *34*, 24–31.

CAIN, A. C. (Ed.). *Survivors of suicide.* Springfield, Ill.: C. Thomas, 1972.

CALHOUN, L. G., CHENEY, T. & DAWES, A. S. Locus of control, self-reported depression and perceived causes of depression. *J. Consulting and Clinical Psychol.* 1974, in press.

DURKHEIM, E. *Suicide.* Glencoe, Ill.: Free Press, 1951.

FREDERICK, C. J. & RESNIK, H. L. How suicidal behaviors are learned. *Amer. J. Psychotherapy*, 1971, *25*, 37–55.

FREDERICK, C. J. & RESNIK, H. L. P. Self-destruction: A national problem. *Social Service Outlook*, 1971, *6*, (17).

HAFEN, B. Q. & FAUX, E. J. (Eds.). *Self-destructive behavior*. Minneapolis: Burgess, 1972.

KRAMER, M., POLLACK, E. S., REDICK, R. W. & LOCKE, B. L. *Mental disorders—Suicide.* Cambridge: Harvard Press, 1972.

LAMB, C. W. Telephone therapy: Some common errors and fallacies. *Voices*, 1970, *5* (4), 42–46.

LEONARD, C. V. & FLINN, D. E. Suicidal ideation and behavior in youthful nonpsychiatric populations. *J. Consulting and Clinical Psychol.*, 1972, *38*, 366–371.

LESTER, D., Suicidal behavior in men and women. *Mental Hygiene*, 1969, *53*, 340–345.

LESTER, D. *Why people kill themselves.* Springfield, Ill.: C. Thomas, 1972.

LITMAN, R. E. Sigmund Freud on suicide. In E. S. Shneidman et al. (Eds.). *The psychology of suicide.* New York: Science House, 1970.

MURRAY, D. C. Suicidal and depressive feelings among college students. *Psychol. Reports*, 1973, *33*, 175–181.

MURRAY, D. C. The suicide threat: Base rates and appropriate therapeutic strategy. *Therapy: Theory, Research, and Practice,* 1972, *9*, 175–179.

PAYKEL, E. S. & DIENETT, M. N. Suicide attempts following acute depression. *J. Nerv. Ment. Dis.,* 1971, *153*, 234–243.

PRETZEL, P. W. *Understanding and counseling the suicidal person.* Nashville: Abingdon Press, 1972.

RESNIK, H. & ZIZMARY, L. Observations on suicidal behavior among American Indians. *Amer. J. Psychiat.*, 1971, *127*, 882–887.

RUDESTAM, K. E. Stockholm and Los Angeles: A cross-cultural study of the communication of suicidal intent. *J. Consulting and Clinical Psychol.*, 1971, *36*, 82–90.

SCHOLZ, J. A. The aftermath of suicide: Reactions of the family. *Life-Threatening Behavior*, 1971, *2*, 86–91.

SEIDEN, R. H. We're driving young blacks to suicide. *Psychol. Today,* 1970, *4*, 24–28.

SELBY, J. W. & CALHOUN, L. G. Social perception of suicide: The effects of three factors on causal attributions. *J. Consulting and Clinical Psychol.*, 1975, *43*, 431.

SHNEIDMAN, E. S., FARBERROW, N. L. & LITMAN, R. E. *The psychology of suicide.* New York: Science House, 1970.

SHNEIDMAN, E. S. Preventing suicide. In E. S. Schneidman et al. (Eds.) *The psychology of suicide.* New York: Science House, 1970, pp. 429–440.

WAHLQUIST, J. & PACK, D. Suicide-evaluation, assessment and prediction. In B. Q. Hafen & E. J. Faux (Eds.). *Self-destructive behavior.* Minneapolis: Burgess, 1972.

WESTENKOW, K. Epidemiology of suicide. In B. Q. Hafen & E. J. Faux (Eds.). *Self-destructive behavior.* Minneapolis: Burgess, 1972.

WHITIS, P. R. The legacy of a child's suicide. In A. C. Cain (Ed.). *Survivors of suicide.* Springfield, Ill.: C. Thomas, 1972, pp. 155–168.

²World Health Organization. *Prevention of suicide.* Geneva⁰ 1968.

A Consumer's Guide to Seeking Professional Help

CHAPTER 12

In this book we have reviewed a series of critical life problems. When confronted with these and other problems in living, individuals can experience a significant increase in subjective discomfort, a decrease in the efficiency with which they meet the demands of every day life, and in some circumstances can begin to perceive reality differently from most other persons. When such situations arise, how can one go about seeking help from professional sources in such a way as to obtain the probability of maximum benefit? In this final chapter we will be giving consideration to the question, "Where and how do I go for help with psychological problems?"

Of course it will be impossible for us to provide a complete guide to professional help-seeking, but we hope to give some reasonable direction for an intelligent approach. With this goal in mind, we will look at the following things in this chapter: (1) brief descriptions of four of the most prevalent approaches to psychological treatment, (2) a look at the question of whether psychotherapy does work, and (3) a suggested way of selecting a source of help.

APPROACHES TO PSYCHOLOGICAL TREATMENT

There are numerous different "brands" of psychological treatment. One recent book on different types of psychotherapy, for the feelings the client is having; it means being able to "walk a mile in her shoes" and being able to understand what the world looks like from her perspective. *Unconditional positive regard* means simply not being judgmental toward the client. *Genuineness* means the therapist's ability to be aware of what her own feelings are and to be able to depend on her own experience in the relationship and not to be "phony."

The interactions between the therapist and client are primarily verbal. The client meets with the therapist, and they talk. The therapist (ideally) is able to be genuine, to have unconditional positive regard for the client, and to empathize with the client. Although there is no hard and fast rule about meeting times and places, the client usually meets with the therapist in his office, and the meetings between client and therapist usually have time limitations which tend to run about one hour or so.

The therapist's primary technique is "reflection," by which the therapist tries to mirror back to the client what the client's feelings, thoughts, and experiences are as seen by the therapist. The reflection approach developed by Rogers ties in with the original assumption that under suitable conditions the client can sort out his own problem. Reflection, undertaken in an atmosphere of empathy, positive regard, and genuineness, is assumed to help the client reach his own decisions and his own solutions to the problem. It should be emphasized that client-centered therapists typically do not use reflection exclusively, nor is the therapist's intervention completely nondirective (Truax, 1966). However, the reflection technique is a key characteristic of what the therapist says and does with his client. The brief example of therapist reflection given here is a hypothetical situation:

Client: I've been married for 20 years now. The kids have all left home, . . . they are all independent now. I've been what you'd call a housewife, I guess, for 20 years. Now that there are no more babies to look after and the housework is reduced, I just don't know what to do with myself. I've tried several things, but nothing is really satisfying. I would really like to find one thing that I enjoyed doing and then become really good at it . . . but I just don't know what.

Therapist: You've reached a point in your life where you have a lot of time for yourself, but it's been hard trying to find one specific thing that is really satisfying for you.

example, listed 10 different types of psychoanalytic therapy
(Kiernan, 1974)! It is clear that we will not be summariz
the available types of psychotherapy and behavior change me
Our goal is to briefly summarize four of the most popul
proaches. The four methods we have chosen to summari
psychoanalysis, Rogerian or client-centered therapy, gestal
apy, and behavior therapy. Our discussion of these
approaches will be in terms of individual sessions, but the
general principles would apply to group therapy conducted i
of these four approaches.

Client-Centered Psychotherapy

The type of approach called client-centered or nondir
psychotherapy was originally developed by Carl Rogers
American psychologist (e.g., 1942, 1951, 1961). Rogers deve
his ideas about the process of therapy primarily (but
exclusively) out of his work with college students. The app
to helping troubled persons developed by Rogers is an examp
a counseling approach which adopts the humanistic perspe
described in Chapter 1.

The main assumption of client-centered psychotherapy is
given suitable conditions, the troubled individual can sort ou
deal with his/her own problem situation. The goal of the
sessions, from the client-centered point of view, is to provide
"suitable conditions" in the interactions between the client
the therapist.

Rogers and a large group of other psychologists (e.g., T
& Mitchel, 1971) have given extensive attention to the "suit
conditions" for good psychotherapy. The procedures employe
the therapist to achieve these conditions can be summarize
three terms: empathy, unconditional positive regard, and genu
ness (Meador & Rogers, 1973). The idea is simply that if
therapist or counselor can be empathetic and genuine and h
positive regard for the client, then the client himself will be abl
make the necessary positive changes to deal with the problen
hand. To have *empathy* means to be able to understand the wo
to see the world from the client's viewpoint, and to underst

The therapist reflects back to the client the ideas and feelings that the client is expressing. The Rogerian assumption is that if it is done under the "suitable conditions," then the client will experience positive change, leading to a solution of the problem situation and to increased psychological well-being.

Carl Rogers' ideas have generated much research in the area of psychotherapy and in a subsequent section we will look briefly at some of that research data.

Psychoanalytic Psychotherapy

Psychoanalytic therapy began with the work of Sigmund Freud around the turn of the century. It was the first major approach to psychological treatment. Freud found that some forms of neurotic problems appeared to be improved through talking; and over the course of working with disturbed persons, he developed a rather elaborate theory of how these disorders develop. The theory, referred to as psychoanalysis, focused on conflicts inside the individual as the principle source of psychiatric problems. As Freud believed these conflicts were often unconscious, the over-all goal of treatment became to help the person become aware of these conflicts.

As the theory developed, three ingredients of therapy became central. These included insight, transference, and working-through. *Insight* refers to the idea that the patient needs to become aware of the conflict and its origins in his/her past. Usually, this is accomplished by the person talking about his life and particularly his early development. *Transference* is a phenomenon in which the patient responds to the therapist "as if" the therapist were another person. Freud assumed that the unconscious conflict had its origin in an interpersonal relationship. In transference, the patient acts as if the therapist were the person involved in that early conflict. For instance, if the individual has experienced a lot of anger in relation to an authoritarian father, the patient may express anger toward the therapist when it is not justified by the therapist's behavior. Typically, it is assumed that the conflict into which the patient gains insight will be involved in this transference relationship. The process of *"working-through"* means the troubled individual applies the insight gained to the transference relationship as well as other current relationships in his life. Presumably, through this form of treatment the individual will be better able to control his responses to present situations.

When Freud began this form of treatment, the troubled individual would come to his office four or five times a week, lie down on Freud's couch, and merely say everything that came to mind. The therapist's statements typically took the form of "interpretations." These were statements that offered potential explanations, e.g., "I wonder if your anger toward your father is being expressed in relation to your boss now." The nature of these interpretations shifted as the person moved through insight, transference, and working-through.

Currently, many clinicians still use a variation of this treatment approach. Most of the time now, the troubled person comes in to see the clinician once or twice a week. The talking is done sitting in chairs on a face-to-face basis. Often the therapy is focused on a few areas of the individual's life. The therapist introduces as little of his own personality into the situation as possible. Thus, he maintains a fairly passive role, primarily listening to what the individual has to say and occasionally offering interpretative statements. This passive role is adopted in order to encourage the transference phenomenon.

Gestalt Therapy

Gestalt therapy is a "brand" of therapy that has become increasingly popular in the last 15 years. Gestalt therapy was developed primarily by Frederick Perls. This type of psychotherapy is a little more difficult to describe than other approaches, perhaps because clinicians and theorists in this area are still in the process of developing adequate theoretical ideas to complement the gestalt therapy techniques.

Perhaps one way of defining this type of therapeutic approach is to look at the goals of this approach. Several goals of gestalt therapy have been proposed (Brown, 1973; Harman, 1974a; Polster & Polster, 1973; Fagan & Sheperd, 1970), and we will look at a few goals here. Four of the most commonly stated are: awareness, responsibility, maturation, and authenticity.

Awareness is the client's recognition of what he is doing, what he is feeling, what he is thinking, and what he is planning. Awareness, for the gestalt therapist, is knowing "what you are experiencing now." *Responsibility* refers to the client's acceptance of responsibility for what he is doing, thinking, and feeling, i.e., to attribute the cause of his feelings, actions, and thoughts primarily to himself rather than to forces outside of himself. *Maturation* is simply growing up; the goal is for the client to be able to be independent without depending on others for emotional support. *Authenticity* is a goal of gestalt therapy that is occasionally parodied on TV programs and in movies. To be authentic is to say what you think and feel, to communicate honestly. Extreme examples of "authenticity" occasionally appear in TV sketches or in movies where an individual engages in a horrendous amount of intimate disclosure to a waiter in a restaurant or to the ticket seller at the movies. These represent extreme examples of the goal of authenticity.

Several techniques have been developed by gestalt therapists to help individuals achieve their goals. We will look briefly at a few of the techniques currently used by gestalt therapists: directed awareness, reversal, empty chair, exaggerations, and making statements (Fagan & Shepherd, 1970; Harman, 1974 b).

Directed awareness is a process in which the therapist simply calls attention to something about the client. The therapist asks the client to focus his attention on a specific behavior, thought or feeling. The goal is usually to simply make the client more aware of his experience.

Reversal is a technique in which the client is asked to role-play the opposite of the feeling indicated by his observable behavior. For example, if the client is smiling a good deal, laughing, and generally looking happy, the therapist might ask the client to role-play the opposite, i.e., to act sad and unhappy.

Empty chair is a rather simple technique developed by gestalt therapists. The client is asked to direct her attention to a chair that is empty and then to interact with people, things, or parts of herself that are imagined to be in that chair. For example, an individual who is overweight and who wishes to become thinner might be asked to talk to his "thin self," which he is to imagine is in the empty chair.

Exaggeration is a technique whereby the therapist asks the client to exaggerate certain aspects of either his verbal or his nonverbal behavior. For example, an individual who indicates he is angry at another person and at the same time mildly clenches his fist might be asked to exaggerate the clenching of his fist and then report on what sort of feelings he was experiencing as a result, what it made him think, and so on.

The last technique of gestalt therapy which we will describe is *making statements*. The technique is simply to instruct the client to stop asking questions and to make statements. In other words, where the client would normally ask a question, he is instructed to make a statement which communicates the same intent. For example, whereas an individual might want to ask his therapist, "Will you work with me now?", the client is encouraged to make a statement, which might be, "I would like you to work with me now."

These are only a few examples of the types of techniques employed by gestalt therapists. In looking at the description of the techniques one major difference between this approach and the client-centered approach becomes clear: The gestalt therapist tends to be considerably more active, more directive, and more in direct control of the therapy session than the Rogerian therapist. As with other forms of psychotherapy, the assumption is that the client obtains benefit from therapy primarily through his *interaction* with the therapist in the therapy session. The relationship and interaction of the therapist with her client, in the therapy sessions, are assumed to be of primary importance.

Behavior Therapy

In Chapter 1 we described a way of looking at behavior that we called the behavioral perspective. Behavior therapy is an approach to helping troubled persons which adopts the behavioral perspective.

Behavior therapy is a group of ideas and specific techniques designed to help people change their thoughts, feelings, and behaviors. The approach has at least two main characteristics: (1) the techniques and methods used are usually derived from research in various areas of psychology including experimental psychology, social psychology, and clinical psychology (Davison & Stuart, 1975) and (2) there tends to be a commitment by the behavior therapist to state the goals of treatment in explicit measurable terms.

Recently there has been much interest regarding the potential misuses of "behavior modification." It might be useful to clarify the difference between the term *behavior modification* and the term *behavior therapy* before we proceed with further discussion. *In general, behavior modification is a broader term than behavior therapy.* "Behavior modification" describes any systematic attempt to apply information derived from psychological research to change human behavior in an ethical manner (Stolz, Wienckowski & Brown, 1975).

The term *behavior therapy* is used to denote the systematic application of psychological techniques designed to help distressed persons change. These applications occur in a clinical setting (the office of a clinical psychologist, a counseling center), most often in a one-to-one relationship between the behavior therapist and his client(s).

What are the goals of behavior therapy? The group of techniques and procedures called behavior therapy do not, in themselves, offer any definition of the goal of therapy. In a sense, behavior therapy does not have any predetermined general goal as do gestalt or psychoanalytic psychotherapies. Different behavior therapists have tried to give their own definitions of possible goals (e.g., Adams, 1972), but using behavior therapy does not imply having any specific goal of therapy. *The goal of any specific instance of behavior therapy is selected primarily by the client*, in discussions with his therapist (Wilson & Davison, 1975).

There is a wide variety of behavior therapy techniques, designed to deal with a wide variety of psychological problems. Procedures have been developed for marriage counseling (Stuart, 1969), for the treatment of phobias (Stamfl & Levis, 1967; Wolpe, 1973), for the treatment of families in distress (Patterson, 1974), bed-wetting (Deheon & Sacks, 1972), sexual dysfunctions (see Chapter

3), overeating (Thoresen & Mahoney, 1974), and a wide variety of other human problems. The specific techniques, of course, vary with the specific problem and with the client's own goals for treatment. There are, however, some general features of behavior therapy that can be described.

The interaction between the behavior therapist and his client probably is the same as the other therapies described here in at least two ways: (1) the therapist and client meet regularly in an office or similar location and (2) the therapist tries to be understanding of the client's views and of his goals for himself.

Some further characteristics of behavior therapy, however, tend to make it unique. The therapist usually conducts a relatively intensive assessment of the problem situation for which the client wants help. For example, if a couple indicate that they are experiencing difficulties with their marriage and that they would like to improve their relationship, the first steps of therapy would involve a rather intensive assessment of several things: what exactly they mean by "marital difficulties"; when, where, and how often these difficulties occur, what happens before, during, and after a particular difficulty, and so on.

Once the behavior therapist has sufficient information, he will help the client formulate a plan to reach his own specific goal. It is at this point that the techniques and procedures derived from psychological research are introduced. What the specific procedures will be varies from case to case, and the procedures vary according to the type of problem. The treatment program will be considered successful when the goals originally specified by the client are reached.

In a way, the behavior therapist has a relationship with his clients that is similar to that of a consultant with his client. The client comes to the consultant (who presumably has expert knowledge) with a problem and obtains expert advice on how the problem can be solved. The client chooses what problems to work on, and the client may ask the consultant for alternative choices in treatment plans. The behavior therapist is an expert who presumably has extensive knowledge of techniques and procedures for helping people change. She draws on that knowledge to advise her client(s) on behavior-change strategies, but it is the client who has the ultimate right to decide on the goals of treatment.

DOES PSYCHOTHERAPY WORK?

Before we begin a discussion of this issue, perhaps it would be a good idea to clarify some terms. For our purposes, we are going to restrict the meaning of the term *psychotherapy* to those types of psychological interventions which rely primarily on verbal interchanges between the therapist and the client and which rely heavily on the relationship between the therapist and the client to achieve the desired goals of therapy. In the examples of treatment approaches we have discussed, the client-centered, gestalt, and psychoanalytic approaches would be considered different forms of psychotherapy. However, behavior therapy will *not* be considered a form of psychotherapy for our present purposes. It should be noted that others have included behavior therapy under the label of psychotherapy (e.g., Adams, 1972; Meltzoff & Kornreich, 1970).

Is the Question Too Broad?

Now that we have provided a general idea of what we mean by the term psychotherapy, let us begin to focus a little more directly on the issue of whether or not it works. The suggestion has been made (Howard & Orlinsky, 1972; Kiesler, 1971; Paul, 1967) that the question, "Does psychotherapy work?" is simply too broad. It has been suggested that the question that needs answering is, "What type of psychological intervention, with what type of client, works for what type of problem?" We agree that this specific question certainly merits attention.

As Meltzoff and Kornreich (1970) have pointed out, however, it also seems reasonable to look at the general question, to get some idea of whether psychotherapy works in general or not. In other words, what is the over-all "batting average" that psychotherapy has achieved in terms of the degree to which it has helped people with psychological difficulties?

Do the Criteria Agree?

How do we decide whether or not psychotherapy has produced

positive results? Do we ask the client, the clinical psychologist, an outside observer? The difficulties are further compounded because different criteria for measuring the results of psychotherapy may not agree with each other (Garfield, Prager & Bergin, 1971; Garfield, Prager & Bergin, 1974; Fiske, 1975; Luborsky, 1970). For example, whereas the client might rate himself as highly improved, the therapist might rate him as moderately improved and the individual's wife might rate him as not improved at all. The issue of who or what (e.g., psychological tests, job performance) is the best measure of the effect of psychotherapy is not within our scope. What should be made clear is that although the achievement of agreement might be possible (Berzins, Bednar & Severy, 1975), indications are that agreement between different measures of the effects of psychotherapy is probably low.

What Do the Data Suggest?

With these considerations in mind, let us now turn to an examination of the data regarding the usefulness of psychotherapy.

There have been strong arguments made that psychotherapy, especially psychoanalytic psychotherapy, is *not* useful (e.g., Eysenck, 1966; Rachman, 1971; Stuart, 1970). The general argument has been that psychotherapy has not been shown to be any better than just letting time go by. The idea is that the people who seem to get better after being in psychotherapy would have gotten better anyway without any professional help, just with the passage of time. These arguments have been supported by research data that seem to indicate that many individuals may in fact overcome their psychological problems without obtaining professional psychological help.

On the other hand, others have argued equally strongly that psychotherapy does in fact produce at least some positive results (e.g., Bergin, 1971; Meltzoff & Kornreich, 1970). The "pro-psychotherapy" arguments are bolstered by just as impressive an array of data as that marshalled by those who contend that psychotherapy has no demonstrable benefit.

So who is right? In our opinion, the data seem to favor the hypothesis that psychotherapy may in fact be helpful in many cases, but not all cases. Meltzoff and Kornreich review a large number of studies that support the idea that psychotherapy can be helpful. Among the studies reviewed by these authors there are 56 studies they consider to have at least adequate methodology. Of these studies, 84 per cent showed positive results for psychotherapy. Bergin (1971) has also reviewed studies that, he suggests, offer some modest evidence that psychotherapy can in fact be helpful.

So, we conclude that there is at least some evidence that some people may be helped by psychotherapy. The potential user needs to be aware that although the data seem to support the idea of the usefulness of psychotherapy in general, *there is no guarantee that psychotherapy will be helpful for any one particular individual.* The over-all "batting average" of psychotherapy is, in our opinion, a generally positive one, but the client of the psychotherapist has no guarantee of improvement.

CAN PSYCHOTHERAPY BE HARMFUL?

Yes, there does seem to be a possibility that in a small minority of cases psychotherapy may in fact be harmful to the client. Bergin (1966, 1970, 1971), Truax and Mitchell (1971), and others have presented data to suggest that it is possible that some individuals may actually be psychologically harmed by psychotherapy (e.g., become more distressed or uncomfortable, have more marital problems). Although it may be possible to argue over the validity of this "deterioration hypothesis" (e.g., Braucht, 1970), it would seem reasonable for the potential consumer of psychotherapy to be aware of the possibility that detrimental effects can occur. The available data indicate that if actual harm does occur, it will be in a minority of cases.

We regard the "deterioration hypothesis" as tentatively correct. The available evidence seems to indicate that although harmful effects from psychotherapy are by no means probable, they seem to be possible.

What Is the Bottom Line?

It must be recognized that the issue, "Does psychotherapy work?" is a very complex one and that our attempts to answer the question in a simple way means that we are missing some of the subtleties and complexities of the issue. Reduced to the most simple factors, however, there seem to be two ways of summarizing the data: (1) Evidence does seem to suggest that psychotherapy can be helpful, but it will not always be helpful; and (2) there is some evidence which supports the idea that psychotherapy may produce psychological harm in a small percentage of cases.

SOME THOUGHTS ON BEHAVIOR THERAPY

Our distinction between psychotherapy and behavior therapy is a very general one, and not absolutely precise. But, as a general distinction can be made, it seems reasonable to discuss these two general types of psychological interventions separately. We focus now on behavior therapy.

There is evidence to suggest that behavior therapy can be highly effective with several types of psychological problems. Among the most notable successes with this type of psychological intervention have been phobias (irrational fears), sexual dysfunctions (see Chapter 3), bed-wetting, and compulsive behaviors. Behavior therapy has been applied with success to many other types of problems, but as with any other form of psychological intervention results are not always successful.

Does Behavior Therapy Work?

At this point the answer to the general question, "Does behavior therapy work?" seems to be a qualified yes. Although a large amount of research on the usefulness of this approach to psychological treatment has already been done, much more research still needs to be done before the answer to the question of usefulness can be answered with confidence (Stolz et al., 1975). The available data indicate that behavior therapy can help in many cases and that the techniques used by behavior therapists hold considerable promise for further development. At present there are no data to suggest that behavior therapy techniques, as used by the practicing clinical psychologist, can cause psychological harm.

However, the issue of "symptom substitution" is often raised in connection with behavior therapy. If symptom substitution actually occurs, it would clearly be a negative consequence of behavior therapy.

The approach in behavior therapy is to use techniques which are designed to deal with the problem situation directly. For example, if the problem is a fear of airplanes, then an attempt is made to reduce the fear directly. As we saw in Chapter 3, in the problem of sexual dysfunction the focus of the intervention is on trying to increase sexual ability and enjoyment. The question is often raised, however, as to whether, the direct elimination of the problem will not result in the appearance of a new problem.

There are data available on the frequency of "symptom substitution." In general, the evidence suggests that as one problem is solved, another problem can emerge (Montgomery & Crowder, 1972). The probability that a new problem will arise would seem to vary with the type of problem and with the adequacy of the original psychological intervention. Something that might be called symptom substitution does seem to be possible.

However, *the occurrence of this "symptom substitution" is rare* (O'Leary & Wilson, 1975). *If "symptom substitution" happens at all, it is in only a very small percentage of the cases treated with behavior therapy techniques.* Furthermore, there are data to suggest that the use of techniques to deal directly with the specific problem will not produce symptom substitution, and may in fact produce other positive changes. For example, the treatment of one specific fear may lead to a reduced fear of other things and to a greater sense of general well-being (Bandura, 1969).

Symptom substitution should not be a worry for the potential user of behavior therapy. Instances of it are rare, and it may be more likely that "snowballing" positive changes will occur.

HELP-SEEKING: CHOOSING PROFESSIONAL HELP

In this section we will very briefly consider some ideas regarding the process of choosing your own source for psychological help.

The Help-Seeking Decision

Perhaps the first thing to consider in seeking professional help is, "Is there a problem?" The general criteria proposed in Chapter 1 (which are based on Buss' (1966) formulations) may serve as guidelines to reach an answer.

The presence of significant psychological discomfort (e.g., anxiety, depression, distress over marital problems) may be an indication that professional psychological help might prove useful. "Is behavior very bizarre or unusual?" For this consideration social rules and norms may serve as general guidelines. "Has there been a loss or reduction in the individual's competence in meeting the demands of everyday life?" Does the individual still care for his own routine needs such as clothing himself, feeding himself, and the like? Finally, a much more simple consideration involves the presence of dissatisfaction with one's own behavior or feelings. If the individual experiences significant subjective discomfort, if behavior is unusual or bizarre, if the individual shows a reduction in the completion of tasks needed for daily existence, or if the individual is dissatisfied with his own behavior or feelings, then professional help-seeking may be appropriate.

We are not suggesting that such considerations mean that an individual is "mentally ill" or that there is some underlying conflict. These are simple guidelines to assist individuals in the decision regarding whether or not to seek professional psychological help for a specific problem.

Available Help Sources

The list of available help sources is long. We will briefly describe only three general agencies and three types of professionals. By no means are they the totality of available help sources, but our short list is representative of some of the available sources.

Mental Health Centers. These agencies usually offer a wide variety of services. Most centers have a sliding fee scale so that even individuals with limited financial resources can get help. The staff of mental health centers usually includes social workers, clinical psychologists, and psychiatrists. Many of the staff members have a master's degree or a bachelor's degree. Mental health centers are available in most cities and in most rural areas.

Crisis Centers. Although the names vary from "Regional Emergency Service" to "Help-line," there are a wide variety of available crisis centers which have much the same goal—to provide immediate help for individuals in psychological distress. The most popular form of crisis center is the telephone hot-line, which is often open 24 hours a day. Individuals can simply call the center's number and talk to a trained counselor. A recent development in crisis centers has been the establishment of rape crisis centers designed to provide immediate support and assistance to persons who have been raped. Where crisis centers are available, the number to call can be obtained by looking in the Yellow Pages under "suicide centers," "crisis centers," or the like. Most telephone operators also know the number to call.

University Psychology Clinics. Usually these clinics are attached to the graduate program of a department of psychology. They are staffed primarily by clinical and counseling psychologists who supervise graduate students in psychology as they work in the clinic. Fees are usually on a sliding scale. Because of their intimate connection with universities, university psychology clinics often offer new and innovative methods of psychological help.

The Social Worker. Most often the social worker who engages in direct psychological intervention has a master's degree in social work (M.S.W.). In general, social workers who have chosen to work in this area have had a good deal of training in techniques designed to help individuals, couples, and families in distress.

The Psychiatrist. The psychiatrist is a physician (M.D. degree) who has received the same general medical education as any other medical doctor and has done his residency in psychiatry. During the residency he/she learns the theory and practice of psychotherapy (and perhaps some behavior therapy). The most unique part of the psychiatrist's training is in learning to prescribe the wide variety of available drugs used in the treatment of psychiatric problems.

The Clinical Psychologist. The clinical psychologist holds a Ph.D. degree. Completion of the degree usually requires four to five years of study. Training includes both academic work and practical experience. One year is spent full-time in a psychology clinic, mental health center, or other similar agency, where the psychology graduate student has a wide variety of experiences helping persons who are psychologically distressed. The clinical psychologist's academic training includes extensive amounts of research methodology, approaches to psychotherapy, behavior therapy, and courses in various aspects of human behavior.

Selecting a Help Source

There is no single way of selecting a help source, but some considerations may make the task easier. Do you know a mental health professional who can refer you to an appropriate source? Although professionals should not take on friends as clients, the professional would be in an excellent position to suggest other sources.

Do friends or family members have direct knowledge about a professional or an agency? They may provide direct information on the therapeutic style of specific professionals.

If no information is directly available, then the telephone book will be a source of names of possible help sources. Mental health centers, crisis centers, and the like will be listed in the phone book. Professionals in private practice (clinical psychologists and so on) will also be listed in the phone book. You should remember that simply being listed in the phone book does not mean that an individual is competent. It is remotely possible that he/she may not actually be what he/she claims to be. In seeking help from an individual professional, you may want to obtain information about degrees and training. A little assertiveness initially may save some difficulties at a later time.

Once you select a specific help source it may be wise to have an understanding of the cost of the professional help. Professional help is expensive, and it is wise to have a good understanding of the fees involved, before beginning sessions with a particular professional.

A Final Note

Individuals who seek professional help for psychological problems should keep at least two things in mind. First, it is necessary to underscore the fact that effective psychological intervention will require some degree of effort and commitment on the part of the client. In most cases, immediate dramatic changes in behavior probably will not occur, they will take some time and effort. Second, you must be willing to give the professional a chance to help you with your problem; however, if you do not observe improvement after a reasonable amount of time (a month or two might be an arbitrary figure), then you should discuss this with the professional. If after discussion with the professional you still are not satisfied with the progress you have made, then it may be reasonable to discontinue the sessions altogether.

SOME CONCLUDING COMMENTS

Although opinions and attitudes are probably changing, it is still possible that seeking help for psychological problems will result in some degree of social rejection (Calhoun, Peirce, Walters & Dawes, 1974; Phillips, 1964). As the experience of Senator Thomas Eagleton in the 1972 presidential campaign indicates, seeking help for psychological problems can lead to negative reactions from others. Regardless of the possible reasons for the negative reactions of other persons (e.g., Calhoun et al., 1974; Phillips, 1964) the individual who makes the decision to seek help from professionals needs to be aware that others who know about the help-seeking may have negative reactions toward the help-seeker.

Although in some circles it is probably fashionable to discuss the weekly visit to the psychiatrist or to the psychologist, the data suggest that most persons will react negatively to you if they know you are currently seeking professional help. The degree of rejection will vary, but negative reactions are predominant. The question arises as to whether or not individuals should freely inform others of their past or present help-seeking, which is a question that cannot be answered with research data. Our interpretation of the available information is that divulging such information *will probably not result in positive reactions and may well result in negative reactions from others.* The negative reactions may be as strong as not giving you a job and as mild as rating you lower on an opinion questionnaire.

In many points in this book we have raised the banner of "remember every case is different," and we will remind you again of this fact. In this chapter we have summarized some general approaches to psychotherapy and behavior change. The current variety of "brands" of behavior change methods is very great, and our descriptions of some of the major intervention strategies is not comprehensive. Our general summaries, however, should provide you with information to assist you in decisions regarding professional help-seeking.

The introductory information presented here should be useful to you. In any decision to seek professional help, we would once more repeat the old phase—*let the buyer beware.*

PROJECTS AND QUESTIONS

1. Contact a professional in private practice by phone. Obtain information about his training and background; ask him/her about the usual fee; find out how long a wait there would be before the first available appointment. Share your information with your classmates.

2. There are data suggesting that females are more likely and more willing to seek professional help than males are. Discuss the possible reasons for this sex difference in help-seeking.

3. As was noted in this chapter, it is possible that some people may react negatively to an individual if they are told he/she is seeking professional help for

psychological problems. Discuss why this may be the case, and discuss how you think you would react if you were informed that a close relative (parent, spouse) was having weekly sessions with a clinical psychologist.

4. In this chapter we have briefly reviewed some of the most popular approaches to psychological intervention. Form a small group and discuss which type of approach you would prefer if you were to seek psychological help—client-centered, gestalt, psychoanalytic, or behavior therapy. Try to arrive at a consensus, and discuss the reasons for your selection.

5. Because of the possibility that psychological intervention may not be success-ful, the proposal has been made that the therapist professional be paid by his/her client only when the intervention is successful. Try to generate as many arguments for and against this proposal as you can. Then, look at both sets of arguments and evaluate them. Which side to you has the strongest case?

SUGGESTED READINGS

Popular Sources

A. E. BERGIN. When shrinks hurt. *Psychology Today*, 1975, November, *9*, 96ff. Bergin discusses his view that psychotherapy can result in psychological deteriora-tion under certain circumstances.

G. T. WILSON & G. C. DAVISON. Behavior therapy: A road to self-control. *Psychology Today*, 1975, October, 54–60. A discussion of behavior therapy as a way for the client to make his/her own decisions and reach his/her own goals.

Advanced Sources

A. E. BERGIN & S. L. GARFIELD (Eds.). *Handbook of psychotherapy and behavior change.* New York: Wiley, 1971. An excellent compilation of articles by a representative sample of authorities in the field of psychotherapy and behavior change.

J. MELTZOFF & M. KORNREICH. *Research in psychotherapy.* New York: Atherton, 1970. A comprehensive review of studies of psychotherapy, through 1970.

K. D. O'LEARY & G. T. WILSON. *Behavior therapy: Application and Outcome.* Englewood Cliffs: Prentice-Hall, 1975. A comprehensive review of the applica-tion of behavior therapy to a wide variety of psychological problems.

REFERENCES

ADAMS, H. E. *Psychology of Adjustment.* New York: Ronald Press, 1972.
BANDURA, A. *Principles of Behavior Modification.* New York: Holt, Rinehart & Winston, 1969.

BERGIN, A. E. Some implications of psychotherapy research for therapeutic practice. *J. Abnorm. Psychol.* 1966, *71*, 235–246.

BERGIN, A. E. The deterioration effect: A reply to Braucht. *J. Abnorm. Psychol.*, 1970, *75*, 300–302.

BERGIN, A. E. The evaluation of therapeutic outcomes. In A. E. Bergin & S. L. Garfield (Eds.). *Handbook of Psychotherapy and Behavior Change.* New York: Wiley, 1971.

BERGIN, A. E. When shrinks hurt: Psychotherapy can be dangerous. *Psychol. Today*, 1975, November, 96–100ff.

BERZINS, J. I., BEDNAR, R. L. & SEVERY, L. J. The problem of intersource consensus in measuring therapeutic outcomes. *J. Abnorm. Psychol.*, 1975, *84*, 10–19.

BROWN, M. The new body therapies. *Psychotherapy: Theory, Research and Practice*, 1973, *10*, 98–116.

CALHOUN, L. G., PEIRCE, J. R., WALTERS, S. & DAWES, A. S. Determinants of social rejection for help seeking. *J. Consulting and Clinical Psychol.* 1974, *42*, 618.

DAVISON, G. C. & STUART, R. B. Behavior therapy and civil liberties. *Amer. Psychol.*, 1975, *30*, 755–763.

DEHEON, G. & SACKS, S. Conditioning functional enuresis: A four-year follow-up. *J. Consulting and Clinical Psychol.*, 1972, *39*, 299–300.

EYSENCK, H. J. *The effects of psychotherapy.* New York: International Science Press, 1966.

EYSENCK, H. J. Note on "factors influencing the outcome of psychotherapy." *Psychol. Bull.*, 1972, *78*, 403–405.

FAGAN, J. & SHEPHERD, I. C. (eds.). *Gestalt therapy now.* New York: Harper & Row, 1970.

FISKE, D. W. The shaky evidence is slowly put together. *J. Consulting and Clinical Psychol.*, 1971, *37*, 314–315.

FISKE, D. W. A source of data is not a measuring instrument. *J. Abnorm. Psychol.*, 1975, *84*, 20–23.

GARFIELD, S. L. & BERGIN, A. E. Therapeutic conditions and outcome. *J. Abnorm. Psychol.*, 1971, *77*, 108–114.

GARFIELD, S. L., PRAGER, R. A. & BERGIN, A. E. Evaluation of outcome in psychotherapy. *J. Consulting and Clinical Psychol.*, 1971, *37*, 320–322.

GARFIELD, S. L., PRAGER, R. A. & BERGIN, A. E. Evaluating outcome in psychotherapy: A hardy perennial. *J. Consulting and Clinical Psychol.*, 1971, 37, 320–322.

GARFIELD, S. L., PRAGER, R. A. & BERGIN, A. E. Some further comments on evaluation of outcome in psychotherapy. *J. Consulting and Clinical Psychol.*, 1974, *42*, 296–297.

HARMAN, R. L. Goals of gestalt therapy. *Professional Psychol.*, 1974, *5*, 178–184(a).

HARMAN, R. The techniques of gestalt therapy. *Professional Psychol.*, 1974, *5*, 257–263(b).

HOWARD, K. I., & ORLINSKY, D. E. Psychotherapeutic processes. *Ann. Rev. Psychol.*, 1972, *23*, 615–668.

KIESLER, D. J. Experimental designs in psychotherapy research. In A. E. Bergin & S. L. Garfield (Eds.). *Handbook of Psychotherapy and Behavior Change.* New York: Wiley, 1971.

LEVE, R. M. A comment on Garfield, Prager, and Bergin's evaluation of outcome in psychotherapy. *J. Consulting and Clinical Psychol.*, 1974, *42,* 293-295.

LUBORSKY, L. Perennial mystery of poor agreement among criteria for psychotherapy outcome. *J. Consulting and Clinical Psychol.*, 1971, *37,* 316-319.

MEADOR, B. D. & ROGERS, C. R. Client-centered therapy. In R. Corsini (Ed.). *Current Psychotherapies.* Itasca, Ill.: Peacock, 1973.

MELTZOFF, J. & KORNREICH, M. *Research in psychotherapy.* New York: Atherton, 1970.

MONTGOMERY, G. T. & CROWDER, J. E. The symptom substitution hypothesis and the evidence. *Psychotherapy: Theory, Research and Practice,* 1972, *9,* 98-102.

NURNBERGER, J. I. & HINGTGEN, J. N. Is symptom substitution an important issue in behavior therapy? *Bio. Psychiat.*, 1973, *7,* 221-236.

O'LEARY, K. D. & WILSON, G. T. *Behavior therapy: Application and outcome.* Englewood Cliffs: Prentice-Hall, 1975.

PAUL, G. L. Strategy of outcome research in psychotherapy. *J. Consulting Psychol.*, 1967, *31,* 109-118.

POLSTER, E. & POLSTER, M. *Gestalt therapy integrated.* New York: Bruner/ Mazel, 1973.

RACHMAN, S. *The effects of psychotherapy.* Oxford: Pergamon Press, 1971.

STAMFL, T. G. & LEVIS, D. J. Essentials of implosive therapy: A learning-theory-based psychodynamic behavioral therapy. *J. Abnorm. Psychol.*, 1967, *72,* 496-503.

STOLZ, S. B. WIENCKOWSKI, L. A. & BROWN, B. Behavior modification a perspective on critical issues. *Amer. Psychol.*, 1975, *30,* 1027-1048.

STUART, R. B. Operant-interpersonal treatment for marital discord. *J. Consulting and Clinical Psychol.*, 1969, *33,* 675-682.

STUART, R. B. *Trick or treatment.* Champaign, Ill.: Research Press, 1970.

THORESEN, C. E. & MAHONEY, M. J. *Behavioral self-control.* New York: Holt, Rinehart & Winston, 1974.

TRUAX, C. B. & MITCHELL, K. M. Research on certain therapist interpersonal skills. In A. E. Bergin & S. L. Garfield (Eds.). *Handbook of Psychotherapy and Behavior Change.* New York: Wiley, 1971.

WILSON, G. T. & DAVISON, G. C. Behavior therapy: A road to self-control. *Psychol. Today*, 1975, October, 54-60.

WOLPE, J. *The practice of behavior therapy.* Second edition. New York: Pergamon, 1973.

Index

Index